CLM

A Science of Martial Art Education

By: Matthew Kyle Powell

Published by 48f Publishing

Copyright © 2020, Powell Industries, LLC.

ISBN: 978-0-9883216-9-4

This Book

When CLM 1 was first created I had no idea that Pramek would grow to what it has become through the years. I had read so many books about martial art that effected my life and I never dreamed I would publish one that effects other people. By the time I got to CLM 4 it was at the tail end of the time that I was actively teaching seminars and my teaching experience changed. I realized two things as I would go back through reviewing the CLM books before a seminar:

1) The base science concepts of the books were still relevant years later.
2) I wanted to add so much more – my notes, my observations, etc.

At first, I thought about creating second updated editions of each, but I realized that this was not necessary – outside of basic editing issues, as they were e-books, nothing really needed changing – it just needed fine tuning. I decided that instead of new editions, I would just combine them all, edit, update, add new graphics, never seen drawings and diagrams, and let this book stand as my contribution to the martial art world. I would create one book that would be Pramek – the passion, the frustration, the challenges, the laughs, the weird concepts, ideas that caught on, the failures. Candidly I'm sure there are some imperfections in this book, but, to me, that is Pramek…perfect imperfection.

This book is broken up into 4 parts and Appendices. The 4 parts are the original separate CLM books, turned into one continuous read through the journey that is CLM. The Appendices are the original dedications and notes. Interspersed into this are images of my diagrams and photos to give the reader a sense of how much we put into Pramek over the years…'we' being myself and others who edited these books and added contributions.

Today, Pramek has changed martial arts and martial artists, even challenging the idea of what martial art is, throughout the world. That change, that challenge, began with the CLM and I hope you enjoy this compilation of what we created.

Yours in martial art,

Matthew Kyle Powell,
Founder, Pramek

Table of Contents

PART 1:

E.fficient P.erceptual L.earning

Part 1 Introduction

This series is the result of the most unexpected of catalysts. I do not want to bore you with a resume, which is public record. My training and experience have led me to a confidence in my ability to defend my life and the lives of others - both of which I have done professionally - but that confidence was shaken the day a former friend of mine was put in jail for randomly shooting someone. The individual he shot never saw it coming. He never knew, on that night, a troubled psychological past, an abusive father, and a drug problem controlled a trigger. Shot as he walked home, on the side of the road, the victim was found dead the next day. He died alone.

Often, martial art teachers discuss 'what if's.' 'What if some catastrophic event transpired?' 'What if I drove down one street instead of another?' I have lived the 'what if's,' in my life. From a middle-class upbringing, my sense of mischief led to questionable activities, which planted me on the path to who I am today. Later on, in life, I was taught to never trust; to survey and scrutinize. I was taught to persevere in violence, watch the watchers, experience, and observe, be methodical, act with purpose, and survive. So, when I saw the headlines and got the call that someone I knew had perpetrated the most random of crimes, while not surprised by the action, I was left in awe of the unpredictable nature of death.

I was left with a feeling that shook my naïve sense of immortality. We can prepare for that time of violence in a job or a certain lifestyle, but if someone wants to shoot you randomly, nothing can defend against that. Statistically, we are more likely to die in a car accident than in a fight, yet we do not train driving every night, we just drive. This led me to a deeper internal conversation: why am I studying martial art? It drew me to thinking about a statement I had recited for over a decade, to myself and to my students: Conquer yourself.

To conquer me: my psychology, my emotions, my past and present, my body, my mind, and my spirit; to exercise control over my body and train my mind. Endeavor to understand why I react in certain ways and learn from those experiences. I work to apply these lessons beyond a training room or seminar, to everyday life. The lessons I learn through the martial arts affect everything I do. I have changed my entire life by studying and analyzing. I have found freedom from those chains I never knew controlled me, and this allowed me to find freedom from injury by an enemy or to learn a new way to move.

People have goals and ambitions: being a scout leader, expertly manicuring the front lawn, winning at a local bowling league. These hobbies are good to have for growth, but they do not help to conquer us. They do not address the fears we face. Such pursuits may give us discipline in their own arena of expertise, but not discipline to face the unknown. Rarely do they harden you while at the same time teach you compassion. Those ambitions do not give you a choice when faced with life or death, nor do they give you the option to conquer yourself and your greatest enemy.

I found, in the end, that I was studying martial art not to learn to fight, but to learn to control myself. And in that control, I was discovering me. I found my own movement, my own limits, my own methods, and exercising the freedom that few others have in their lives. One can build a deck or hit a softball, but can they control their own body, mind, and spirit in those lessons learned from those ambitions? No. And in controlling your body, mind, and spirit, you gain freedom from the constraints of the world, of injury, of age, of fear, of an enemy.

I'm fortunate to feel free when teaching, training and when developing martial art. I am a bit of a mystic about it – I can ably defend myself– but within this study, I found a way that was different: a way that freed me from others' instruction, as I looked for methods that worked best for my students and myself. In teaching I am free to create, change, I adapt, evolve, and so does what I started: Pramek. In this, I find freedom from constraint as I rely on myself, and the knowledge about my actions, and how I can change to be who I want, not who a teacher wishes me to be.

I began this series because I have, for a decade, labored to find that freedom, for others, within martial art. This gift we are given, be it in traditions one thousand years old in katas, or the camaraderie of a training class on reality-based methods. It is a gift we martial artists of every stripe feel, and those outside the world only see. This series is my interpretation of that gift, a different way of sharing that gift with others, from the most experienced instructor, to the new student off the street. To look beyond the classroom into those who inhabit our classrooms every day; they are the true focus, as they look to us for education and guidance. With the methods in these manuals, we can perhaps hand them something they will find more applicable than a punch or a kick.

We can help them find how they become who they are and teach them to control and decide who they will become.

In friendship,

Matthew Powell

Founder, Pramek Systems

Chapter 1: A Philosophy

The CLM series should both educate Pramek practitioners and martial artists of every stripe about how to learn, how to test, and how to teach. The theories expressed have been exhaustively researched, tested, and have evolved over a decade of trials that have led to this method of teaching. This is not an orthodox teaching method; it is balanced upon the neurological reality we face in learning and teaching combative skill.

The primary goal of any martial art training is to acclimate the student to the unknown and then to conquer it. The most mortifying situation that can befall man is that of a combative scenario in which they, or a loved one, can be injured or even face death. To remove fear of injury and death and allow the student to operate under this circumstance speaks to the core of our purpose in a martial art: survival. A martial art is not about dance, or it would be called dance. A martial art is not about competition, or it would be Olympic swimming. Instead, a martial art, from its historical roots to its modern expressions, is primarily about the defense of the body against injury, while creating injury in the body of an enemy. Working from this base, the student can decide the avenue to utilize these skills, be it sport or movement and health.

Proper training is the first line of educating a student in survival. Survival, over a timeline, is not only about fighting. Survival is about quality of life. Nowhere in the realm of sports or fitness outside of martial art can a student receive an education on surviving. They can go to a gym, but they would be given fitness instruction. They can go to a dietician, but will only learn how to improve upon their diet. They can visit a physical therapist, or a psychologist, but they will only receive therapy. A student will not acquire some of the most important survival tools needed; tools such as fighting skill, understanding, and self-discipline unique within the martial arts. These tools, over the career of a student, will increase their ability to survive physical altercations, which are a primary threat to man. These skills can also increase their quality of life as they work towards a lifetime goal of mastering a subject that challenges them in all aspects of existence: mentally, physically, and spiritually.

This thought process is not every martial art, or every school or instructor. Sadly, many schools focus on punching someone in the nose, but not the hallmarks of a good education, such as mechanics of the motion, or how to teach it. Without full spectrum instruction, we are left with a student who has some of the building blocks needed, but not an adequate supply to sustain survival. Like a house built on sand, without the proper foundation of learning, the student would lose his footing and risk loss. Appropriate teaching of the student begins with fundamentals, such as recognizing how best the student receives instruction. These fundamental elements of education guide and set the standard for the relationship between teacher and student. If such fundamental subjects are not understood by the instructor, the transfer of knowledge may be ineffective. When one takes on the role of a teacher, as someone who will bestow their knowledge of martial art, they assume a responsibility beyond just instructing a punch. They are adjusting the neurological wiring programmed through millennia of survival by the human species. With that responsibility should come great reverence

This is not an easy task and is far too often overlooked when they day to day grind of class comes into play. Too often, the true nature of what is being taught becomes lost in the business, and the responsibility a teacher assumes is shrugged off. Effectiveness in application or technique gets demoted and replaced, or more commonly, diluted into something that is more marketable but less effective. This kind of attitude encompasses little moral or ethical consideration to what effect it may have on the student. The nature of what, and why we teach, becomes lost.

In adjusting and changing the neurological wiring that governs fight and survival, one is providing a degree of freedom the student may not find within the confines of a gym, therapist, or a dietician. In Pramek, combative training is viewed as instilling the confidence in the student that they are not victims, that they can master an enemy, or the self. It is not fair to have a student who will freeze when they should move, or move when they should freeze, thus placing them in harm's way. It is not fair for a woman to be taught methods designed for military men, twice a week, against an attacker twice her size. Nor is it fair for a student to be repeatedly injured in training, robbing them of the one element they may need for self-protection. This is not freedom; it is control. Control by the nervous system, the self, an instructor, or a method that puts a premium on brawn instead of intelligent training.

The world's greatest striker is useless with a broken arm. He is a slave to his injury, his training methods, and his teacher if an environment was created that encouraged it. Is a man at fifty-five, who is a lifetime martial artist truly free if he cannot bend over to pick up his grandchild? Is he free when he is unable to get out of bed due to injuries from training in his youth? Is a woman free if her martial art teaches her methods that would be ineffective or inapplicable against a determined aggressor?

In Pramek, we would argue that none of these examples are freedom.

A martial art under any name, from mixed martial arts to reality-based self-defense, is about giving students the ability to free themselves from injury or any other factor that limits life. Pramek is about giving access to the student, the option to act beyond their natural fighting instinct, which may put them at a disadvantage. A wild animal will fight, but that animal is not taught how to fight; it's nature is to survive. The animal may adapt to surroundings based on experience, but it will naturally fall back on what it is born with: teeth, claws, speed, and weight. It may win, or lose, but it does not possess the conscious ability to choose a new method of fighting its opponent. The animal will innately fight death out of instinct, with the advantages of experience along the way.

This separates man from animal at our base level. Mankind has survived through time by the ability to use the items in the environment; sticks, which became clubs, slings that became arrows, plants became cords used for netting. Without utilizing tools, the survival of man is unlikely within the natural world. Our enemies are everywhere and hold many advantages over us. A seemingly loveable large sized housedog, such as a mastiff or a German shepherd, can kill the untrained. Why else would they be used by the police and military? A full-grown dog has greater power to weight ratio than a man, and will fight accordingly, without conscience, without regard to injury, or disadvantage. Man's survival, from tigers to the little dog attacking the mailman, is governed by his ability to use knowledge of his environment and tools within his experience.

While the animal will use innate instinct, man will use experiential awareness, and this gives man the evolutionary edge to build civilizations and survive in the world today. We are not faster than a wolf, we cannot see at night like a wild cat, nor do we have venom like a viper. It is man's ability to manipulate the wolf or wildcat to do his bidding in nature that allows him to survive as well use knowledge and technology to even our odds against these predators.

Is a martial art so different?

Martial art is essentially a study of anthropology as we look at technology throughout thousands of years. We have adapted to fight with technology, and it is through that knowledge that man can survive to continue to make those adaptations. Our ancestors did not exercise to build upper body strength. They hunted, most often in teams and used rudimentary weapons they fashioned themselves and their strength was developed around these activities and their available diet. Today, we exercise on machines and use weights to increase our strength.

As technology changed, man changed.

An example is the introduction of gunpowder. This weapon altered the landscape of battle forever, and allowed civilizations to thrive and dominate, by creating efficiency in battle. On both land and sea this technology led to range and damage increasing, meaning the surrender of those without this technology. This led to some societies surviving while others did not. At the root, it is the process of education, adaptation, and the ability to flourish long enough to be duplicated that enables civilizations to thrive, while those without become stunted. It is the use of new weapons and technology that supports these civilizations to create better farms with healthier animals, leading to stronger soldiers and refined thinkers who design more competent technology, and so on. We have seen in our lifetime the evolution of anthropology and society in the use of martial art skills we teach daily.

Much like the ability to adapt and change technology to suit our needs, man should strive to make decisions about self-defense. Over time these decisions are passed down to others and imitated, systemized through reproduction. When people ponder the question of the origin of martial art, it is systemization through reproduction that is the answer. This process increases the likelihood of passage of amount of information to the next generation. In many ways this process changes the very evolution of man, as stronger civilizations prosper, their changes surviving on, while others do not. Man is born to fight like an animal to survive, but through martial art he can learn more specialized and sophisticated techniques of fighting. Within martial arts, we find true freedom from our perceived neurology and psychology. Just knowing this is a possible reality results in the chance to move beyond limitations and leads to greater adaptation. We find through martial art training the ability to control these parts of ourselves that seem uncontrollable. When viewed this way, as it is in Pramek, martial art is the freedom to adapt knowledge and technology instead of technique or drills.

An example of this is Pramek classes focusing on street intelligence and survival. In these classes we use the example of a street criminal that has one method to employ:

1.   engage the target [strategy],

2.   distract the target [tactics],

3.   attack the target in one move [method],

They do this because it has proven successful in accomplishing the crime [goal]. This attack methodology is displayed repeatedly in the news, in debriefs, and based on results is more effective than the most skilled martial artist. This is when the confines of training, regardless of scope, can adversely affect the student as situational experience outweighs technical skill. The criminal picks a target and applies the method, free from the confines of belt driven technical skill. When they are victorious it is because of the knowledge of what works for him versus what does not. That knowledge is built upon a foundation of success and failure under stress unseen in a dojo. If one took this concept and applied, it to martial art it would appear that emulating a criminal's methodology would be more effective than the techniques of an experienced teacher with multiple blackbelts. Sadly, many street self-defense methods are taught without this mindset.

Without copious amounts of techniques man is free to choose their own course. If he can read a physiology book, he can gain the knowledge to harm and heal. Even against a trained opponent, the eye gouge will work because it is basic physiology. A trained enemy is still subject to the laws of equilibrium. The proverbial 'criminal' understands that a target's psychology, when manipulated through strategy and tactic, can outweigh technical skill. Freedom to use this knowledge can set the basic student apart from the trained master. It can be difficult to ascertain if masters of martial art know these things or they may not, which is why we created the CLM. In many ways CLM is a student's insurance policy – it is a methodology based on the supremacy of science over the master. Within the CLM a basic student discovers from the beginning a better way before they are steeped in the rigors of discipline and ritual. CLM is the book to the lecture, the guide to understand the master. But, when no master is present, the student can still gain in skill because the possibilities are endless for self-instruction. As we discuss later in this book in the CBTM process, a 'master' or 'guru' is not even needed for martial art learning

These manuals are not about punching someone in the nose or about wrist grabs.

This is a series guided by the realization that martial art can create a path to personal revelation and evolution unlike any other study. In these days of marketing, contracts for training, or the latest and greatest 'super-secret' fighting methods, the Conceptual Learning Method is the recognition of freedom and the promise a martial art can hold in its basest form: that of survival and the individual decisions that affect it. CLM exists to assist the student and the teacher. This knowledge can help teachers create contracts worth entering by using new adaptive methods of instruction. It can help market what people really want: to feel a sense of self-worth and accomplishment on their own. The compliments of a teacher or a belt will only push and motivate so far. On the flip side of the coin, it acts as a warning that freedom can be found, taught (in methods like this series lays out), and that students hold their own destiny. This freedom will overcome those obstacles, which would seek to limit their ability to survive and enjoy a greater quality of life.

Chapter 2: How We Learn a Martial Art

Traditionally martial art teaching is made possible by a method of learning recognized as Procedural Based Learning, or PBL, and most martial arts rely on a form of this. This method, composed of rules, skill sets, and techniques, is typically governed by what could be considered an 'if=then' equation of thought. In PBL a student is taught action based on 'If the enemy does X, I do Y.' This eventually leads to more complex 'then' statements and longer chains of actions, for example, 'if the opponent does X, then I do Y-F-R-A.' This minimizes adaptation and maximizes following learned behavior. In this manual we inquire as to whether this is the most effective overall method of learning combative skill, and if not, what may be? Additionally, considering the popularity of PBL, we seek to explore if there another way that can supplement procedural based learning, perhaps even replace it?

To find this answer first we should understand how we learn martial art skill.

The Nature of Procedure

No one is born with martial art skill. Martial skill is acquired through learning in a way that is not very different from learning to use a spoon or solve a math problem. First, we must understand the concept we are being taught, which is most recognized as the cognitive phase. In this phase we examine the method through experience, pay attention to detail, and try to understand the concept by developing patterns of association. These patterns are rudimentary and flexible as we draw associations from the cues and the context of the environment around us and actions we take. Sometimes these are strong patterns because we see the cues in a variety of situations, versus rare cues that draw little association and generate little in terms of pattern recognition. An example of this would be a strike, which is common versus flying leg scissors; a technique so rare that it provides little ability to draw associations and pattern recognition.

In a martial art, the best way to think of this is when first learning a strike. A jab is seen so commonly it forms a strong pattern of association, associated with a memory and repeated exposure. These patterns and types of associations vary. Imagine for a moment the association a student would draw in the following situations:

A. student is taught the jab by throwing the jab;
B. student taught the jab by being hit in the face with the jab;
C. student taught the jab by watching but not participating in either above;

In each they would form different associations.

Which do you think would create the most powerful association and have the longest-term effect on a student's learning?

The larger, more powerful associations become greater patterns. These patterns create a powerful memory. These are termed schema. Whether students know it or not, they are governed by scheme from the earliest part of the martial art training (and in their everyday lives). As the patterns of association become more grounded, what used to be assumed as unpredictable becomes more predictable. This predictability leads to our developing a memory based around it. A student looks at the material presented and begins to develop a mental construct of what information is being processed. The student learns how it is enacted, breaks the information into smaller clusters of ideas to learn. Now we must develop a physical association between our patterns and their results. This is where the associative phase begins.

In the associative phase we take the mental and visual concepts we are taught and physically manifest them through recreations of the pattern. This phase is what the layman may refer to as muscle memory, as the student repeats the skill over and over. In this repetition the student is creating their own method of performing the pattern. The student will leave out movements they find do not work for them individually until the pattern is internalized. Individual students will leave out individual parts of the observed pattern to develop their individual pattern.

Their nervous system will interact with the environment and draw an association between the cognitive understanding and the physical action. In other words, there is a big difference between watching someone throw a jab (cognitive) and throwing the jab and hitting someone with it (associative). The more complex the skill, the longer it will take to 'automate', or internalize, as the mind and body must put segments of the schema together. Over time, movement is refined through experience, as the schema become more specialized and we create a more accurate association between X technique and Y technique, the movements connecting them, and our responses.

Martial artists in this stage become conditioned to a response. This conditional 'if=then' programming which in the cognitive phase was general becomes greater conditioned through movement repetition and associative patterns. Over time, smaller movements comprising the 'if X = then Y standalone responses' become 'if X pattern = Y pattern responses' as the small ideas of clusters blend and create larger clusters. In other words, the first time you throw the jab it is a small idea of clusters, but the more you do it, and the more successful, those smaller clusters become bigger and bigger. Soon, one jab against a stationary target becomes a jab on the move against a moving target.

How does this happen?

Movements which are unneeded are discarded as the martial artist repeats the movement and pattern over and over, refining the schema further. Whether the schema called upon is an exact match for the situation is not as important as recalling it, and students begin to move faster and use a variety of complex patterns. The more complex a skill, the longer it takes to practice removing unneeded movements, thus more practice is required. This is characteristically the difference in what we would call a 'white belt' and a 'black belt.' A black belt has had a longer period to practice more complex skills.

When a student has repeated the skill enough times, it's called motor learning and the student begins to reach the autonomous phase. Motor learning is the third part of procedural based learning, in which the skill or procedure is repeated repeatedly. A technique is a procedure governed by schema, our recognition of stimuli, and our ability to recall schema in relation to stimuli. The best way to think of this is 'If X, then Y, then if J, then G, faster, faster, and faster'. In many ways martial art PBL style techniques are the same concept as multiplication tables where a student practices a mathematical problem repeatedly, learning short cuts and tricks. This repetition combined with short cuts and tricks reduce the amount of time for completion.

When the student sees the multiplication card, they process it not as multiplication, but as an experience and memorized solutions corresponding to boxes and numbers. The student may have to take a moment to read the numbers, which could be differently patterned or placed in decorative boxes. These are distractions for the task at hand: repeating learned memory. Remember this example, as we will come back to it in differentiation.

In a martial art, stimuli are adapted to as the student finds small obstacles in the way of learning the skill, such as varying angles or levels at which it is performed. These stimuli can increase the time the student it will take the student to repeat the patterns. The movement skill, or technique, is repeated in the same pattern through motor learning, where the movement is performed many times, resulting in a skill which is performed without a conscious effort - it is what might be considered automatic.

This occurs because in the brain, motor memory is separate from declarative memory. Declarative memory is conscious, meaning we consciously have thoughts to recall facts or memories, such as a birth date or to remember to perform a task, like going to the doctor. Procedural based learning is how we get to the doctor: we drive the car. Motor memory is turning the keys in the ignition while putting on your seat belt, then placing your arm over the passenger seat and looking back after shifting the car into reverse. In the autonomous phase, the body has repeated the skill, the process we have discussed previously, to the point it has dropped unneeded and ineffective movements and the process has become automated. It is part of the neurological pathways in the brain, on the motor side, as opposed to the declarative side, which is a thought like the capital of your state.

Most martial artists wish to attain the autonomous state with their skill, where they have a large number of techniques in their 'muscle memory' (which is the neurological programming and pathways developed of time and repetitions), which they can add together with other patterns of movement. These are generally considered to be complex techniques often seen in advanced drills. After a period repeating the complex movement patterns, like combinations of strikes, become neurologically imbedded like a simple movement, such as a single strike.

Their skill becomes autonomous.

Unfortunately, there is a problem - the ability of the practitioner to learn technique after technique contrasts with their ability to learn other skills in life. In our experience, and that of many studies, a student will need to repeat a movement pattern over 5000 times to move from associative to autonomous. This high number of repetitions is why a student will get into their car and perform the same "ritual' with the seatbelt, or throw a simple strike, but not perform flying leg scissors or complex submissions under pressure. In this example, the student may perform two of those motor patterns, such as putting on a seatbelt or throwing a right cross, in life daily. These repetitions add up and the student is advancing those toward habits of movement.

Advanced joint manipulations are not an everyday movement and skill set, and they rely on fine motor skills. As such, the student's ability to practice is limited to martial art class. A complex submission will also have various stimuli the student has to work through, versus putting on the seatbelt, and these will draw away from the student's ability to perform the task the same way in the same pattern many times. There are training methodologies shaped around these challenges, for example, shadow boxing. This method is utilized to overcome complexities in motor movements, such as chains of strikes, and can be done to build on repetition but they only account for half of the equation in training complex motor movements for combat. Complex submission requires a training partner. Yes, you could use visualization, or you could even roll around with a dummy and pretend – but you need another human to have an associative experience with complex submissions. With everyday tasks taking more precedence in the brain developing new neural pathways for motor memory, the student can be at a disadvantage from their first class in developing true mastery of a martial art.

Gross Motor Skills

Humans learn by procedures and schemas. The more complex a movement the more likely it will take to move from cognitive to associative to autonomous stages in procedurally based learning. To overcome this challenges, gross motor skills are routinely learned first and then employed by most martial artists. Rolling over, standing, walking...these are gross motor skills adjusted by fine motor tuning, as opposed to picking up a fork and eating, which is a fine motor skill. Gross motor skills are large ranging motor patterns learned in early childhood that we continue to build upon as we age. We take basic gross motor skills and apply them in different situations. In general, gross motor skills should be defined as being based upon large muscle groups accomplishing work and performing whole body movement. To gain a better understanding of this working definition let's begin with our first gross motor skill: standing.

Gross motor skills are typically based on posture, meaning the body must be for the most part aligned to accomplish them. Muscles develop to assist the body in these endeavors, so for example, as an infant grows stronger, they can hold their head up. The head is vital to postural control and the muscles controlling the skull, which houses the eyes, must develop to steady the head and allow the eyes to develop perception and track objects. There is a natural progression between strengthening the neck muscles and supporting the head. This progression allows an infant to start tracking objects and interact with them. As the infant grows stronger, they will reach for objects, developing the muscular-skeletal posture, or 'structure'. Structure gives shape to the infant grabbing objects and creating closed structures with them. For a definition of 'closed structure' please refer to Pramek's other works on biokinematics.

As the infant grows stronger, they pull themselves up, aligning their spine. This alignment eventually gives away to standing and walking. As infants become toddlers, they strengthen their biomechanical structure, and interact more with the world...grabbing, holding, and carrying objects. Over time, these gross motor skills give the infant the ability to reach out for the world and transition to large motor groups being coordinated to perform tasks. The difference between an infant walking and an adult running is time, muscular, and spinal development. A child picking up a toy is no different than an adult lifting a weight; it is a matter of gross motor control and strength development over time and experience in a lifetime.

Posture control, or 'structure', also affects us in combat. Many martial arts will focus on manipulating an opponent's 'structure' for two reasons. First, to affect the equilibrium of an opponent, controlling the position of the center mass and manipulating it to outside a load bearing area. The other reason for this is creating difficulty in tracking objects, as the head is unable to steady itself to track a fist, for example. This manipulation and control restrict the ability of the other person to track targets like a fist or knee when the head is controlled.

Having covered gross motor skills for how they develop one must also ask why they decline. One issue consistently shown to be an obstacle in gross motor skills is age. The body begins developing gross motor skills to operate at a young age and progresses throughout life. Unfortunately for us, around the time the human body reaches the age of 30 gross motor skills begin to decline. As people grow older, they do not run, roll, sprint, and lift weights, due to daily life. They do not have the freedom of childhood to play and develop motor skills like in climbing a tree. People place themselves into a box where daily lives contribute to utilizing gross motor skills less and less until the body ages to the point where it can no longer use them as effectively as they did when they were younger. A common example of this is an adult who has not ridden a bicycle since childhood. They say riding a bike is a skill one will never forget - yet the motor skills required to pilot a bicycle degenerate over time. You can try this yourself – if you haven't ridden a bike in a long time – attempt what was easy as a child. You will most likely find that standing on the seat, ride without hands on the handlebars, and other tricks easily performed as a child now have become exceedingly difficult.

Studies also illustrate consistent exercise by groups over 30 years of age will slow the decline of gross motor skills. Experience begins to combine with these skills, and as people age, their experience in operating their body can allow them to perform at the same levels as their younger counterparts. With proper utilization they can even perform at higher levels of individuals younger than themselves. Experience counts in law enforcement, teaching martial arts, military service, or for those who stay active in physical culture. This understanding of what role experience plays in retaining skill is why Pramek combines a focus on the physical state with mental exercise, leading more refined movement based upon efficiency as opposed to effectiveness.

The internet has created a culture where martial art is more accessible than ever. The fear of walking into a class full of kids subsides with online learning through videos follow by seminars. This new accessibility means any times we find that students come into martial art at an advanced age. When one looks at martial arts, those interested in a scientific system like Pramek typically have developed motor skills and if over 30, will be in their declining phase. This is important for teachers to understand – expecting new students over 30 to pick up skills requires a special touch. It is up to the instructor to utilize safe physical exercise and make good use of experience, promoting efficiency in all students as a goal along with effectiveness. This will allow older students to become more efficient over time with their limited gross motor skills meanwhile assisting younger students in becoming efficient from the beginning. As younger students reach the period in their lives in which gross motor skills decline, they will have a head start. Having a long term view is why the Pramek concept of Theory + Movement = Application places a premium on the efficiency of a student as much as their martial effectiveness. Efficiency isn't about a shortcut, it's about putting the least amount of work in to get the most output, like a machine lifting a box, or a vagus nerve strike instead of a prolonged wrestling match. It is the goal of Pramek to look at these measures of efficiency and use them as a basis; using the body as that machine to lift an object, or utilizing the 'miss by an inch, miss by a mile' principle to push students to become more efficient.

Fine Motor Skills

While gross motor skills are large movements, fine motor skills are small muscle movements. These small motor movements can occur with or without eyesight, while still accomplishing the same general tasks. Think of fine motor skills as for example using the fingers, and as we develop and grow older, the fingers are used to grasp objects as opposed to holding them in our palms. Fine motor movements are defined in writing and grasping smaller objects. Fine motor skills, as opposed to gross, require a different category of strength, motor control, and when using the hands, dexterity. It is this level of dexterity and fine motor control which, in many ways, separates humans from other mammals and allows us to use small tools, while other mammals do not have the ability to manipulate them.

While our hands and finger are the primary area of study when talking about fine motor skills, these skills are not just the hands. In Pramek, we often illustrate a principle in which the arm is the same as the leg. It's the same overall structure, and therefore subject to the same general laws of biomechanics and mechanics. One search of the internet for the use of feet and the foot to accomplish tasks otherwise done with the hands (writing, putting on diapers, tying knots, etc.) shows that fine motor controls we think of as reserved for the hands and eyes can be utilized by other parts of the body.

In Pramek, we exercise and develop fine motor skills in our wrists and our ankles, elbows and knees, shoulders, and hips. As we say in Pramek, 'If you have movement, you can still fight'. Movement control allows a user to move the body through their joints and extends freedom to create openings and accomplish mechanical tasks without the use of the hands. Grabbing the legs and kicking them may seem strange, because we use the term 'grab' when speaking of the hands. It is possible to grab the leg with a foot, manipulate and rotate it, and then move it. One need only view their lower body the same way they view their upper body. To practice this, a Pramek student can try using their foot to accomplish tasks like opening a door or drawer, utilizing the range of motion in the foot and ankle to accomplish these tasks while the hands operate separately.

Coordination creates efficiency to direct the body toward biomechanical efficacy. Within a large motor pattern, there are kinematic elements such as the elbow, a wrist, or a knee. These can create complex movements within a large movement pattern. It is these fine motor movements which the body develops toward efficiency while using a large movement pattern. In training, these patterns are routinely used so they are accessible when the body begins a large movement. An example would be a grab and throw which is a large movement pattern, but a fine motor movement would be the way a jacket is grabbed or utilizing the wrist to strike while in the grab, etc.

Fine motor skills are perishable skills and should be developed and maintained. Simple exercises can be utilized to keep these motor skills in better accessible condition. These exercises are where martial art can educate the non-martial art world. While many people might not want to go to a boxing class, they can benefit from the hand-eye coordination drills that come from boxing. Learning to use simple drills, such as dropping small pieces of paper and having a partner catch them, is excellent for developing hand eye coordination. These exercises also serve two purposes: one combative, in training hand eye coordination and fine motor skills for better striking and grabbing. The second is more subtle, keeping hand-eye coordination skills which are non-combative in nature in useable condition.

How Many Techniques Can One Learn?

The number of techniques one can recognize cognitively is unlimited... but the associative and autonomous phases are a different story. One can learn an innumerable quantity of techniques in the cognitive phase. As simple as watching television, most students have learned millions of ways to disable an enemy, take away a knife, throw a punch, or do a 'crane kick.' We look at the concept and see what action a person is making, understand the concept of why they are doing it and what response it elicits from another person. We develop a general pattern of recognition the technique has an outcome but move no further because we do not perform the task repeatedly or experience it.

For a martial artist, this cognitive phase is the beginning of training as they strive for the autonomous phase where the conscious becomes unconscious. So, how do we get to that phase? First, we must determine how many times one must repeat a movement for it to develop a neurological pathway. The problem is - no one really knows. Estimates range from 5,000 - 10,000 repetitions to enter the autonomous phase. 5,000 for simple, gross motor skills - versus 10,000 for complex, fine motor skills and combinations or transitions between gross and fine motor skills.

These are high numbers of repetitions for one to master a 'technique' and these quantities beg the question: with this many repetitions, how many techniques can one learn? We estimate, based upon research at the Krasnodar Polytechnic Institute when studying for the patent for the Kadochnikov System, the body without extreme stimuli (external distractions or obstacles) can enter the associative phase of learning 300+ techniques, or movement patterns categorized as procedural 'if = then' responses for martial art. The student can then transition these to an estimated 70 autonomous techniques, or responses to non-life threatening environments with minimal stimuli and arousal. In threatening, high level intensity and multiple stimuli environment, the student may only access as many as 35 specific responses.

An example would be an advanced sport fighter who is placed into a real-world situation against an unknown opponent who fights using unfamiliar methods. Combining nervous system responses, added with transition from fine to gross motor skills, the number of neurologically accessible techniques becomes limited to the techniques that have repeated the most times and have imbedded the strongest neuro pathway.

There are exceptions to these general guidelines, as we are basing our idea of what technique is and what we have as our 'natural' fighting skills. Humans are 'hard-wired' for a functional set of evolutionary combative methods. It means we, with no martial art training, will fight like animals, using our claws, weight, speed, teeth, autonomic nervous system, and intelligence - all of which are neurologically hardwired as a part of our autonomic nervous system - as much as tunnel vision, increased heart rate, and adrenaline release. Hence part of our body is termed the autonomic nervous system because it is automatic within the brain. We are born with "fight, flight, or freeze' as neurological programming. Each of those states have techniques programmed to them.

Imagine for a moment being given an older computer as a gift. While older, it still performs the functions you need it to perform. You load new programs on to the hard drive in the computer, some of which do not exactly match the operating system on the computer itself while others take up a lot of memory. The immediate memory, or RAM, becomes incredible slow and cannot perform simple tasks. The long-term storage on a hard drive becomes corrupted. Perhaps the fan on the computer gets dusty, the power cable is frayed. Soon, the computer runs slower, or it crashes, and becomes difficult to deal with and the issues become impossible to solve without re-formatting the drive.

Now, imagine your body is that computer, your mind is the memory, and the nervous system is the operating software. The brain is preloaded with operating software for survival that has worked for thousands of years. This operating system is tried and true, even if outdated. Anyone around IT knows that many times older operating systems are used because they are so well explored, their vulnerabilities and capabilities knowns. It's this ancient operating system we build on top of. We repeat strange techniques that conflict with the operating system, with the RAM, and then we become upset when we can't recall a technique or perform it well. When we can't perform it well or remember, what do we do? We attack with size, speed, claws. Even when given the most advanced weapons, in hand-to-hand combat the human will fight like a caveman fought thousands of years before him when weapons are removed.

We were never truly built for this replacement of our operating system, substituting flying head scissors and arm bars in place of the primordial reptilian brain form of fighting. We have so many other things we need to do to eat, build shelter, find water, and in today's modern society, drive massive vehicles that weigh a ton at high speeds. Within this paradigm we find why the best fighters in the world, the most skilled, spend the most time perfecting their art. They spend their time developing neuropathways around fighting while non-martial artists spend their time developing neuropathways around driving.

With evolution as it's code writer, our basic operating system, RAM, and computer for fighting and survival is rather good. In fact, it is so good, we stopped having to focus on it long enough to gather and farm food, build civilizations, reach for the stars. As far back as man has fought man and beast, our genetic predispositions toward everything from bone density to muscle fiber has placed the fighting man where he naturally belongs from the pike man to the knight to the archer. Martial art replaces this evolutionary design. If you're naturally lanky and built for striking, martial art makes you grapple and wrestle. If you're short and stocky and built for grappling, martial art has you doing high kicks. With this recognition, be weary of loading the wrong software on the wrong machine, because once loaded, the machine (you) will try to use them automatically.

What is meant by this?

Be careful what you repeat.

Autonomic Skills

The autonomic skills are strongest neuro pathways created through repetition. The more you do something, the stronger the neuro pathway and the faster you can recall it without trying to remember what you are trying to recall. In terms of motor learning, the 'now how did I do that?' question becomes a training issue more often with small, complex movements. Larger, simple movements are easier to program so you don't ask 'now how did I do that?'. A student is more likely to practice a technique that always works, hastening the transition from associative to autonomic programming of technique. With positive feedback brought on by physical success, such as an effective throw or punch, a person will repeat the same techniques because they 'work,' prompting an endorphin release that brings pleasure as a reward. As is human nature, the process will be repeated to gain positive feedback. With this process, a technique is born.

This process of motor learning, success, and feedback means what works most of the time is used the most. Students will exhaust what they know best, what is easily accessible, first. A combatant may have certain methods that work for them and will utilize them. When these techniques are exhausted, they will transition to associative level skills, skills they have done but not done repeatedly to great success. After associative is the cognitive phase, where they try techniques they've seen but haven't associated with a success. Even the most skilled fighters rely on the most basic of techniques. In the highest level of professional fighting to combatives, most fights are fought with basic striking, kicking, and grappling. What is the differentiator? Combining these techniques with natural attributes such as weight and mass, experience, and psychology to win a fight.

Fighting results in autonomic nervous system responses such as increased heart rate and tunnel vision making fine motor skills difficult to neurologically access. It is only when the fight slows that more advanced fine motor skill methods are made readily accessible again. When broken down to a neurological and mechanical level, fighting becomes an ebb and flow between fine and gross motor skills. Fight duration and physical exertion eventually limit capabilities to gross motor skills. In sport, as the time of the fight goes longer, it increases the duration of physical exertion, exhausting the body. Only the most defined, strongest neuro pathways are accessed. In street combat, the higher levels of bioenergy being used in stress situation leads to quick feet becoming sloppy stiff legged movement and accurate punches devolving into wild swings.

With the knowledge of what is neurologically occurring in combat, one can see the differences between the cognitive phase, associative phase, and autonomous phase physically manifested. Coaches often notice that a student is not using everything they know in training, and sometimes the coach will ask, 'Why is he/she not doing what they do in training, and just throwing the same punch?' Rarely is neurology examined within this situation. If it were it would become transparent why basic skills are being used instead of newly acquired ones. Focusing on neurological training would mean a training regimen that looks very different from traditional methodologies.

Drills in training commonly revolve around basic combinations of kicks, strikes, knees, and take downs - which are gross motor skills. Once the take down occurs, the reliance upon fine motor skills is heightened. But, if these are not trained through repetition, combined the demands of performance in sport or combat, then the most basic ground techniques will become the most neurologically accessible. Students able to demonstrate advanced techniques in demonstrational training, while have difficulty recreating them in stress situations, are demonstrating the associative or cognitive phase. This is why single sport fighters, such as boxers who spend large periods of time with procedural drills based on combinations of hand and arm work, have a distinct advantage over a fighter who has trained in a variety of arts, but has not mastered any. The single style master may not have the wider range of martial art techniques, but the neuro pathways to what they know are highly defined and accessible. This neurological accessibility translates to more options in combat the longer the fight goes on.

In judging a martial art or artist we must look beyond the terms like 'mastery' 'intermediate,' and 'novice.' We must examine where the student is on the scale of the procedural based learning system upon which their techniques are based. How many repetitions and challenging scenarios has the student been exposed to, to develop schema and motor learning? What phase are they in with their techniques in terms of neuropathways? What is the level of exposure to stress and time of study? When these matters are considered it is clear why older practitioners can hold 'master' levels, as they have had more time to repeat movement patterns and use those movement patterns to gain experience. In terms of gross and fine motor skills, seasoned or longer-term practitioners hold an obvious advantage over younger practitioners or those who have had less time to study and transition from cognitive to associative and autonomous phases.

Challenges force the student to refine their technique and associate reactions to their technique with alterations in physical employment. The longer time a student must perform repetitions, for example katas, and then refine them in application, or a tournament, the more techniques transfer between cognitive - associative - autonomous states, increasing the number of techniques neurologically embedded. This answer creates more questions: what if the opponent or enemy has more techniques? What if they have spent more time studying and in more tournaments? How does one expect to learn something that may save their life in a short period of time if they must repeat a technique 5,000 times (without external stimuli) just to embed the technique? What if one 'chokes'? What if one comes up against an enemy who uses a method of fighting that the technique set cannot address easily, leaving massive grey areas in the motor learning process?

In one view, this occurred with the arrival of Brazilian jiu-jitsu in the UFC. It wasn't that the Gracie BJJ program was superior as an art form, but it challenged the neurology of the opponents and destroyed the accepted strategy for mixed martial arts at that time. Opponents were in the associative and autonomous phase with striking and kicking. But, on the ground, they were cognitive and associative. Physically they were unprepared for that level of ground combat, transferring any ground motor skill sets back to cognitive in application. What if 70% of one's technique skill set relies upon the right arm and someone ties up or injures their right arm, relieving them of 70% of their techniques? What if the opponent has 20 techniques in the autonomic phase, and a student only has 10 techniques that are autonomous? Obviously, this presents a dangerous challenge for a student and their teacher preparing them for combat. As well as a challenge, it presents a unique opportunity to develop a training methodology that addresses these short-comings.

Chapter 3. E.fficient P.erceptual L.earning

Reality poses unique challenges in training a martial artist. A high rate of injury and muscle fatigue related to combative training pose unique challenges for martial art students. Operational conditions for a user (exhaustion, intoxication, high elevation, allergic reaction, constricting clothing or equipment, injured teammates, or family members) create a level of challenge not found in other pursuits. Combine the previous elements of challenge with Murphy's Law and we find that training can be a blessing and a curse that can reduce the likelihood of attaining the autonomous phase of techniques. Against an untrained opponent, students with a higher number of autonomous phase techniques will have an advantage so long as they are working within the technique motor set. But with operational conditions or against an enemy who is better trained, this advantage can dissipate. With these situations in mind, full reliance upon procedural based learning can be a weakness. Notice the words 'full reliance', and as we move forward, it is vital to remember that procedural based learning has its place in a martial art training environment.

Pramek has developed, over a decade, a method of teaching and learning that makes use of more universal principles in addition to procedures; as well as concepts such as '1 tool for 8 tasks,' as opposed to the procedural principle of ''8 tools for 1 to 8 tasks.' This methodology, Efficient Perceptual Learning, or EPL works to take a student through the stages of perceptual learning, with a student given tools instead of procedures to resolve a task. Words are important, which is why we use the word resolve, not solve, and not fail at solving - resolve. The goal of EPL is not to create the perfect throw or punch, but to allow the student the ability to resolve a physical interaction like combat using tools based on principles. With this method, the student is views combat and movement from a conceptual basis, applying universal principles to the task at hand, instead of imposing techniques which may or may not work.

This may seem difficult, but in practice it is not.

Pramek does not rely on technique. This is not to say Pramek does not teach technique at all. Pramek procedurally teaches directed, purposeful techniques for combat. Our goal is to be without many 'techniques'. Instead in Pramek we teach principles to students and allow them to express that theory through their movement, and then choose an application. The student doesn't perform a procedural block to answer the question of 'if x, then y'. Instead, the student performs a wedge, which will address y…and z, t, f, or w. We can then test the effectiveness of that theory through Pramek's DPT, or measures of efficiency (heart rate, respiratory measurements, etc.) and movement (how long engagement lasts, how far engagement has moved in distance).

What is learned by a student if not technique?'

First, one must adjust their understanding of what a technique mechanically is versus what a technique accomplishes. One does not perform a submission, which is a goal, one performs an arm bar to gain a submission. A student does not have to perform a technique thousands of times to understand what it is, how it works, and its primary goal. A technique is not a strategy. A student educated on principles, tools, and concepts will understand and have exposure to procedural techniques but will view them differently than a procedurally based student.

Pramek expects a student to use a tool or concept to address a situation. Take for example a wedge or a lever which are physics principles. A Pramek student will form a wedge to cut force or hold open applied force; or a student will look at a release from a grab as a lever and function around the lever instead of the 'grab.' The student will take body parts and make them into physics principles to address the situation they are confronted with. These machines of efficiency are matched by a student becomes biomechanically efficient. Pramek uses specialized exercises to become efficient in a biomechanical sense, utilizing the various systems in the body (muscular, skeletal, vascular, etc.) to create powerful coordinated movement that does not waste energy to best apply the principle.

In Pramek, hand-to-hand combat is a biomechanical interaction. The body is a machine operated by systems like the brain and the nervous system interacting with the world through the muscular or skeletal system. When two bodies engage in combat it is an interaction between two machines. The two bodies interact like machines when viewed mechanically. Grabs are levers, punches are impacts, or throws are removals of equilibrium. The machine can be damaged by impacts just as the machine can run out of energy. If one removes the concepts of style or system from combat, they begin to view combat for what it is: a mechanical interaction between biomechanical machines. If the reality of combat is that it is a mechanical interaction between two biomechanical machines then what makes the difference is the operator: the brain, nervous system, and how efficiently the machine operates. The student must first understand how their own machine operates, combining all the internal systems into a coordinated efficiency to better operate in combat.

Once this is understood and acted upon Pramek then educates the now biomechanically efficient student on combative decision-making and how combative interactions are mechanical in nature. An example may be teaching the student the basic simple machines of efficiency in physics. The student then incorporates their biomechanically sound movement to create a machine while in combat with another person: an efficient lever to release a grab. This level of education creates options, which as we discussed earlier, is important in using motor skills in combat. Most students of martial art have heard of joint locks being called a 'lever'. What they do not realize is that there are three classes of levers, as well as force couples and compound levers. Armed with this knowledge, a student does not need a technique, but an example, and then the knowledge to create these machines with their own movement. In Pramek the question is asked: if a technique is physically created from levers, force couples, and compound levers - then is it not more effective to teach the student what these principles are and then allow them to create methods that work for them?

Learning Without Techniques

A student will often train repeatedly in an art and learn several techniques. As stated earlier this is not a 'bad' thing, it is an element of training. But when you are procedurally based the likelihood of a situation arising that challenges everything and render it useless rises. If one is trained based upon 'if x, then y' then any circumstance that greatly affects the elements of y can create fundamental disadvantages for using fundamental disadvantages for using y as a technique.

The primary basis of Pramek combatives is procedurally based techniques within a framework called the BCB, or Basic Combative Concepts. A right cross, or low kick, is not theoretical and must be taught mechanically and procedurally to understand how to use them within combat. These techniques are rarely ends in themselves and must fit within a framework based on a goal. BCB is based upon theory and movement, and then applications, which are individual. The BCB can be broken down into digestible sections, and then built upon in a progressive manner. The student does not have to learn 15 procedurally based techniques and responses, but the theory behind the techniques, and then decide using their own movement how best to apply the theories.

The BCB is comprised of:

- Basic Combative Tactics
- Striking - basics striking concepts
- Kicking - basic kicking concepts
- Grappling - basic grappling concepts
- Grabs and Clinch - basic grab and clinch concepts
- Throws - basic throwing concepts
- Weapons - basic common weapons and concepts behind use
- Improvised Weapons - basic uncommon weapons and concepts behind use;

along with the following areas of study:

Mechanics of Combat:

- Screw
- Lever
- Wedge
- Inclined Plane
- Pulley

Human Biomechanics

- Efficient Movement
- Human Equilibrium
- Locomotion
- Basic Kinesiology

- Human Servomatics

Physics of Combat

- Force and projection of force
- Force couples
- Equilibrium
- Impact and Contact

Human Physiology

- Basic anatomy
- Human nervous system - Central, Sympathetic, Autonomic
- Nerves and pressure points
- Human Function Systems -Vascular system, Respiratory System
- Sensitive targeting (eyes, throat, groin, etc.)
- Design and composition of joints

Human Psychology

- Effects of the nervous system on psychology
- Combative psychology

Strategy

- Basic combat strategy of offense and defense
- Combative ranges
- Strategy based on fighting styles

These sections combine into a framework, called T+M=A, or:

Theory + Movement =Application

In combining theory with efficient movement, a student can create an application such as a strike, grab, or throw that is mechanically sound. A 'punch' makes the student conceptualize a strike or throw as a mechanical and biomechanical principle. Thinking in terms of real life application, such as an injury, if a student learned a 'punch' as subject to the laws of technique and motor pattern repetition, everything they have learned is now altered by the injury. When striking is taught from the viewpoint of the projection of force and impact and targeting, the type of strike develops based on the student's movement. Once a student can understand projection of force, impact, targeting, and biomechanics they can develop their own means of striking. This is not to say that basic strike education is not necessary but should be complemented with T+M=A to create a more adaptive approach to striking.

Another example would be a student who has not trained in throws but learns human equilibrium and force couples, and combined with understanding points of contact, can create a throw. This throw may be unorthodox, but it will be within the abilities of the student - their understanding of theory and movement, and experience with application. Thus, the longer a student trains, the more adaptive a student becomes. Additionally, if a student is already educated in strikes and throws, the knowledge of theory provides them greater flexibility in their tools.

Within these concepts we find the macro-level subject of the CLM series: conceptual learning.

'Conceptual learning' can seem challenging to those educated in a procedural based thought process. If viewed at its purest form, a grab is a point of rotation with force being rotated around it. A grab is a lever. In Pramek it makes logical sense to teach the concept of the lever as opposed to the rehearsal of a procedural technique as it leaves a student more adaptive instead of restrained by procedure. For example, the wedge is a body movement expressing a physics principle and is not a technique. A technique addresses a technique, but a principle encompasses multiple techniques. For example, a student is taught a block for a certain strike and then is taught a block for another strike. But, if a knife were involved, the student would use a different technique. The student could instead use a mechanical concept, such as a wedge to address all three situations.

A wedge is a physics principle the student uses, and it is adaptable to many situations. It is not governed by technique but instead the theory of the wedge, the student's movement, and the application it should be used within. In physics, a wedge is a wedge - it does not hold conscience, does not ponder if it must be used against a door, to hold open a space between two objects, or to lift an object higher. The wedge is applied mechanically to the situation. By using the body to create a wedge, the student can cut through force, hold open force, and project the base of the wedge (ex., the body of the user). Using concepts, the student is only concerned with the end result, which is not being hit and moving the strike off its target, whether that the incoming strike is a fist or a fist holding a knife. The student can then utilize other concepts or techniques such as vital targeting, perhaps removal of equilibrium, or a choke technique to follow up after their use of the wedge.

Chapter 4: Learning Perceptions and Concepts

What is perception, and can it be used in training? If you, the reader, were to define perception, what would you define it as? Definitions are important, so that a common understanding of a topic is created, which is why we lean on definitions in the CLM manuals. To understand perceptual learning, one must first understand the definition of perception: interpreting input through individual experience. Interpretation, experience, instead of repetition and procedure. Procedural based learning, for this discussion, is task based. A technique is a task, and the user gets better at the technique through repetition. As the demands of the task and stimuli increase, they distract the user from accomplishing the task of completing the technique.

In perceptual learning, the task is not a technique, but an actual task to be accomplished. For example, in taking an opponent to the ground, the task is removing equilibrium, not a technique-based throw. Perceptual learning within Pramek, the EPL method, lets the student apply theory through their perceptual system and develop experience based on this interaction. Application is accomplished through the utilization of the sensory organs and making an observation about the environment. This information is then processed by the mind to make decisions about the environment...and thus, create a relationship with this environment. The relationship has no connotations, it is what it is, and this may be a positive, negative, or neutral relationship. The eyes look at the environment and then the mind processes the information about the environment. The student can then decide which methods of applying theory are best and then enhance their application based on this experience.

For the following section we will look at a strict procedurally based methodology, understanding that not every scenario is similar. While it might be simple to teach a deflection as 'technique A,' this would mean the deflection must use motor repetition, which is a long term process. One method of deflection let's say for example, X, is neurologically embedded as a technique to be called up for use by the user if Y is observed. Should unexpected stimuli happen, the deflection may not operate according to how the user wishes or another method that is neurologically embedded, such as a block, may be used. As a student, or a teacher, you may have seen this, when a new student uses a punch block for a kick, or a kick deflection for a block. When a student relies only on procedural technique the mind can get 'confused' as it tries to figure out which X matches what Y. Regardless of time in training, this embedding process may create a lag-time as the user draws upon experience and determines what technique to use. This is an example of why many times multiple punches are thrown and ineffectively blocked before the user can determine the most suitable technique for the job. The person's neurology must catch up to the situation and begin using techniques that are accessible but applicable.

In the ever-changing environment of combat, lag-time could be harmful to the user as they are set upon with a variety of attacks that overwhelm a limited skill set in defense. A technique is an end in itself, a task to accomplish, then a new task is assigned based on the general 'if = then' programming of techniques. This change in the stimuli forces the user to transition to another technique in reaction to what is observed. For example, if a knife or club is introduced, the user must then access other techniques to defend against the attacker and the objects, meaning new neuropathways associated with knife defense and different motor skills. As a fight progresses the student will transition neurological pathway to pathway, techniques, motor skills and skill sets and, as they these pile up possibly develop a greater lag-time.

In a purely procedural based model, the person with the least lag-time wins.

Within Pramek, principles are utilized to develop a multi-purpose tool mindset. A deflection is a matter of physics or mechanical principles as opposed to a technique. In Pramek, a deflection is a physical outcome of a principle, such as a wedge or screw, used in the defense. It is a deflection, for use anytime, not just in reaction to technique W, D, or Z being observed. The user applies the principle to the incoming attack based on what it is within the laws of physics, which means a beginning point, a delivery system, and a weapon, which has a trajectory and target. Whether they use a screw or a wedge or an inclined plane the result is the same: deflection, or as the adage reads, 'miss by an inch, miss by a mile.' A deflection is just a result of the student's action using a principle and brings the student close to their goal instead of a technique that must be used, repeated to develop an 'if=then' response.'

Another way to view this is looking at the perception of what is being accomplished, or what the goal is. The goal is not the deflection, or technique X, instead the goal is to not get hit and have the incoming strike not impact a target. If the goal is to not get hurt, does one have to repeat a technique 5,000 times when learning how a deflection works, or will it accomplish the same task if they create a deflection with the body? The result is the same: not getting hit by the strike. The difference is that one method requires 5,000 movements and that movement may not be correct depending on how the strike occurs; the other method requires the student to understand a principle and then utilize the principle. The student should not worry about what kind of strike is occurring, just to worry about making sure it does not reach its target. In this method the student's 5,000 movements can be experience and scenario based instead of procedural repetition based.

I know it may seem I've oversimplifying it…but are you overcomplicating it?

CLM, the EPL process requires a paradigm shift for the student.

The student takes the concept behind, for example, a screw, then utilizes it in a defensive movement, and then adapts the principle as need be. Adaptation allows the student, regardless of the attack or the weapon being used, to incorporate the principles of the screw to address the incoming attack. This method differs from a technique which would seek to address each individual attack or weapon. After experience, instead of rote repetition, a student could use a wedge to defend against a strike, then a knife, and then a stick in quick succession and without knowing what the incoming attack and weapon will be. In other martial arts, the students would have to stop, prepare for a knife attack scenario, and then use a technique against the knife attack. If a stick is brought in, or the attacker switches back to a fist, the defense must be reset to address different techniques. Pramek sees few differences between the fist and the stick - only a matter of principle application.

Conceptual Learning

EPL allows the student to look at the reason behind what they are doing and understand their goal? Technique is replaced by working toward the reason they are there in the first place – a throw, versus making the opponent kinematically fall. Those complexities that make up a larger unit have concepts behind them, and instead of techniques the student examines concepts.

Think for a moment on mathematical equations. When taught procedure, the student learns to identify problems and then use an equation to solve the problem. In this example, a procedure would be to subtract, multiply, or divide to solve the equation. Mathematics is looked upon as a set of procedures to solve problems. This is vastly different than the concept behind subtraction or division. This is best explained as taking items and putting them on paper through writing, versus putting physical items on a table. Conceptually, imagine demonstrating subtracting 1 from 4 by writing an equation versus taking a table out and removing one of the 4 legs. These methods are well known in classrooms throughout the world when dealing with mathematics with such a record of success, Pramek applies them to retaining overall memory of perceptual methods.

The procedure of division is different than the concept of division. Division is an action, think of the example of the table above, as opposed to a procedure on paper. While procedures fade, concepts do not as we utilize concepts in our everyday lives, from recipes requiring mathematics or basic problems in a corporate or work environment. Think of multiplication tables you used in school – versus multiplication you use in measurements in cooking or in construction. Consider solving paper equations versus dividing up gifts based on recipients, magazines, and holsters to personnel, or working on a conveyor belt removing items in the sorting process. The physical concept outweighs the paper procedure when it comes to realization of division.

The term, Efficient Perceptual Learning, is based on the need to efficiently educate a student in a rapid manner without the use of motor patterns which take time, schema, and training. Principle based learning creates a concept, such as the wedge. The student learns to accomplish a result, the lever instead of the complex joint lock, which is the goal of martial art if it is viewed through the prism of survival.

It is commonplace in martial art schools to hear someone say, 'Hold on, let me remember how to do this throw' as opposed to moving toward the goal of removal of equilibrium. Understanding concepts does not take up neuro pathways in the same manner that techniques do as they are stored differently in the brain. Retraining movement to be biomechanically and kinematically efficient in nature accesses different parts of the brain for autonomous action separate than strikes or complex throws because these become nervous system habits, as opposed to neurological pathways developed through procedural based learning. By understanding the concepts behind combat and principles that govern these concepts, students are not able to 'forget,' they use their movement to achieve a goal, which is governed by a principle.

Technique-less martial art

When a 'technique-less martial art' is discussed in contemporary discussion, most of the time it is discussed within the confines of a movement based learning method. Students copy a teacher's movement and then begin to mimic it. Sometimes they learn new movements, or modify existing ones, to assist in the effort behind this movement based art. This is common in arts where the instructor was not taught the full physical meaning, such as mechanics, behind what they are teaching so they parrot what they have learned and work toward creating reasoning where reasoning may not exist. This is procedural based learning, as students see a technique in the cognitive sense, and then begin motor pattern repetition in the associative phase to mimic the teacher. After enough feedback and repetition within training the student begins to aesthetically appear the same as the movement based instructor.

In Pramek, it is important to remember there is no 'wrong' or 'right', only efficient, and inefficient and whether the effort has achieved its goal. The movement based training style is inefficient, meaning it does not reinforce large motor patterns through repeatable motor patterns, nor does it engage fine motor controls systematically to create autonomous methods. The student is only mimicking movement, which while removing technique, it reinforces that which creates technique: repeatedly rehearsed motor patterns but many times without purpose or organization a student can follow.

This is not the same as the idea of being without technique within Pramek. Our idea is based upon learning theory combined with movement, resulting in an application, conceptual knowledge, and perceptual learning processes. Throws are, in principle, removal of equilibrium first, a technique second. Grasps are a lever and mechanical connection with a fulcrum; blocks and deflections are wedges and screws and only then techniques. Techniques drive fast reactions of learned behavior to stimuli (see CLM 4) but are not the end in themselves. By perceptual we mean in identifying how to operate, develop receptors for operation, address the stimuli presented by the enemy which prevent achieving the goal, and then if need be use those stimuli to address the goal. Over time, the perceptual changes become second nature, or assimilated, and become an adaptation.

The student becomes conceptualized.

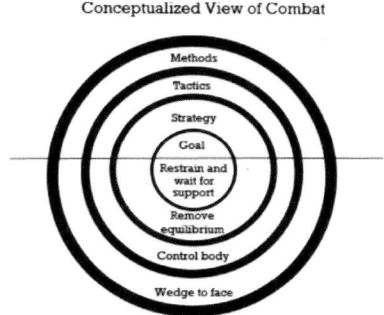

Conceptualized View of Combat

Through conceptualization we can change the way the student looks at the world and what was once complex. In conceptualization, combat develops a structure and a path toward a goal. But, for procedurally based students, combat can still be seen as complex, requiring the use of techniques to address other techniques or momentary adaptations accomplished through movement. Often, this is reflected in the 'I don't know how it happened' comment after a technique combination that has not been taught or seen before. At first, we can see performance decline, as they attempt to address the environment perceptually, to look at a goal and base our decision making process on the goal, and not base our goal on the decision making process.

If left to its own devices the brain can often spin out of control in thought and the possibilities of what 'may' occur. Think of sitting quietly in a room and how hard it is at first to meditate – now add in combat. So, why would we allow control by this unfocused brain in combat when it could think up associatively ineffective techniques to use and what might happen with infinite possibilities. Instead, we can stop, decide a goal, and put the brain to work on how to achieve the goal using what it knows. At this time, it becomes valuable to understand the difference between procedural and perceptual and how they can work in unison for a student.

The Cone of Experience

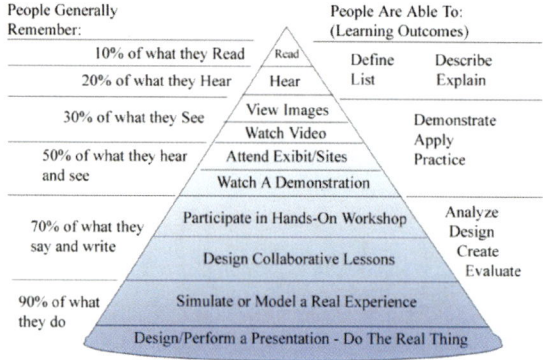

Dale's Cone of Experience

Graphic courtesy of University of Alberta

http://www2.education.ualberta.ca/staff/olenka.Bilash/best%20of%20bilash/dalescone.html

As one looks at the difference between perception and procedure, 'how' the student learns plays a strong role in how information is absorbed. The above diagram, based upon Edgar Dale's 'Cone of Experience,' was created to show various learning methods, and how much is remembered based upon the learning method. The cone was devised to show how each level, from reading to performing, builds upon the other, and each level is rarely exclusive. As discussed in depth in the CLM section The Teacher and the Student, students will fit into learning profiles, those being visual, auditory, or tactile profiles. Individuals learn differently from each other - some by hearing, some by doing, some by seeing, and some are a mix. Using Dale's 'Cone of Experience' in this chart, we see that each learning profile has its own strengths and weaknesses, and they build upon each other. Within teaching and learning combatives, one should remember that just because they are doing something does not mean what they are doing is working or realistic.

Which would seem to be more practical in combatives training? Reading a book, or physically performing a task? It would seem the physically performing the task. But, if a student reads something so powerful that a student need only use that knowledge to win a fight then, in terms of the 'Cone of Experience', 10% is incredibly powerful. For example, reading about how to distract the eye using psychology and strike the vagus nerve…and effective 10%. This 10% is in opposition to presenting 90% of the time, such as breaking boards with one's head. Such skill has little to do with the ability to win a fight consistently, but it is activity of performing. Activity does not always translate into productivity.

Just because one is being taught a theory or a technique does not mean it is effective. One must temper their knowledge with practicality and realism. This is where it is important to engage the eyes, ears, and hands in training. One can see the theory, hear the explanations, and then develop experience in hands on practice, combining all levels of the 'Cone of Experience' in their combative training. This is the key to conceptualization. There is much to be learn in books, which can refine movement and fighting skill, and then the 90% to remember because is much more effective. This is how students move from procedure to conceptualization, as they see that if one makes the above about a goal, instead of about a technique, the training is sound. The purpose would be correct, and knowledge read, heard, seen, and done becomes that much more powerful.

The Two Directions

In EPL, the student is taught in two directions: the science behind what creates an application, and the science behind efficient movement. We accomplish this through the Pramek Basic Combative Concepts (BCB) curriculum. Once the student learns these concepts, they understand why humans move the way they do. They understand what mechanical couples and machines are created in combat or in interaction with the environment. The student understands the weaknesses of the body and the overall strategy of combat or application of force. They learn the laws of biomechanics, kinematics, as well as physiology. Understanding the systems of the body (muscular, skeletal, respiratory, circulatory, neurological, nervous, etc.), the student is shown how to combine these systems together to create efficient movement. The respiratory system is coordinated with the muscular and skeletal systems, while the neurological is engaged to control the nervous system. In combining and coordinating these systems of the body, the student can integrate the systems into accomplishing goals. For example, the student may use the respiratory system to control the circulatory system and conserve energy when cold, or the student may use the respiratory system and nervous system in coordination with the muscular and skeletal to project a stronger, more forceful striking movement.

The student will be continuously learning efficient movement while learning only sections of the theoretical basis behind Pramek. The student should be learning to move efficiently and function efficiently; while concurrently learning the concept behind removal of equilibrium or a grab release, which is a lever. At higher levels, an example may be joint physiology and the physics based 'machines of mechanical destruction' to create a joint immobilization method. Over time the student begins to see combat not as strikes, but as mechanical interactions and outcomes based upon mechanical coupling or manipulation of an enemy's psychology or physiology. The student moves beyond technique and then uses efficient movement to achieve their goal.

☐

Getting to Conceptualized, or,'1.'

Pramek EPL

$$\left(\begin{array}{l} \text{Attention Weighting} \\ \text{Imprinting} \\ \text{Differentiation} \end{array} \right) + \text{Unitization} = \text{Conceptulization} \quad \text{'1'}$$

With procedural based learning, students must identify a threat, decide of how to defend themselves, and then utilize techniques that do so. With enough motor repetition, techniques will be utilized which are practiced as the student has been exposed to identifying a stimulus. An example of a stimulus may be an extended arm, giving the students a chance to move from side control to an arm bar. This is typical in sport fighting, as the interactions are controlled in a well-lit, timed environment.

In reality-based combat, this is rarely the case. A student must make a threat determination, then use gross motor patterns to defend against an attack or initiate the attack and overwhelm the enemy. This requires large amount of bioenergy and is governed by range of motion and general strength. A determining factor, as we have seen, is autonomous access to neuro pathways, or how many techniques the person has access to between the associative phase and the autonomous phase. Should the person be overcome by an advantaged opponent (which is common in female vs. male or malnourished third world combatant vs. nourished first world soldier), the disadvantaged lose at the most basic of levels. While this may be reality in many decisions, in Pramek, leaving the survival of the organism up to luck, number of techniques, or body size and stature is unacceptable. It is this idea of unacceptability in methods of self-defense that is the parent of the EPL process.

The EPL goal is to expose the student to as many stimuli over time to get to 'one,' where the student no longer recognizes technique, emotion, or attack style by an opponent. At the 'one,' or conceptualization, the combat which was originally techniques, emotions, styles, etc., are one single unit addressed by the means of principle and goal accomplishment, versus a prolonged battle to accomplish the goal. This is a long-term process of training. With procedural based learning, it is motor repetition to get the student to the autonomous phase. With EPL, the goal is exposure to events, both static and dynamic, to expose the student to a variety of scenarios in which theory may be applied.

Chapter 5. How to Teach EPL - The Training Stages

It seems like we have covered everything but putting this into the training room. EPL is about distinguishing the distractions of combat to get to the root goal of combat and then accomplish this goal. Thus, the training stages are geared toward selecting a goal and then working toward that goal in a progressive, understandable path. The training stages are specifically designed to take a student from no knowledge to full knowledge without wasting time. After these lessons are learned then other subject matters could become the topic of the EPL - but for the beginning stages, the goal is the simplest means of surviving.

Survival. It is important to remember this phrase, the training method, refers to the previously mentioned Pramek BCB. While this is Pramek specific, any art can use this method to educate students or to hone skills. In many cases, one should utilize their own goal in a fight, such as pulling to the guard or a single leg pick up, and then place this within the training stages of EPL. EPL is as universal as a wedge or human equilibrium. Like anything else in Pramek, if a 'theory' cannot be quantified by knowledge found in a book in a library or classroom in a university, then it is avoided until it can be quantified, or students advance in their ability to draw correlation between something not quantifiable with its applicability. For example, to many chiropractic science or acupuncture is not certifiable medical science, but this does not mean they are not applicable. The student must draw a correlation between applicability and scientific knowledge. Within the EPL, Pramek BCB concepts will be used but if the reader does not know the wedge the reader should substitute their own methods and names for these methods.

Training Stage 1: Attention Weighting

In the first training step of the EPL the student must pay increasing attention to the important features and principles of their work, or Attention Weighted. By weighted we mean the student is directed to important stimuli constantly instead of momentarily. There are overarching physical and psychological stimuli, which affect combat more than others, and attention is weighted toward these principles as opposed to swinging fists and wrestling. One example of these is the removal of equilibrium. As the student begins to train using this principle, they can be guided to concentrate on focusing on the kinematics as opposed to using techniques. The primary goal in the Attention Weighting phase is to remove distraction from the student so they can work toward what is most important in the task before them.

In this process the student moves toward a singular goal and receives a positive reward under controlled training methods. This ensures the student will continue to work with such overarching principles and achieve their goal. The reward ensures the student is learning how a principle operates. The student should be allowed to focus their attention on the principle, as opposed to being concerned with resistance such as being struck, injured, or embarrassed. In the attention weighting stage, the student can succeed at first with minimal interruption from their training partner other than light, non-forceful attacks.

It is during this time the ability to learn is in a flexible state. Considered 'perceptual plasticity,' the student can make correct and incorrect decisions based on achievement of their goal and come back to their basic core principles as a base to work from. This is in opposition to a technique, which can be executed correctly or incorrectly as determined by a coach or the experience. The perceptual plasticity state differs between these two methods...one is based on experience in situations and one is based on the experience in doing a technique 'correctly'. In procedural based learning, if the movement pattern is incorrect, or the motor repetition is changed, the student can have a larger gap between correct and incorrect technique due to repetition.

Imagine for a moment teaching someone how to eat with a fork, and then after a few days putting objects on their plate they cannot penetrate, then teaching them a different way to hold the fork. Technique based training is often no different. If the motor repetitions are substantially altered, the student can be affected detrimentally or develop a hybrid between correct and incorrect motor patterns to accomplish tasks. An example of this is common in a kicker who was never taught to pivot their foot on the base leg. While this may seem simple, it is the first sign of a properly educated kicker. After thousands of repetitions the student's base instruction can still be seen. To correct this is not a long process, as the body has most of the correct mechanics, but the student will still have to complete hundreds of repetitions to program this. Depending on the age and willingness of the student, this may never alter to the generally correct method of kicking with a pivoted based foot.

Perceptual plasticity is different, as it ties the student to correct or incorrect outcomes based on the experience and the reward, versus the motor repetition. A student who works to remove equilibrium (as opposed to performing one throw) 1,000 times in various scenarios will find numerous ways to remove equilibrium while programming few motor patterns, which are the result of positive feedback from the training experience. This student once trained with basic defensive principles against strikes and kicks will be much more effective in combat than a student who has taken the same amount of time doing single kick repetitions improperly. It is the plasticity, or the ability to bounce back, of the perceptual learning method that allows a student to explore the principles. Simultaneously the student can stay away from motor repetitions of technique that will be limited by a limited number of neuro-pathways. These pathways should be utilized for imprinting, which will be described as developing shortcuts.

This plasticity adapts the usage of the principle by the student to the tasks at hand. The student must look at larger principles, such as removal of equilibrium, breaking the structure of the spine, and damaging the internal support structure of the body instead of strikes or roundhouse kicks. Strikes and roundhouse kicks are procedurally based techniques, not overarching principles. This is not to say these techniques cannot be figured into employing principles in combat, such as a knock-out or concussion. If this is the goal of the student, then the student should be trained on the physiology of a knock-out and then trained to attack the physiology using a strike or a kick. This is a far cry from teaching someone to strike for the sake of striking. Other examples of principles are the application of the six machines of mechanical efficiency; impact and shock concepts; open vs. closed structure, etc.

In EPL the student should look at the overall principles and patterns they utilize in combat. First, the student should be educated on ICM's, or 'Initial Combative Movements'. ICMs are a stance and initial projection of force against the student such as a strike or kick. The student must learn to 'read,' but not be distracted, by these ICMs as they are attaining their primary goal. Stimuli which are unimportant to achieving the goal are considered 'DS,' or 'Distracting Stimuli.' Distracting stimuli, the most common example being feints, can often be skipped or not addressed as they are unimportant. While feints have a place in sport, in high paced reality based combat, boxing style-feints have little effectiveness and are an example of DS.

ICMs are filled with DS and the student should learn to differentiate the two. An example of an ICM may be bringing both hands up to form fists and then widening the feet. The ICM will provide the student access to an opening to achieve their goal. The hands have no bearing on equilibrium, but the wide feet positioning does, thus one is a DS and one is not in terms of the goal of the student. If the goal is the removal of equilibrium, then the student must decide to work against the points of friction with the ground, the foot position, which will force movement from the opponent. This foot position will lead to more openings for attack and not limit the options of the student. The student will start to focus on what is important (foot position) versus what is not (hands at the ready), as opposed to procedural based learning, which would teach the student to assume a stance and prepare to fist fight. Attention weighting drives the student to instead focus on their goal.

When the student decides what course of action to take, they are operating at a higher level than someone who's body reacts to create a course of action. It is a matter of importance versus unimportance and the weight of the student's attention should be placed, in this stage, upon those stimuli that are important, such as moving the center mass outside of the load bearing area, as opposed to those which are not, such as round house kicks.

In teaching class, examples of goals should be broken down into topics to ease learning and allow the student to weight attention. In this stage, these goals should be recommended so that limited distracting stimuli are recognized, and the student can focus on these particular stimuli and the reactions they create, and then focus on the principles at hand which utilize the scenarios to train to effectively use a principle.

Here are some common examples of goals within the Pramek BCB:

- Psychology - distraction, use of emotional intelligence
- Mechanics - levers within grasps, screw movements, wedge movements
- Physics - open vs. closed structures, point fixing, force coupling,
- Physiology/ Nervous Reaction - vital points (eyes, groin, throat)

A student must also realize that sometimes the stimuli are not external, but internal based on previous experiences. A student should work through these internal stimuli (like a flinch or a tendency to make a previously injured arm rigid) and understand they can be in control if they weight their attention on a goal and work toward it using their movement. The student must continue to work toward movement efficiently, developing and recognizing schema, and working toward what should be demonstrated as the most effective use of attention weighting and goal attainment. The primary purpose of the attention weighting stage is noticing goals and working within a demonstrated pattern to achieve the goal.

Speed and Tension within EPL

Beginning with the attention weighting stage, impact and speed must be addressed. Eventually in later stages the student will be faced with high speed and high impact attacks. In the attention weighting stage, the student is learning a vital concept...to pay attention to the goal at hand and the strategy they have chosen to achieve their goal despite light resistant stimuli. Often referred to as 'soft work' or 'lite rolling' in other systems, this stage should be varied in speed with a particular focus on slow speed and light impact. The student should not be concerned with high speed or high impact from the beginning as this will force the student to pay attention to stimuli instead of goals. This will take place under subsequent training stages, which will be addressed in the Directed Perceptual Testing, or DPT, section of this book. In this phase speed should vary with the needs of the training and their attention. Speed in training should vary from Low ($> = 25\%$) to High ($> = 75\%$).

The most important aspect of this type of speed training is development of attention to goals. The student can observe the situation in slow motion, and then able to look for their goals. When the student is put into slow speed training, the focus is on mechanics and attention to goals. The student should not be overwhelmed with distracting stimuli (strikes, kicks, etc.) at high speeds. The speed should be slow so that the student can pay attention to their goal and move toward their goal using the principles they have learned.

Both the student and training partner should be moving at the same speed relative to each other. This should be completed with a few speed tests, working from slow to the agreed pace so that both understand the speed at which to work. This can be done in a progression, or the two can agree on what speed and then begin at this speed. At no point, unless agreed upon, should the students work at disadvantaged speed. This will take place in other areas of training. The overall purpose is the attention to goals, not how fast can one move or defend.

In this stage, it is acceptable for the student to use rudimentary, natural, or prior martial art experience, to address the incoming attacks while working toward a goal. A student should not be told 'correct' or 'incorrect.' The student should have their goal and work toward that goal only while paying minimal attention to incoming attacks…to see what is happening and make decisions based on their goal and not the defense except for minimal methods of defense.

The student begins to learn in this stage, at this speed, that incoming attacks are not as important as the goal. If one can step to the side of an attack and remove the equilibrium or execute a sweep or gain the side and move to a rear choke, then why spend large amounts of time defending against DS. If a method or technique is repeatedly unable to achieve the goal, it should not be executed, as it will only waste the time of the student in terms of learning.

Training Stage 2: Imprinting

Imprinting is the repeated testing of the weighting stage so that a student develops individual methods of addressing combative interaction. As the student progresses through the attention weighting stage and gains experience, receptors or actions develop that are specialized for stimuli or parts of stimuli. In using the term receptors, we are referring to the tactile, visual, auditory, and nervous system. The student is taught methods and sees examples of applications or movement within the attention-weighting phase. In imprinting the student begins to make such applications their own.

As the student becomes familiar with the various principles and their own movement, they will develop their own methods of how to do it. As opposed to techniques, which through motor learning develop neuro pathways, imprinting allows access to a means of applying principles their own way to the whole of combative interaction, versus a technique for a specific method. When the student enters the imprinting stage, they recognize methods that will operate effectively, perform tasks, and achieve their goal.

Obviously, there are situations where a lever or wedge is much more applicable than a wheel and axle, and sometimes affecting the psychology of the enemy will work best. In the imprinting stage, the student begins to recognize these methods and develops receptors to begin making principles work on a consistent basis based on their own movement and employment. An example of this would be a student consistently rotating a training partner to affect equilibrium, as opposed to pulling the opponent and attempting to trip them. The rotation affects all three planes of human movement and directs the center mass outside of the load bearing area, as opposed to a pull and trip, which would affect only two planes of movement. As the student becomes more proficient with the principle, they can be educated on the methods of applying their theory against different styles, stances, or in defensive and offensive movements.

Imprinting is primarily about experience over a period and number of scenarios. The student will begin to address the distractions ignored within the attention-weighting phase; as opposed to the associative phase of procedural based learning is centered on motor pattern repetition. The imprinting stage of perceptual learning, which is based upon exposure to scenarios to develop experience. Through exposure, as well as positive and negative feedback, the student will have more experiences upon which to draw. Addressing distracting stimuli, with this experience receptors and actions are born, both reactive and proactive. The student moves, the theory and the application become their own versus copying a teacher or repeating a movement with purpose.

With this in mind the training should focus on using high numbers of scenarios, angles of attack, variety of training partners, etc., to create more experience within which receptors will form and the student will better imprint their own methods of utilizing principles and theory through their movement to create an application. As the reader, consider this methodology as opposed to showing the student a technique and asking them to repeat it over and over in the motor repetition of the associative phase.

It is important to recognize that generally accepted forms of combat fighting should be used to begin an imprinting scenario. Put simply, if a student has an extremely low likelihood of facing an opponent that uses a rare art, the student should not be exposed to that rare art. Additionally, distracting stimuli should be used that the student should have to address in reality. In attention-weighting the student ignores an incoming punch as much as possible, maybe even take the punch to an extent, to achieve the goal. Now, in the Imprinting phase, the student should defend against the punch.

While students will work to achieve their goal through principle, they will create what is considered 'feature imprinting'. They will become familiar and recognize certain features of methods of attacks. This should be encouraged and pointed out. With a group or instructor, consistent weaknesses in certain attacks should be explored. An example would be a kicker who does not pivot their base foot as opposed to one who does. The base foot on a front roundhouse kick is a feature of that kick and should be noted. The students will develop, through their own means, or through guidance by the instructor or group, how to attack this feature and it will become part of their method of, in this example, addressing kicks. Another example may be a lead hand for a boxer that allows the student to grab and manipulate it, or wedge past it. Such features of many accepted fighting methods of opponents should be features the student can develop receptors around, giving the student an acceptable short cut to get to their goal.

The primary goal of imprinting is to test the lessons learned in attention-weighting. In attention-weighting, the student has a goal and works toward that goal in the manner they are shown, while having lite to medium speed DS come at them. The student then ignores the DS and works toward the goal. Imprinting is about doing this over and over, gaining experience, developing an individual method of utilizing principles methods, learning features of DS, defending against DS. Imprinting is internalizing the lessons of attention-weighting and using experience to reinforce the ability to work toward the goal.

During imprinting, each scenario offers a chance for the student to gain experience and develop their own methods of dealing with opponents. The student should place a premium on efficient movement and effective end-results. The moment the student becomes engaged in other tasks, like drills, the period should be stopped and brought back to the beginning, so the student keeps their goal in mind.

Development of ICM's while Imprinting

One primary goal in this stage is to work with the student to develop basic methods to use which will act as short cuts to the goal. There is no reason for a student to get into a boxing match if their goal is to gain mechanical advantage and control the opponent through a joint-lock or a choke. The student most likely at this point have developed personal ICM's to deploy, as experience has taught them some methods and stances work better than others. This is an example of why experience in imprinting is important: the student learning from trying a variety of stances, ICM's, defenses, hand placements. Experience in imprinting, when done properly and for the student's benefit, allows the student to find their own way and not copy the way of the teacher. As the axiom says, 1 tool for 10 jobs, with ICM's and imprinting the student is developing their individual tool. A student's experience will assist in developing their own ICM's, for example, to achieve an initial goal, act as a means of defense, or create openings to the enemy.

An example of this is to educate the student on an ICM that attacks the eyes while using a wedge or screw, and then working toward their goal. At this stage, the student can develop procedural motor patterns through experience. One challenge with procedural techniques is they are designed around an art which has created these techniques to address another technique. There is a pitfall here, as the student must not be allowed to experience the same attack or defenses too many times as they begin to falsely rely on one ICM, which becomes a technique. Instead, the student should view stimuli as over-arching. The student's ICM should be a method that performs a task, such as preventing an incoming attack (ex., through stopping or disrupting an attack), accomplishing a secondary goal (ex., blinding an attacker while using the wedge to defend themselves), and then moving to their primary goal (ex., gaining mechanical advantage to affect a joint lock). This is one movement that addresses multiple issues confronting the student and is offensive and defensive in its nature.

In closing, within the imprinting stage, the student will develop these ICM's on their own through experience – a proper teacher should guide them and educate them on what they are experiencing, and work with the student to show them what they are not seeing.

Training Stage 3: Differentiation

Let's review. In the attention weighting and imprinting stages, the student is educated about their primary goals and overall strategy. The student in those stages moved from achieving a goal to addressing limited distracting stimuli in the path to their goal. Once the student can achieve their goal while addressing limited distractions, the student moves into the differentiation stage. Now it's time for a new phase, differentiation.

In the differentiation stage, distracting stimuli that were once whole and fused become separated. In this phase, the student can be focused to differentiate the distractions from their primary goals in combat.

- Strikes (DS) become separated from equilibrium (goal)
- Kicks (DS) become separated from throws (goal).
- Words used to excite the emotional responses (DS) are separated from a screwing movement to the face (goal).

Most martial art students view combat as the techniques being used, instead of the goal they wish to achieve. This is the cognitive stage of procedural learning taking over as the student seeks to develop association between the techniques and the goal. The techniques are obvious, but the goal is subtle. In our view, many of these techniques are not of consequence to the student if they wish to achieve a goal, like removal of equilibrium.

The techniques being used are not the goal.

The goal is the goal.

The goal being the goal is the 'why' in Pramek's EPL differential stage. This stage works to show the student that other methods are distractions from their primary goal and how to address these stimuli to get to their goal.

Differentiation training should be used in a progressive manner. First, the student must be put through complex engagements to test their imprinting, which is whole stimulus differentiation. The student should pick a goal, then work toward the goal while being confronted with a variety of stimuli. This should be completed at varying speeds, from 25% to 75% relative speed. This should be done repeatedly as explained within the DPT as stress and fatigue training. As the student comes under a variety of attacks, they will develop internal obstacles, and the opponent will create external obstacles, to their goal. Now that we know the structure, let's look at some category training based on general movement patterns.

These categories are as follows:

- *Long range: strikes, jabs, kicks, swiping or jabbing movements with a knife, spitting, throwing objects, etc.*
- *Medium Range: elbows, crosses and hooks, repeated jabbing movements with a knife, knees, stomps, attempts at joint manipulation, extended arm chokes*
- *Close Range: elbows, shoulder strikes, upper cuts, close rapid thrusting movements with a knife, hip tosses, single and double leg take-downs, headlocks, joint locks, close range chokes*

The instructor should categorize stimuli then the student addresses the stimuli based on principles and methods that have been learned. Problems and obstacles within the training session should be categorized down so the student can see the differentiation between DS and their primary goal. Once a student has shown proficiency in how to address defensive and offensive applications through principles under varying speeds, the student should be retested in whole stimuli sessions. This will be a repeated training cycle, as the student shows an inability to deal with various attacks and must be brought back to categorized training to look at their goal and work with the stimuli to achieve the goal.

At certain points, 'paralysis of analysis' can overwhelm a student. A student will develop a sense of frustration and will analyze what is happening, creating complexities in categories while forgetting their primary goal. This is what happens in real life combat, as 'plans' go out of the proverbial window. The goal must be the same as the attention weighted stage - the universal concepts that govern combat and human movement and targeting these. A teacher must be aware in this process. When a student begins to over-analyze troublesome stimuli, they will look for one solution that works or at least functions consistently. Regardless of effectiveness, when this scenario occurs, the student will become stressed and fatigued and will often time attempt to develop a technique. The training partner must also be watched and not allowed to 'let the guy win' because they feel uncomfortable with the stress or fatigue their training partner is undergoing. They must be honest with their partner about whether something works or does not. A lack of being candid will lead both partners to develop motor repetitions due to the feedback loop when something works repeatedly.

Is this bad?

Is it 'correct' or 'incorrect'?

If the method or technique is unrealistic and cannot function under medium speed testing, it is not bad as much as mechanically incorrect and defeats the purpose of the use of adaptable principles. The method developing would be unreliable or unrealistic. If the student develops a consistently effective method of addressing this issue, one that works repeatedly against different people, then it should be allowed to pass – it is an adaptation. If it is based in frustration and is unrealistic, it must be stopped. To address this, first the student should be brought back into whole stimuli stage and the trouble stimuli should not be used. This will enable the student to feel accomplishment and receive positive feedback to alleviate psychological frustration. In other words, if the student is always getting caught with the uppercut during the takedown, remove the uppercut, get everything else right, then come back and address the upper cut – in other words, differentiate between the take-down and the upper-cut defense. Do not allow the upper-cut defense to become the take-down method instruction because the student is frustrated. This kind of scenario should also be avoided because the teacher is frustrated with their own level of instruction – just because the student is frustrated doesn't mean the instruction is bad. Move back to the EPL, look at what is happening mechanically, change things up, move on and come back a month later to overcome initial frustration.

Once a student has overcome their frustration, they should be redirected to the stimuli which posed a psychological and physical obstacle to the student's progression. At this point the student should be placed into a slower speed training stage that will allow the student to understand the principals involved within the category. 25% to 50% relative speed is the optimal speed for this training level. This speed leads to learning various short cuts (such as hooks instead of grabs). A student may see, as the opponent works slowly, that one form of methods and application is better in the circumstance.

As the student begins to adapt to these stimuli the speed can increase, or other stimuli can be introduced. An example may be combinations of punches. The student may become adept at working against three punches at speed, but the fourth or a knee may pose a problem. It is best to back down to differentiate between what needs to be addressed and what does not. We cannot emphasize this enough: do not let a problem become a drill that distracts from the goal, as the drill will become the goal. The goal is the goal. If a student is 6'6' tall, defense against long range attacks may not be a focus as this student will most likely outrange most opponents and attackers will attempt to close to medium or clinch range or affect take downs. This should become the focus. Certain categories may be given more emphasis than other categories, long vs short, which may not even be of consequence if the student has their attention on one goal. Another example may be that a particular stance may make the need to defend against long-range attacks become irrelevant because the student can attack their goal from the onset.

Take a moment here – reread what was just written. CLM is about the goal, the why, the reason behind activity. There is an ever-present tendency to work against what the other person will do, to trade punches or kicks, to wrestle when the other person wants to wrestle. This is often because students learn techniques to address other techniques. Students become distracted by stimuli and address those stimuli using trained technique - instead of using principles to work to their goal. When there is a reliance upon technique and drills, the student can become easily engaged in drill reproduction and technique matching, instead of working toward the goal. A high-level enemy will know this and play to this weakness brought on by procedural based learning.

A high-level enemy, someone who fights to live instead of fights for fun – the robber, the mugger, the enemy soldier, the saboteur – they can 'feint' their way to victory.

The student in the differentiation stage must be able to identify their goal, then recognize and quickly categorize stimuli. This is the categorization of what is dangerous and will cause great damage as opposed to what is ineffectively projected at them and will cause little damage. One example of this would be that feints should be recognized and categorized as not dangerous but what they produce (a follow up strike that is unexpected) should be prepared for. In this, the feint can be skipped, even attacked, and the incoming attack preempted.

Priority must be placed on differentiating between these stimuli, their goal, and the work needed for the goal while minimally addressing the distracting stimuli. This may seem a strange stage, but it is best tested by asking a student, unbeknownst to their training partner, to touch the left ear of the partner while their partner attacks them. 'Touch their ear' is a common refrain in Pramek. It's a goal, a small goal, a micro-goal – but it's a goal and a focal point in the confusion of combat. Give the student a goal and the student will see how quickly they can achieve a goal by moving around the stimuli and just focusing on their goal. This is the goal of the differentiation phase – to differentiate between distraction and goal, understand the nature of the distraction, and work past the distractions to the goal.

Training Stage 4: Unitization

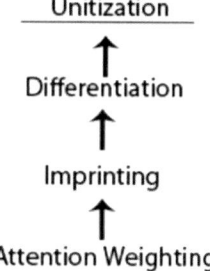

Pramek EPL

Perceptual Learning

Unitization

↑

Differentiation

↑

Imprinting

↑

Attention Weighting

The concept of no technique, being formless, or being constantly adaptive seems to be the perfect state of martial art practice. From the Chinese masters to Bruce Lee, an Alexei Kadochnikov, the rare modern UFC fighters, and professional boxers – those special practitioners where being without techniques is often view as the highest form of martial art. Candidly this is an abstract concept rarely understood, much less achieved. It is for wall posters and reserved for those moments that make on-looker's and students gasp at mastery, when luck, combined with technique and an accident sometimes combine to create something that looks like it was created from thin air. Or it is the combination of associative understanding of so many styles and techniques that the procedural regurgitation seems to be so seamless as to be combining so many arts and methods the practitioner appears to be without technique. 'Formless', or 'technique-less' is a goal, to be as formless and adaptive as possible – it is that rare state of just 'being' in the fight, neither acting nor reacting, just doing all the right things to win.

In Pramek's CLM, the concept of the 'absence of technique' acts as a catalyst for the student to accomplish a goal, instead of worrying about which associative or autonomous motor pattern to utilize. When Pramek states, 'Do not fight against style, fight against the human being using the style' this is shown in EPL. Throughout the training stages, the student must be educated on basic methods of defending themselves to accomplish their goal – e/affect the physics, mechanics, psychology, and physiology of the opponent.

The unitization stage, or 'getting to 1,' is where a student begins to view a complex unit as several parts. As stated, most students begin training in martial art thinking combat is a complex, overwhelming unit. Think of how the layman views his automobile. He views a car as a car, while a mechanic sees a car for its parts and how to work on each individual part...and how those parts affect the overall performance of a vehicle. The Pramek student should endeavor to look at the overall vehicle that is combative interaction, it's individual parts that make it up, and how they can be used to achieve the goal instead of their previous view of combat as complex.

Strikes are just strikes, to be used to remove equilibrium (goal).

Kicks are just kicks, to be used to remove equilibrium (goal).

Ranges are just ranges, to be used to remove equilibrium (goal).

The goal is the goal to be used toward achieving the goal.

Combat is complex, but also rather simple.

In the differentiation stage, stimuli like kicks or strikes are seen separate from a concept like equilibrium. The student learns to address these stimuli and work toward the goal. Within the unitization stage of training, the kick or strike is seen as connected to the goal. Mechanically, a fist is connected to the elbow, the upper arm, connected to the shoulders. The shoulders are connected to the center mass and the center mass is connected to the hips. The hips are connected to knees, the shins, and the feet. Within Pramek, this connectivity is viewed as stepping-stones. If the elbow is moved, then the body part connected to the elbow will move as well because no part is separate in the kinesiological chain of the body. Each of these parts is related to a range in which the student has worked with, toward a goal and a principle.

Suddenly, magically, moving the elbow just a little bit throws the opponent. Does this start to sound like formless? Does this sound like mastery?

Unitization forces the student to look at what they originally viewed combat as, techniques like strikes, kicks, etc., and see a single unit representing gaining a goal. Stimuli may be addressed within a strategy or skipped, and the end goal be worked toward. The student no longer needs to worry with specific techniques as much as choosing what end-result they wish to achieve and then work within the interaction to achieve this goal. Combat becomes unitized in nature, comprised of single pieces allowing the student to achieve specific tasks.

Within the unitization stage, the student must learn that while complex, the human machine, from the hip to the mind, is predictable in its efforts and movements connected. Telling an opponent what action will be taken can create an assumptive response in the body as the opponent registers the threat and then considers the defense. A feint can elicit a response. Throwing an item on the ground can elicit a response. In each of these scenarios a strike has never been thrown but the opponent has already lost the ICM fight. Neurology means the body will move in patterns and sometimes the body will move unconsciously, the response can be attacked.

These complex, separate units provide the ability to achieve their overall goal and adapt. This stage can be micro or macro in nature. A student may be trained to look for removal of equilibrium. An example of a student like this may be a grappler; the student's primary goal is removal of equilibrium and therefore, other categories matter little as a grappler will not use long range, but primarily medium and close range. A striker on the other hand will use strikes, and these strikes can be used to achieve the goal of removal of equilibrium. Techniques or ranges are steppingstones to achieve a goal, and not the goal themselves.

In the end of the unitized stage, the student has moved beyond procedural and perceptual knowledge of combat to a new realm of conceptual knowledge. Now they understand the concepts…but to become a better teacher, student, and practitioner, the student must gain conceptual knowledge of combat.

Stage 5: Conceptualization

As we have learned, at first, our general view of combat is confusing, if not overwhelming. The conceptualization stage is the combining all the training stages in an actional path to goal achievement. With attention weighting, the perception becomes adapted to the goal by paying attention to important stimuli, developing schema, and features of the achievement of the goal. When moving to the imprinting stage, the student develops receptors specialized to the achievement of the goal, as the student makes the method their own and uses it within their abilities physically and mentally. The student then tests their own developed methods against basic defenses and identifies the various ways that an opponent can move and use techniques to prevent them from achieving their goal.

Differentiation pushes the student to identify once indistinguishable stimuli to become separate and categorized. The student learns that they do not have to address every stimulus presented and can work toward a goal separate from the stimuli presented. Within the unitization stage, their goal is a complex configuration of movements, interactions, psychology, and other interactions they once addressed or avoided - now the student uses these to accomplish their goal.

Take a moment and reflect on the words written earlier:

In Pramek, theory + movement = application.

By understanding the theory and then moving efficiently, the student can create an application, so, for example, a student with an injured arm is no longer subject to the laws of technique and motor pattern repetition. A strike is taught from the viewpoint of projection of force and impact, targeting, and then the type of strike is developed based on the student's movement. A student can understand projection of force, impact, targeting, and biomechanics and then develop their own means of striking. A student who has not trained in throws will understand human equilibrium and force couples, and combined with understanding points of contact, can create a throw. This throw, or that strike, may be unorthodox but it will be within the abilities of the student - their understanding of theory and movement, and experience with application. Thus, the longer a student trains, the more adaptive a student becomes. Here we see the result of conceptual learning.

After the conceptual learning method, the student sees their own knowledge and movement as a means to achieve their goal. The longer a student trains the more the student will learn to adapt. The longer a student works through the imprinting stage, the more they will be able to express the principles through their movement. The more times a student is in the attention weighting stage, the more often they will be able to select an efficient, effective goal to achieve. The more times the student is within the unitization stage, the more they will learn to use the opponent's stimuli as a means to utilize their theory.

Conceptualized View of Combat

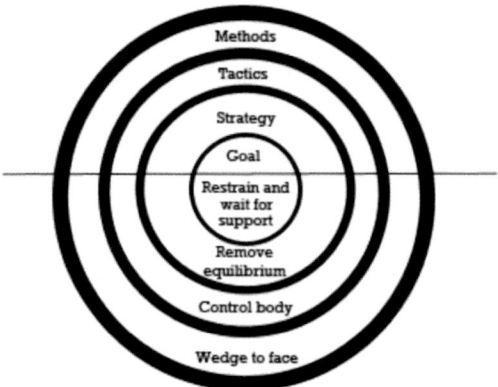

Pramek's CLM is about conceptualizing action. The conceptualized view categorizes the information and shows the student how to organize it into three steps. The student decides a 1) goal; 2) develops a strategy; and 3) uses tactics and methods to achieve that goal. Because of the BCB, they understand the nature of the psychology of violence, so it is not random. Students learn the physiology of injury so they know what they should be aware of, for example, targeted knife attack versus wildly flailing arms. The student develops a clear mind regarding approaching combat. The EPL is that it removes the unpredictability of combat through experience, altering the schema, and giving a conceptualized view of combat. Using this conceptual knowledge to control, manipulate, or change the combative interaction adaptively will allow a student to create their own tactics and methods, as opposed to being controlled by the neurology of technique.

Chapter 6. Changing the Light Bulb

Once a student has moved to the conceptualized state, the student should feel free to train with any number of scenarios and utilize their learned method of fighting. At this point the student has begun to make their own method of fighting. No, the student is not creating their own style – they are making the style their own. The student should change the variables, keeping the goal as the constant. The student should also feel comfortable taking a step back to the various phases...stepping back is not bad. No one wants to be held back a grade in school, demoted in a job or in their belt system. Often, going backward in training methods is seen as a negative.

In the EPL, going backward it is actively encouraged.

This taking a step back develops an understanding of more stimuli, schema adjustment, and new methods of achieving the goal not used before. The EPL is a safe training environment for exploration, not governed by the fear of being hit or choked out. The EPL is a light in the dark.

Conceptualization is a high state but must be viewed as an evolving, ever-growing state as the student becomes more adaptive. The student will become a better teacher within this state as they work with junior students and educate them due on what they have seen in their time in EPL. But conceptualization also means the student should have a high knowledge of combat - mechanics, movement, psychology, physiology, etc. The student may make these kinds of concepts their goal within the attention-weighting phase or employ them as a secondary goal. If a student sees a new technique, they may use the EPL to learn the technique, breaking it down, and then make it a secondary goal in addition to their usual goals.

Learning is perpetual within the EPL; each time a student thinks of a new method, they can become a student all over again. The student can make that method their focus in attention weighting, imprinting it to find their own way, then differentiating to see what filters and defenses stand in their way and get past them. A practitioner can then use these defenses to achieve the goal in the unitization phase, and reach conceptualization again and understand the concept behind this new method they thought of. There is no substitute for experience; within EPL, the experience is how conceptualization happens.

Combat is a problem-solving exercise, so training should reflect this and lead to 'light bulb moments.' The bulb will dim at first and may need replacing, or perhaps the outlet itself is out...but if there is power, and the current regulated by the teacher, the bulb will burn. When the student is attacked in higher-level EPL training, such as at a faster pace in the differentiation phase, a teacher may tell the student they must work slower than the attack. In other instances, the teacher may say the student may only use limited number of methods. As we will see later in this book sometimes, the teacher must remove themselves as a 'teacher' completely to teacher the student.

With each challenge the student is more apt to use the mind instead of the body, looking for ways in which the attacker can be manipulated in a direct manner instead of a prolonged manner. At this level, the 'thinking' part of the system is revealed, as the student must use sensitivity to address threats instead of physical force. At this level, the student is creating a hypothesis to test. While the student is analyzing the situation at a certain level, they must test applications against various attacks, and then uses the situation test it.

Our Bulb

Often, the lessons learned have little to do with survival fighting, but more with discipline...discipline by nature assists with the trials of fighting. We cannot always scenario test students to the reality of a real-life situation and some students cannot stand the rigors of repeated scenario driven training. But the student cannot be sat in a room and told to point spar the entire day and expect to advance either. When this happens, as is address later in this book, eventually boredom or frustration will form in the student's mind and the student will leave. There are so many questions in training that we are faced with: What if the student fails repeatedly? Is there a way to adjust this failure? How does one learn what their student can really take mentally?

The EPL shows us the light to find these answers – that we can learn differently and just as effectively. But the bulb that has now brightened must be tested to see if it will work. Many have heard the quote by Thomas Edison, when he said, 'I did not fail, I only found 10,000 ways that did not work.' Edison used a new kind of filament to create a longer lasting bulb, but it took time and tests, and experience to create a stronger bulb. The men before him had reached a time of nearly 14 hours for their bulb to burn bright…but Edison had models that reached 1200+ hours. He did this through trial and error. He tested the current, the filaments, the gases…everything that could be tested was tested.

The proverbial 'light bulb' above our heads in looking at aspects of the EPL must be tested, hypothesis formed, dogma shattered. Our training current must be lowered when we have had enough information and then turned on to its highest level when our spirit must be pushed to its limits. The student must be progressively broken and repaired, their knowledge assaulted, their defenses brought down not against a punch, but the defenses of the ego which tells the student they can do that which they cannot without luck…but they can learn to do with skill: survive.

Only then can we get to the nature of what survival is…solving problems.

Then we must test our perception of what of that nature is.

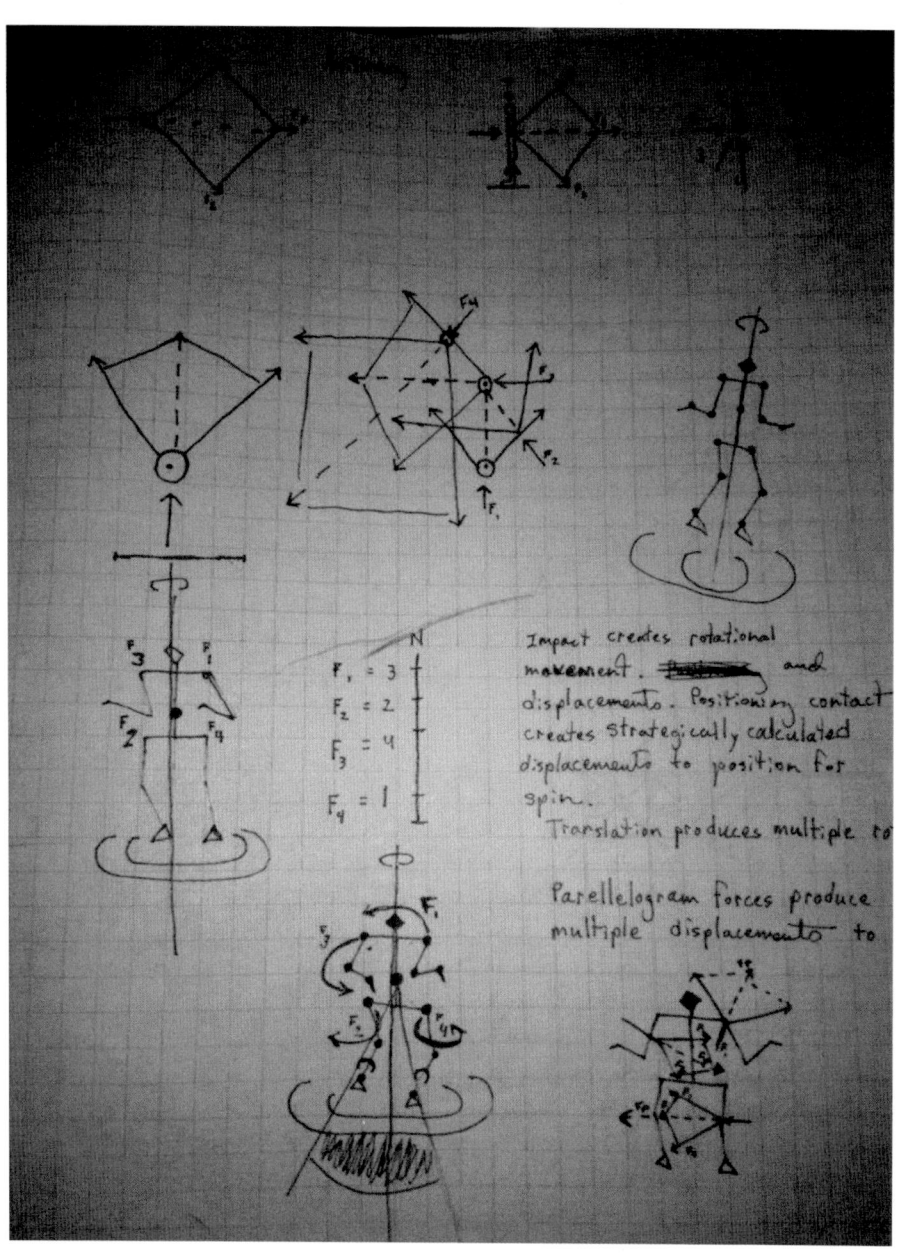

Impact creates rotational movement. ~~and~~ and displacements. Positioning contact creates strategically calculated displacements to position for spin.

Translation produces multiple to

Parellelogram forces produce multiple displacements to

$F_1 = 3$

$F_2 = 2$

$F_3 = 4$

$F_4 = 1$

Notes on human rotation

70

Bio-mech basics -
    Body as structure - w/ internal links
    Body as levers / pulleys / etc - types (bones, joints, tensile)
    Bio mech link - chain
    Open chain vs closed chain - examples

Human movement theories -
    Spatial - Space
        3 planes - movements in all 3
        0 placement in space
< Angular motion vs Linear - impulse facilitate rotation
    Rotational - fixing 3 points
    External forces & Internal forces support
    Creation of CM
    CM
    Equilibrium

Exercises - combine physical + mental
    Gen ex - physical - strength, coord, motion → Body - eye & hand
        mental - flush ca.

    Bio ex - efficient - build tensile & assimilation + coordination
        ① ROM
why   assimilate healthy + nurture +
          energy - generate & project energy
          timed, expel heat, lymph etc
    ① build up outside in, inside out comb..
    ② preserve cap libr um - 60/40...

Early notes on the basics of biomechanics

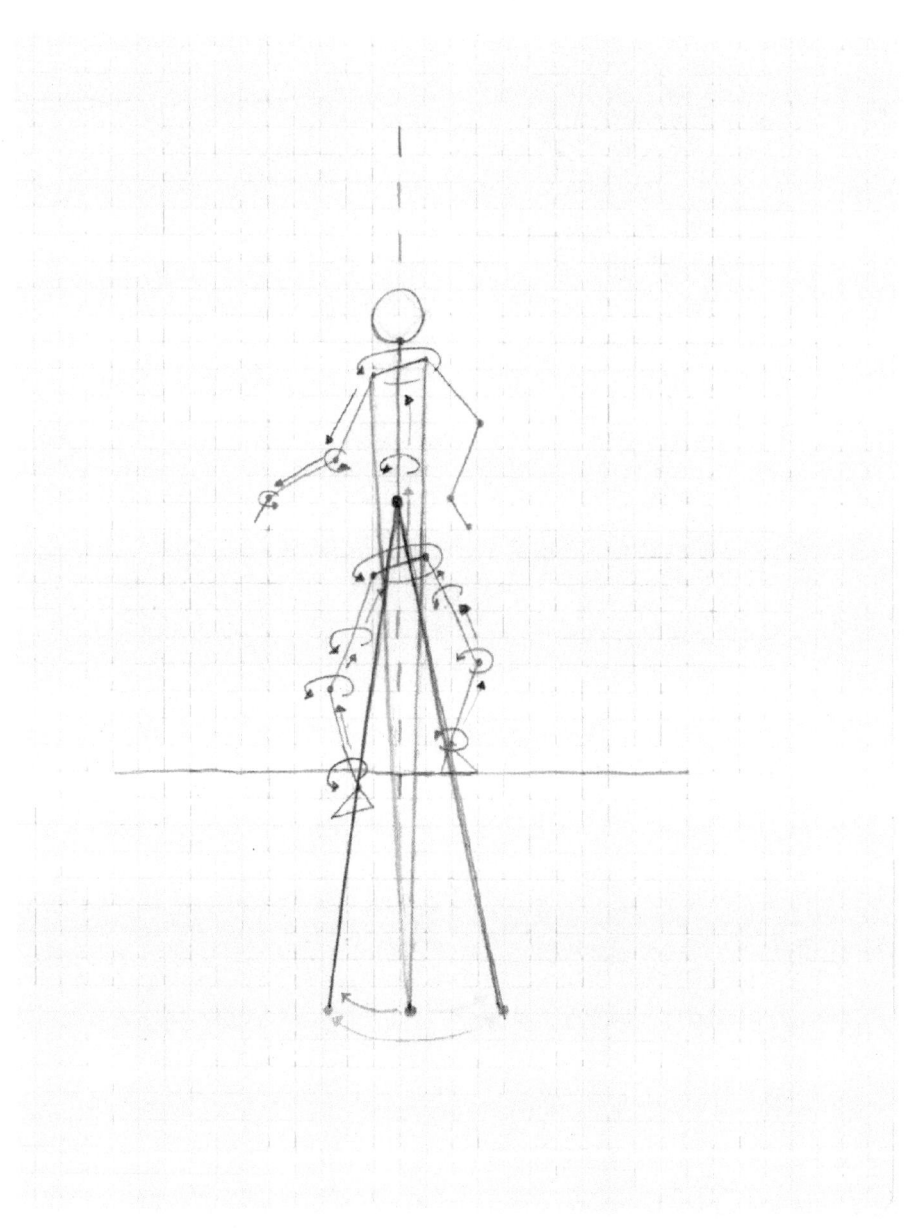

Early notes on the theory of human equilibrium

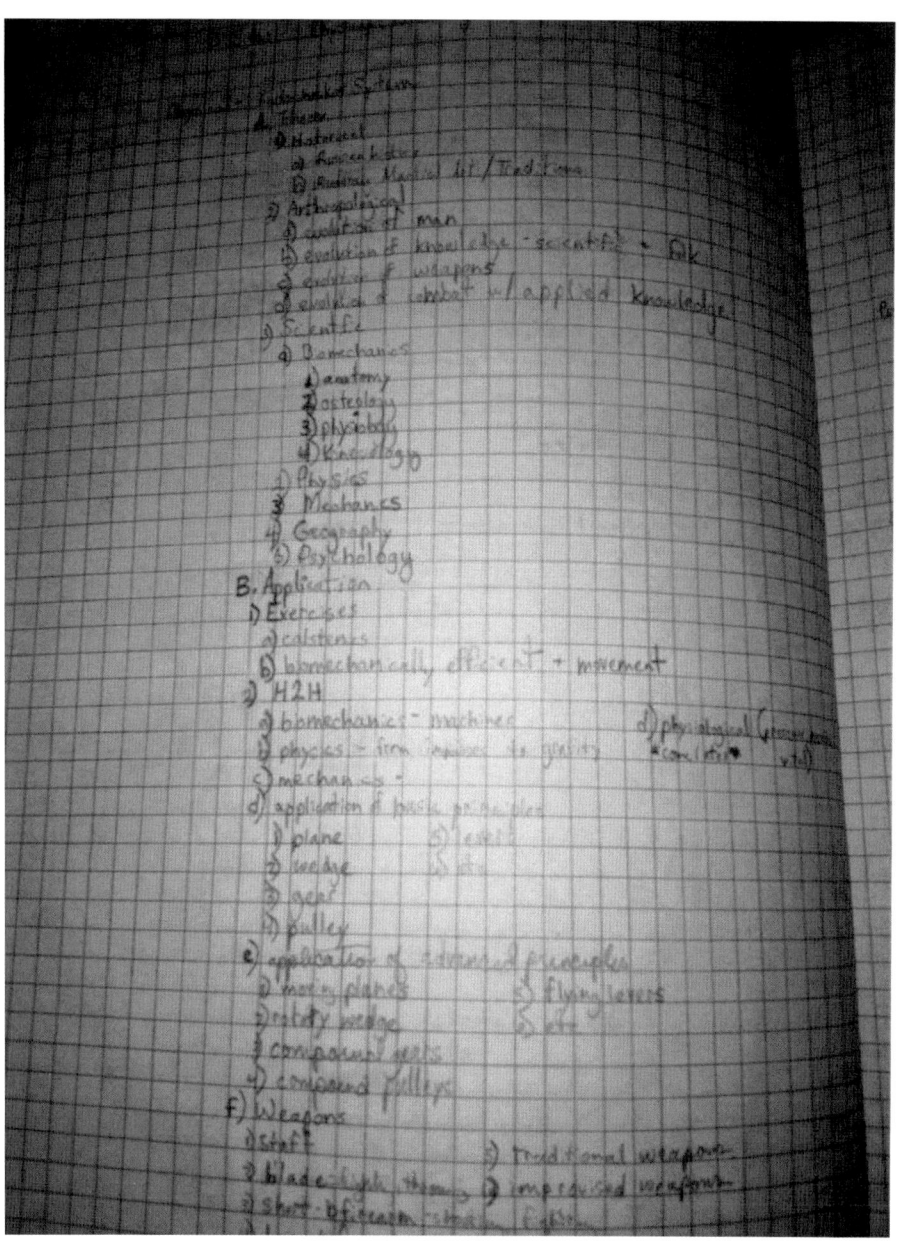

Early notes on courses of study

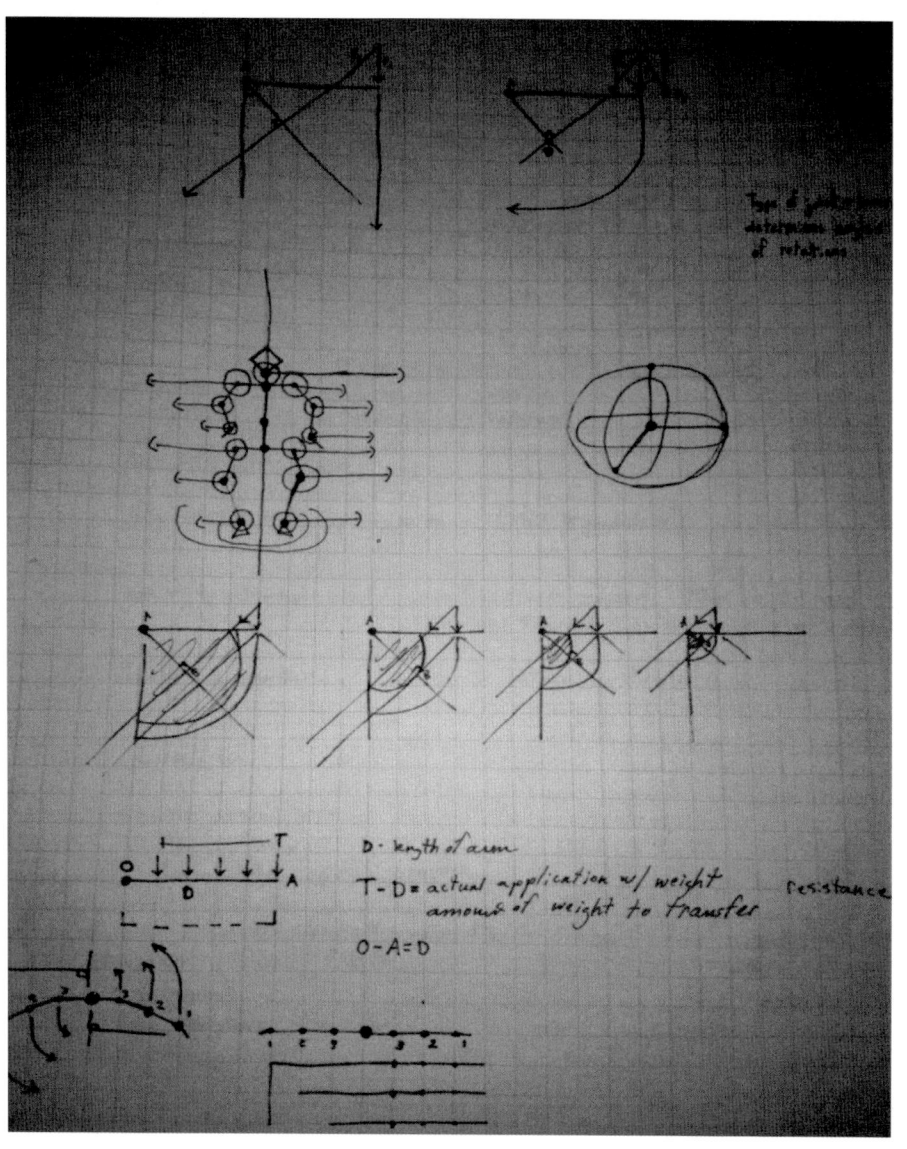

Notes on leverage

Combat shooting

static

Movement - To Ground - back, forward, side

Transitions

On Ground - back, forward, sides senstivity

- In place   Strings

Forms - back

- stomach

- crawls

- buoyant movements

Strings

Dynamic & Transition movements — ? (4)

back, forward, side

Strings

To Standing

- back, forward, sides

Strings

Drops/Falls

back forward sides

Strings

Theoretics

- Hips

- Ways to create power

- Ways to create torque

Notes on combat shooting

75

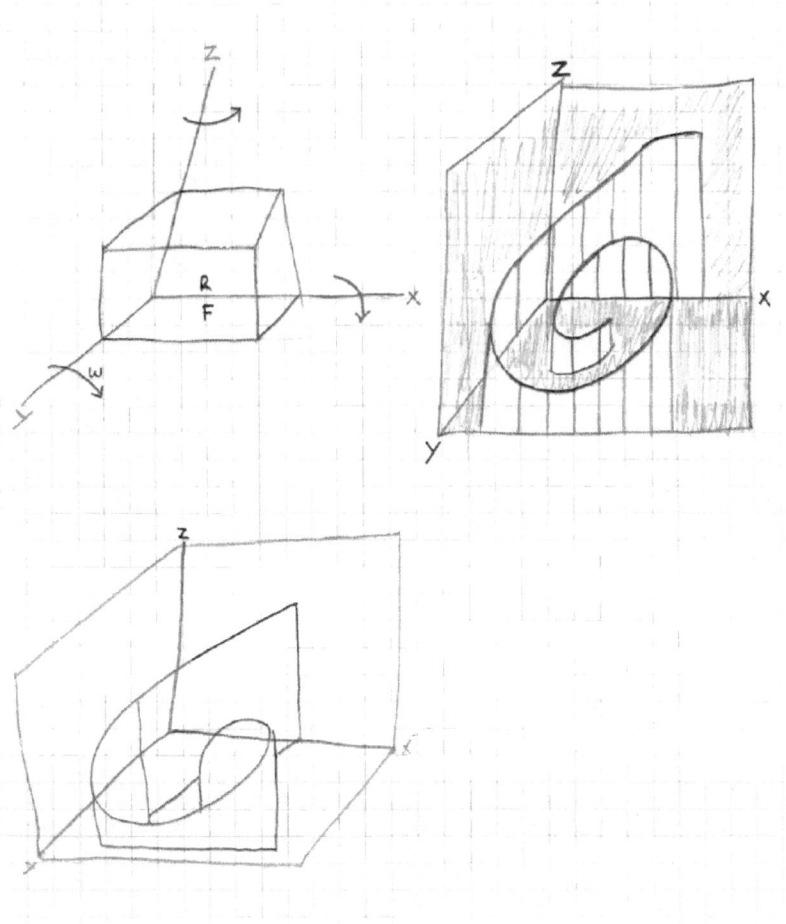

Early notes on understanding three dimensional movement

Elasticity $v < .03 \times \bar{z}$
                              $v > .03 \times \bar{z}$

   Displacement : v

Deformation - displacement field, not one displacement

Any displacement is not single point, but creates a field
   of deformation.

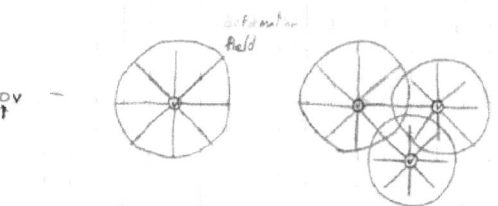

Could displacements be combined through fields and add +ve properties...

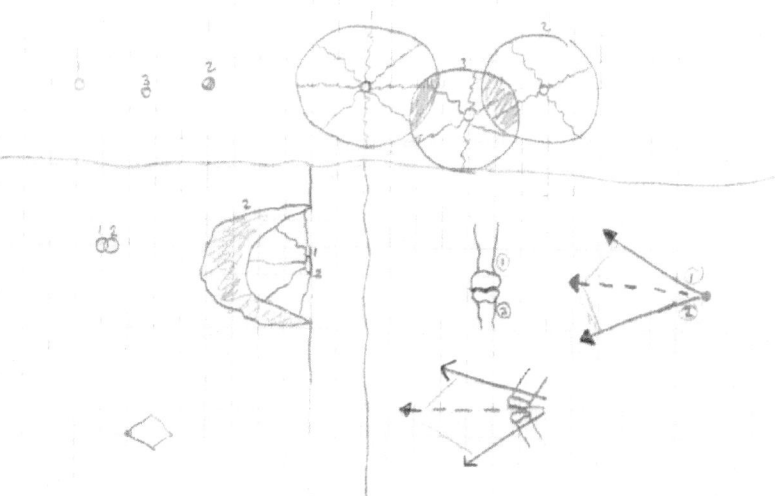

Early notes on displacement versus deformation in strikes

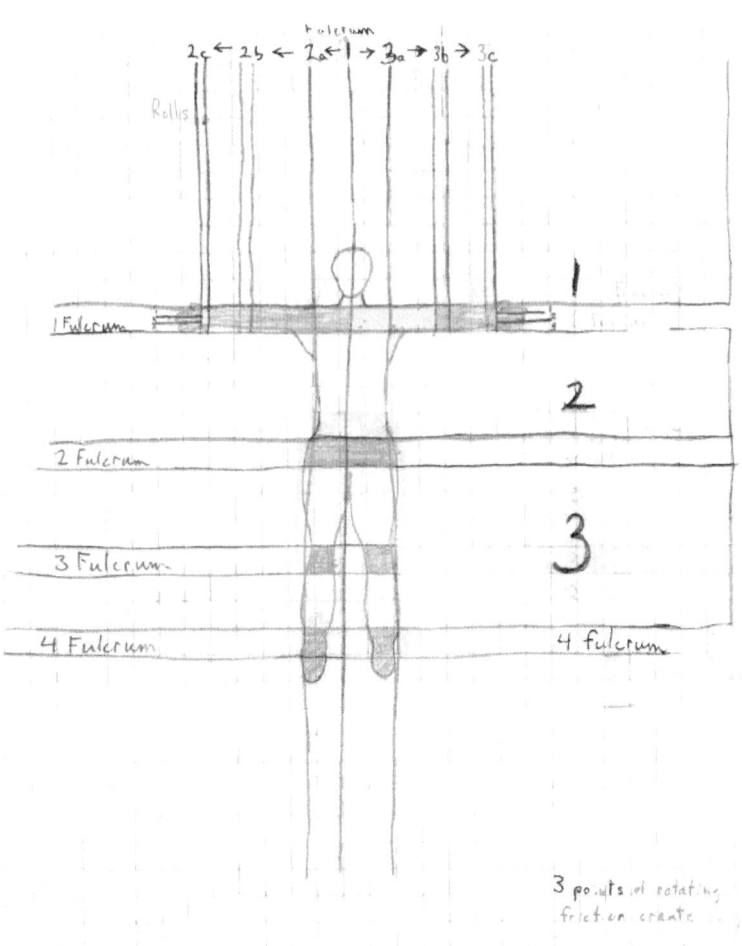

Notes on the 'gear' and ground movement

Machine of leverage + efficien

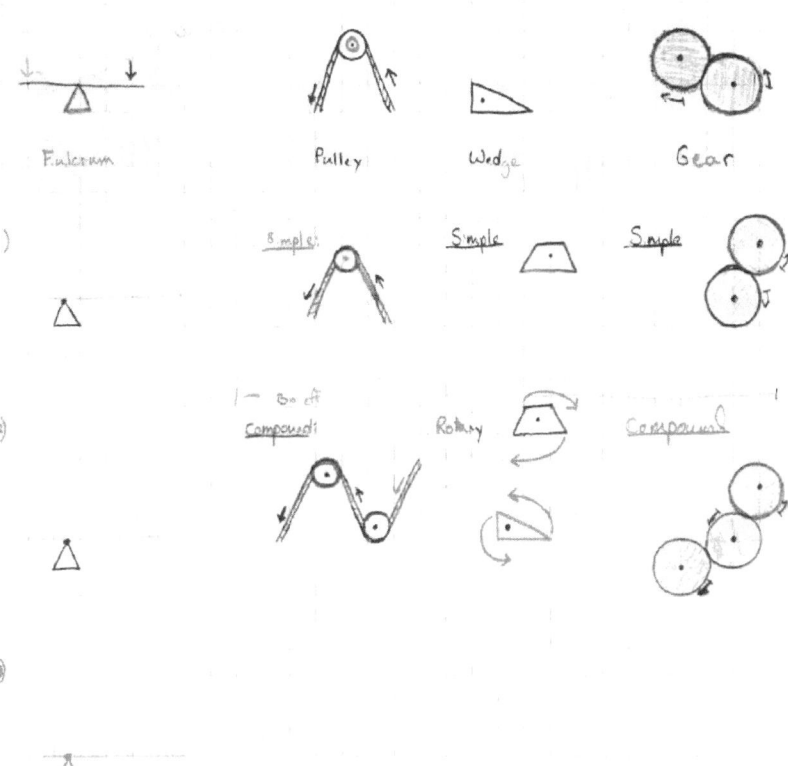

Fulcrum   Pulley   Wedge   Gear

Simple   Simple   Simple

Compound   Rotary   Compound

Notes on the machines of leverage

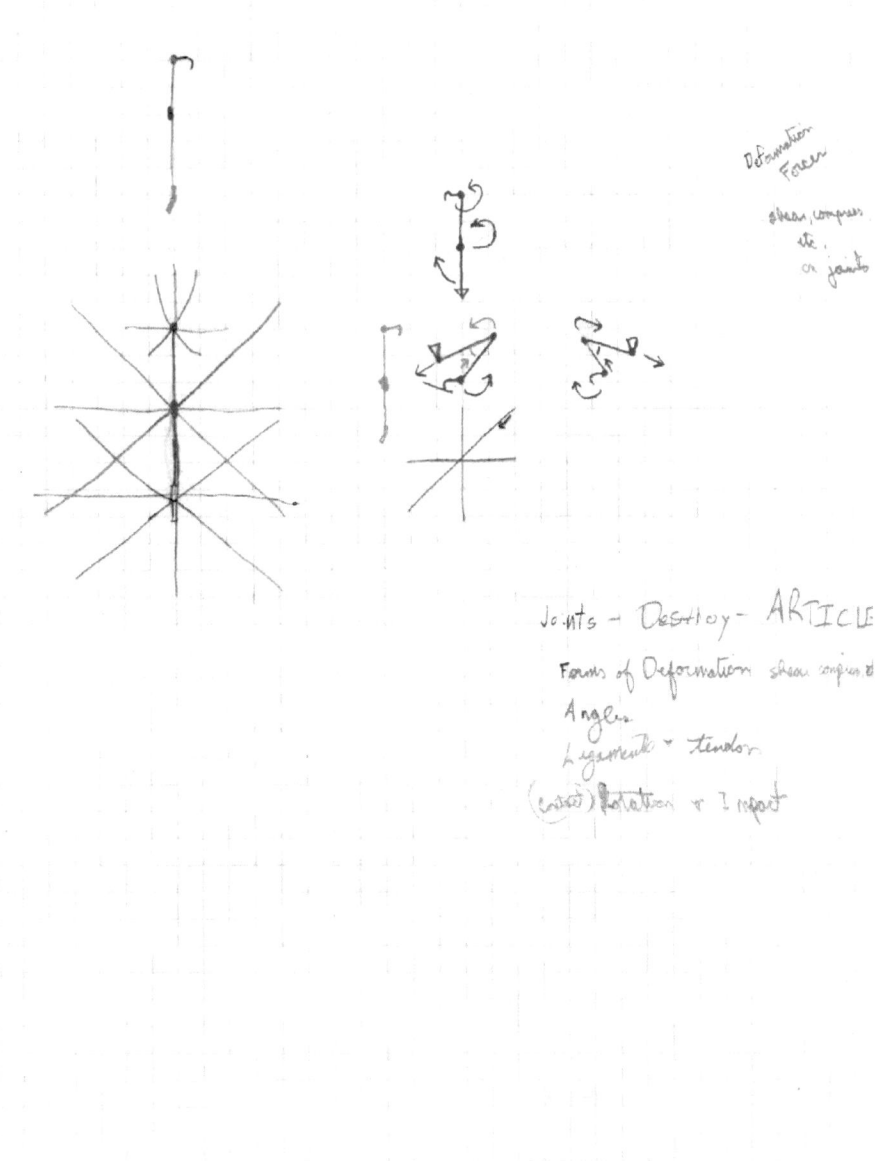

Joints — Destroy — ARTICLE

Forms of Deformation shear compressed

Angles

Ligaments + tendon

(cross) Rotation + Impact

Early notes on joint manipulation and deformation

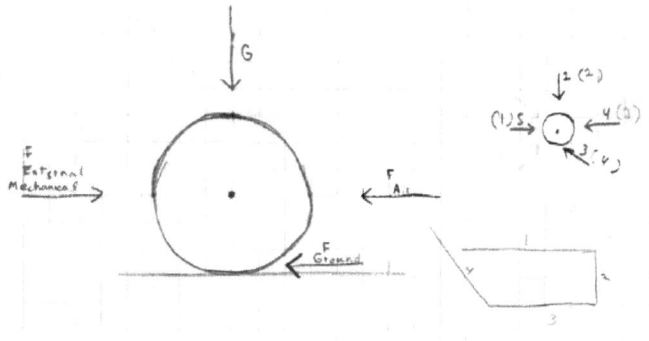

Friction redirects
Ball only as stable as forces acting on it.
If any force's action is ≠, ball is unstable
Friction force with most force will determine
direction of ball - same as with body

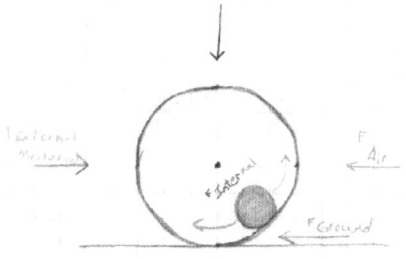

Notes on stability

Mechanics

Newton's Laws - 1, 2, 3   (M4, 5) (A 223)
    └ Transmissibility M4
       Force
       Inertia - Gravity, and Gravitational Forces, Weight M3
       Equilibrium Types M19, M108, M151
       Elasticity and Displacement - linear is rotational

Force Types of forces
    └ Parallelogram M5, 6

Periodic Motion

Work and Energy M133.

    - Machines to create energy   Energy
        └ Coupling M15   └ Kinetic M251,
        └ Gears   └ Potential M255
          └ Torque   └ Power M260
                                           └ Collision - Elastic & Inelastic
                                           └ Moments M13

        - pes   and Strain
           └ Load
           └ Tens
           └ Compression
           └ Bending
           └ Shear
           └ Combination
        - Hooks Law

    - Friction - M84
    - Pendulum's

Machines of Mechanical Efficiency
    - Levers - Classes (Fulcrum)
    - Pulleys
    - Gears
    -

Notes on mechanics

82

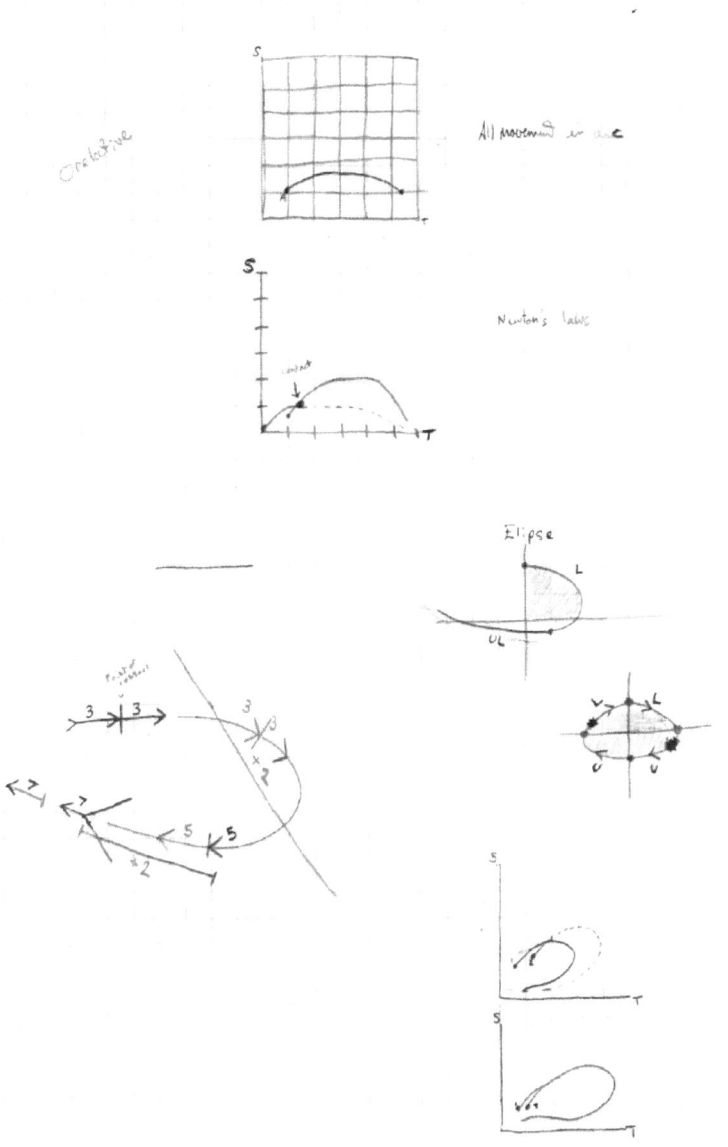

Notes on movement and arcs, later became the 25% rule

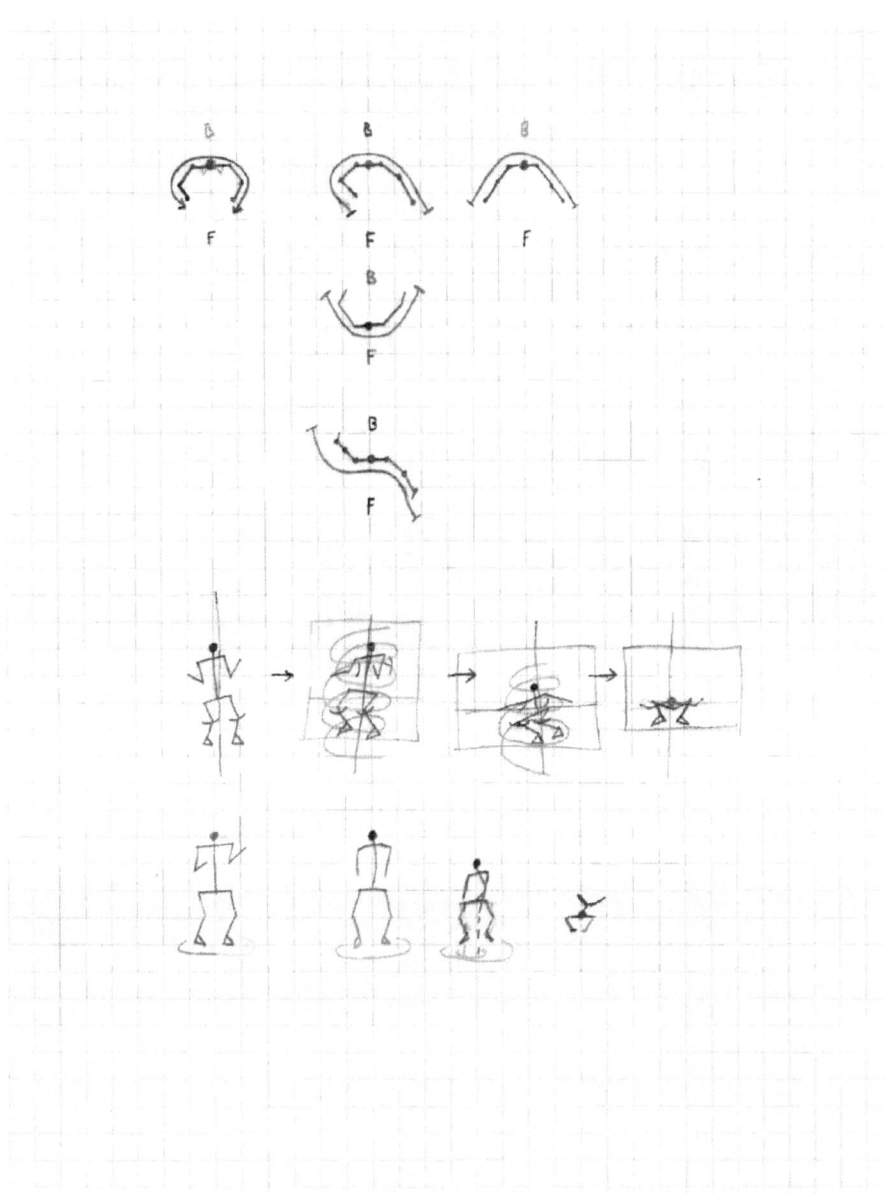

Notes on a student's movement

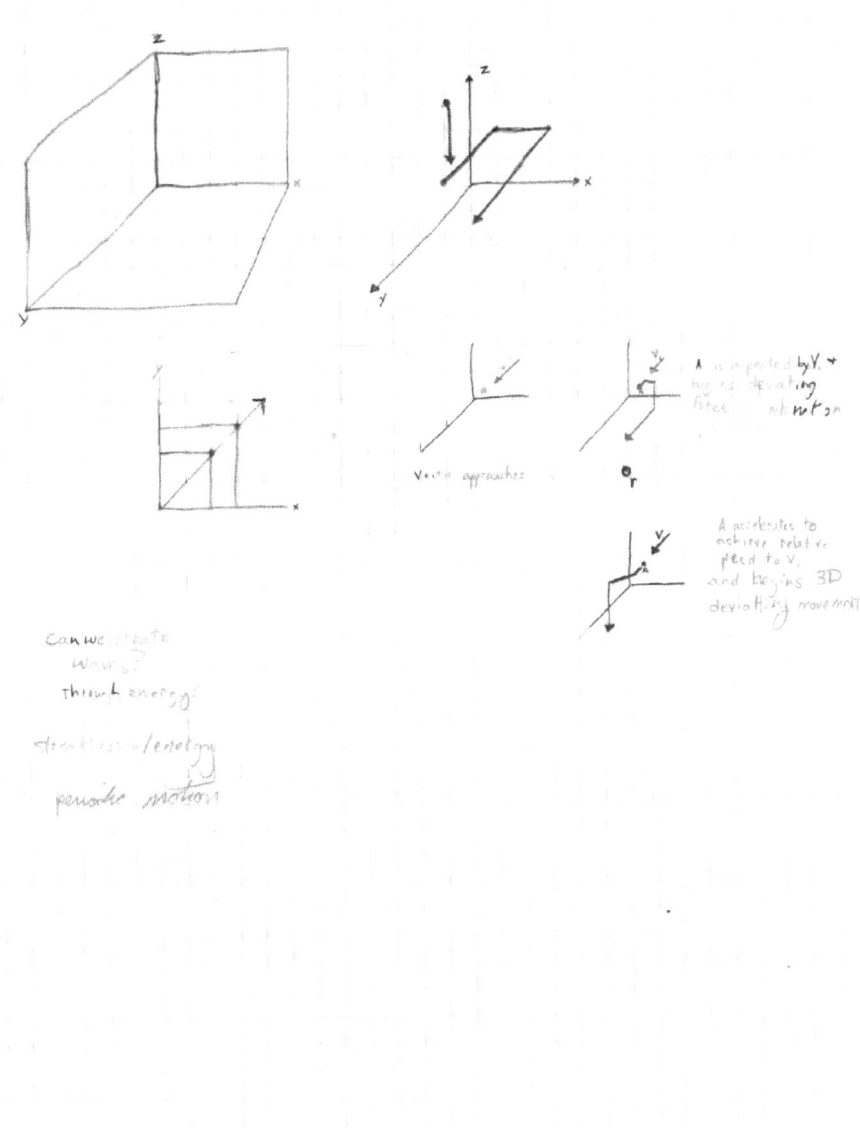

V still approaches

A is impacted by V + has its deviating force minimization

O_r

A accelerates to achieve relative speed to V, and begins 3D deviating movement

Can we create waves? Through energy?

storeless w/energy

periodic motion

Notes on vectors

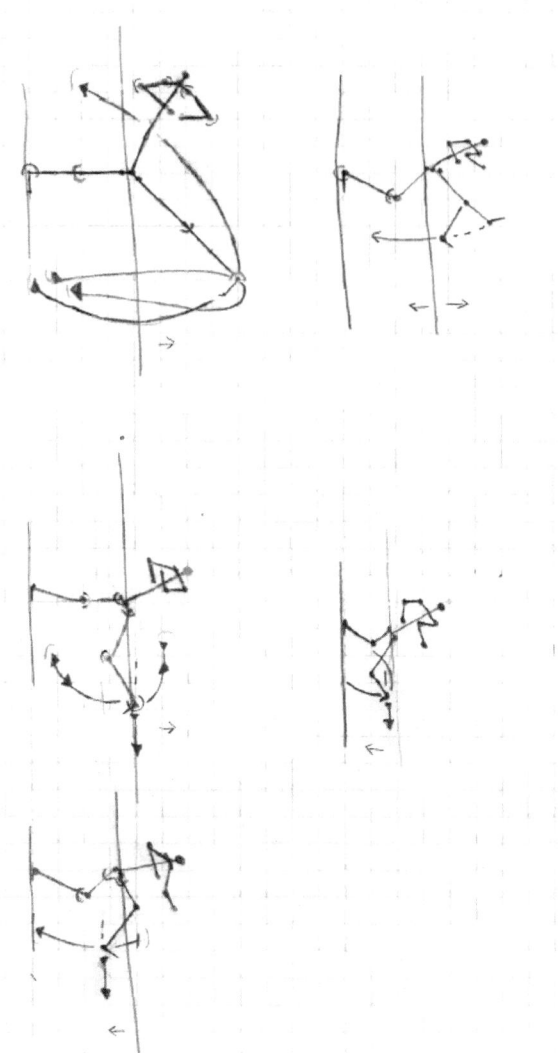

The kinematics of a kick

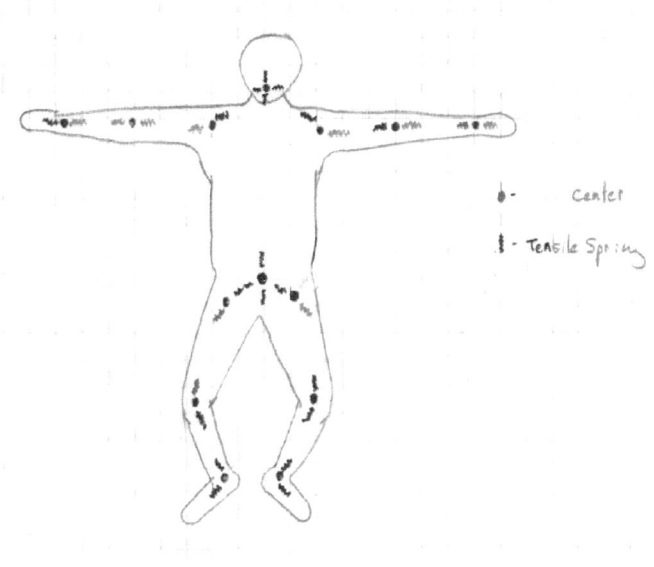

Center

Tensile Spring

Tensile strength in the body

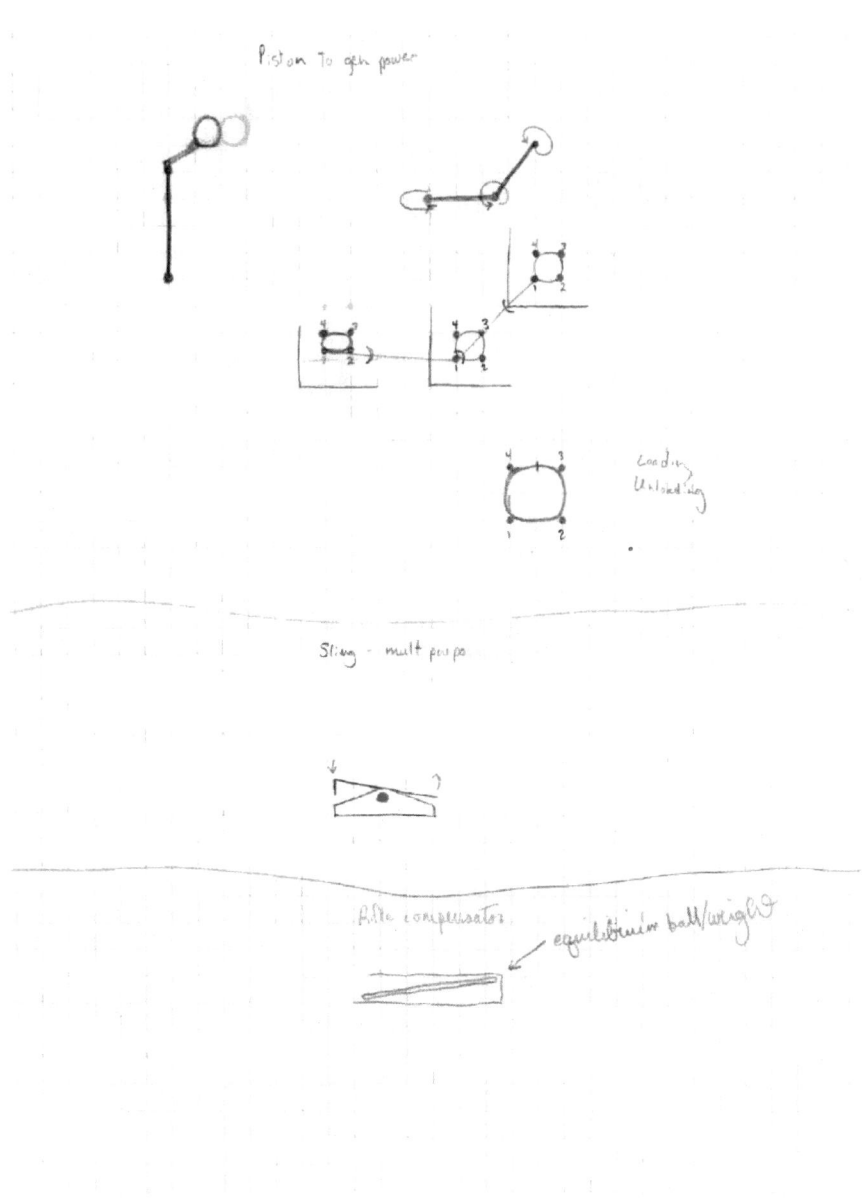

Piston To gen power

Loading
Unloading

Sting - mult porpo

fine compensator

equilibrium ball/weight

Pistons and power generation

88

Quadrant 1

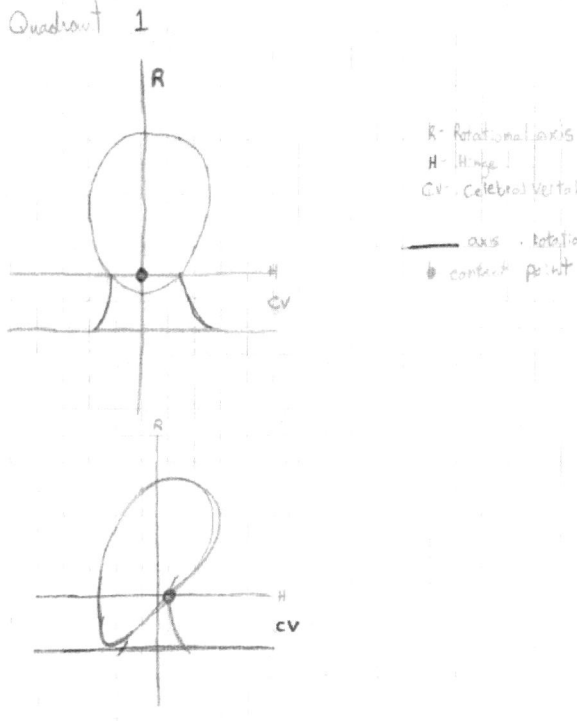

R - Rotational axis
H - Hinge
CV - Celebral vertabrae

——— axis · rotation
● contact point

The axis of the head and neck

89

PART 2:

DIRECTED PERCEPTUAL TESTING

Part 2 Introduction

Every day the human brain is tasked with solving millions of problems.

The only way to solve a problem is to test the problem – to form a hypothesis, to look at the problem from different angles, and to make decisions that can lead one to success over the problem. The EPL is a method of solving a combative equation. This equation must consider the environment, the student, and their enemy. All these variables create a problem that the user must solve – a problem with the enemy and his tactics. Even a problem within the user such as a lack of experience or disadvantage due to position or injury. Martial arts, shooting, knife work – all these subjects are means of solving a problem that the human being is confronted with – survival. But many times, these are tools available when there are no other ways of addressing the problem confronting the user.

When you are a hammer, everything is a nail. This is why many martial arts create for good fist fighters or great grapplers, but not thinking warriors. In a way, a warrior is a fighter – but over a longer timeline. Anyone can be a fighter by wishing to fight and being willing to put themselves into harm for a reason. But, over a timeline, a fighter is trained, taught by teachers and experience on the battlefield. They see reasons for what they do and why the battlespace changes around them, how to interact with it as it is, and make it what they wish it to become my making decisions that affect it. The fighter who once wanted to fight becomes an experienced warrior in their command of the fight ahead of them.

A warrior is challenged by the problems that lie ahead and will actively work to confront and face them, gaining valuable knowledge and intelligence about perhaps a certain enemy, as a boxer knows much about other boxers but little about grapplers and their tells. A point sparring fighter is not ready for 360 degree actions with firearms, and some soldiers may feel uncomfortable with the confines of the rules.   There is a difference in how these problems are addressed and how they are viewed. A fighter will box with a wrestler, or work within the rules of the ring confinement and fighter. But a warrior will make use of the confines of the ring for their strategy because time has taught him or her to do so. A warrior, even in loss, will learn valuable lessons on how not to lose again. A fighter is tough, but a warrior is hardened. He is built from a different cloth...and that cloth is made from the strongest tensile fibers in the world: tested experience.

Combatives is problem solving like anything else in life. There is a problem – you must solve it. If you have a problem with the computer, you don't give up and never use a computer again. You troubleshoot and solve it, and if you can't – you ask someone to help you. If you are under fire, if your knot is not properly tied, if you are out of water, if you are facing three people when you thought you only would face one...these are problems.

These problems will not go away. They must be confronted with the experience of the person confronting them. Using his or her own knowledge, the problems are confronted and either overcome the person, giving information on how not to do something...or they are overcome by the person, giving information on how to do something. The dividing line is the willingness of the person to engage the problem honestly and put his or her honest best against the problem presenting itself.

Problems that we cannot solve have a way of quickly disrobing us and showing who we are.

We become participants and interact to solve the problem, or we become spectators watching the problem solve us.

What differentiates the willing participant from the spectator is the participant will engage the problem and work to solve it. They will train to get it right so when they get it wrong, it is more right than the other guy. And when they are unsure, they will ask for guidance. The spectator will watch the participant, will remark at their abilities, perhaps even attempt it – but if they are not psychologically dialed in, if his or her physical prowess is not to a level of being able to solve the problems; if he or she does not have the neurological tools that allow them to think and act simultaneously, then he or she will rarely win repeatedly. If the person will not ask for help: then that person will perish or be left behind as fighters, as the warrior who wants to learn will push on, pitting his or her experience against environment, and asking for help along the way from others like himself or herself, who have experience and have tested it.

Within the EPL, we have learned how to gain experience.

The spectator may have knowledge, but knowledge without an able user is just knowledge. Knowledge with an able user is applicable knowledge – it becomes experience. Think for a moment on a surgeon from a rural area and a surgeon in a major city hospital. They have the same medical knowledge from school. Each has knowledge, but experience and how it is gained is a dividing line between these two doctors. One may have a better bedside manner, understanding certain ailments, while one may have a better understanding of stress and physical trauma. Both are far advantaged from a student in medical school, who receives high marks in their anatomy class.

Knowledge without experience withers quickly under the bright light of application. When one is forced to apply their knowledge, if it is not tested by experience it will quickly fail. But in health, fitness, martial art, shooting, and other endeavors, far too often the inexperienced are viewed positively. One with experience obtained more than thirty years previous, but has not tested it since, is still viewed as relevant experience...even as the entire society and battlefield around them has changed. Students with advanced belts with no street-violence testing are viewed as capable of teaching about street violence, when in reality, their experience withers quickly under great psychological testing.

Wide ranging experience takes a fighter and makes them into a thinking warrior. It must be the goal of every instructor to become a thinking warrior, a problem solver – and view their own teaching as a problem to solve, to make it better. To view their students as problems that can be solved, can be worked through, and the more student, the more experience, the better the instructor.

The EPL can create a fighter. It can show a fighter new methods of achieving goals, of focusing their attention, of making methods their own, how to look at threats and not be distracted. Within the EPL the student has gained much experience, but that experience must be tested. In testing the EPL through a progressive manner, the fighter who has experience can discover whether that experience will stand up to the physical, psychological, and neurological rigors of combat. By gaining knowledge and intelligence about the problems they are facing, fighters learn about themselves and the rigors of the testing harden their toughness.

This can only be done through testing the experience, creating a thinking warrior...a problem solver.

Chapter 7: Testing the EPL

In the beginning, when a student first entered Pramek's EPL, the general view of combat is that of confusion and complexity. A student's first fears of combat are that of injury, how random it is, or how disorienting it can be. They have no concept of combat beyond a filter that is based upon years of experience, fear, and misunderstanding. It is through this filter that the techniques are employed. Students begin with a fear of injury, at the randomness of violence, and are then shown techniques to use in combat. The primary issue in training in a martial art is understanding the nature of violence - either one can participate in its randomness, or one can decide to respect it but ignore it, and then work toward a goal. This goal can be anything from not being caught off guard to how to execute take downs and control another human being. EPL is designed to remove the unknowns, as much as possible, from the student's world view in relation to combat.

Conceptualized View of Combat

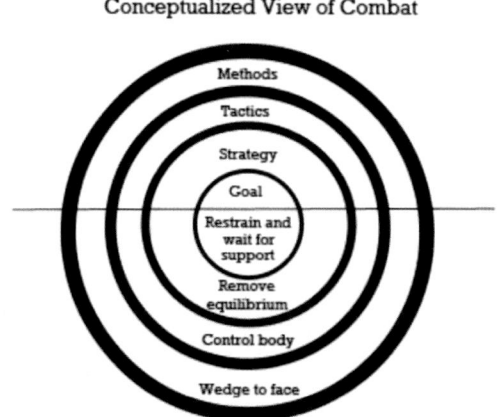

As opposed to the general view of combat, the conceptualized view categorizes the information and shows the student how to organize it into three steps to achieve their goal. The student decides a goal, develops a strategy, and then uses tactics and methods to achieve that goal. Because of the BCB, they understand the conceptual nature of psychology of violence so that it is not random and the physiology of injury so they know what they should be leery of (for example, targeted knife attack versus wildly flailing arms). Then, the student has a clear mind approaching combat and views their techniques, or in EPL, methods to achieve a goal. One secondary function of EPL is that it removes the unpredictability of combat through experience, altering the schema and giving a conceptualized view of combat. Understanding and controlling the concepts behind what is occurring in combat is the end result of the EPL learning phases, but this must be tested.

At this point in training, the student has been educated and worked through the phases of EPL. The student has demonstrated their aptitude and understanding of theory + movement = application and has shown that it has been imprinted and unitized, then conceptualized. Within Pramek and EPL, the student must now move to having their aptitude truly tested within combative training. This testing is directed at measuring the adaptability of the student to a variety of obstacles. Success is not governed by how hard the student can hit, but how accurate the student can be to achieve a goal under varying levels of duress. This testing most accurately shows how well the student understands the subject matter.

This testing does not have to be for everything at once. If a student has shown general aptitude in how to perform the wedge and remove equilibrium, then this must be tested under more extreme, targeted scenario training. This leads to the next phase of Pramek's CLM: the testing phase or Directed Perceptual Testing. Here, the student can be graded accurately on their ability to perform under varying levels of duress up to scenario driven training. In this section, we will move through phases of training leading to a student who can perform under the most stressful of hand-to-hand combat situations, giving them access to '1 tool for 10 jobs' that is an efficient, adaptable, and well-honed application. It is of paramount importance to understand that theory + movement = application in Pramek. As such, we must strive to educate the student on each and show them their strengths and weaknesses within the testing phase.

This testing is called Directed Perceptual Training (DPT) for a very specific purpose. It calls into testing every phase of EPL; it questions the perceptual abilities of the student. It challenges the student to take each lesson learned and then directly tests them. Typically, in martial art testing is just having two people spar after learning a technique. The DPT will usually make procedurally trained students highly uncomfortable as it tests for perception and does not test for procedure. It checks the adaptability of a student to difficult stimuli that will test the overall aptitude of the student. Procedurally based students quickly find that under the DPT guidelines they are in a state of disadvantage in terms of adaptation to stimuli. The perceptually based student, who has been taught to adapt and achieve goals, and adapt his or her strategy to the goals, will find the tests demanding initially, but eventually will not be insurmountable.

The DPT is designed to be one of the most difficult testing methods that is applicable to any martial art. Procedural based systems can utilize the DPT without alteration and will greatly challenge their students to perform techniques, whereas EPL based schools will find the student adapting under the weight of the DPT to achieve their goal. Here it is vital to remember - EPL and PBL methods are not incompatible. They can be blended, as will be discussed later in the manual.

Progression

A student should never be barnstormed into any phases in training, especially the testing phase. We caution to avoid using the term testing without explaining to the students the nature of what the test is. There are not passing grades in combat, only getting home alive, whether it is a grade A and there is not one mark on the student; or a grade D where the student sustains injury but prevails - they have still survived, passing life's testing. The problem forms when students feel the testing will inhibit their ability to move forward in training, which is not the case. Testing should not act as a barrier to progressing, but a springboard to learn and jump from. Within EPL an infinite number of methods can be trained and then tested with the DPT. These phases of testing are not one-time deals; they are learning labs for the student and the teacher. While they are progressive in nature, they are no different than practicing algebra to brush up for a calculus class.

☐

Chapter 8: DPT Level One: Tension Testing

The first goal of testing a new method is to test it against an opponent who is providing tension against the method application. This is not the same as fighting, as fighting brings a new state of nervous system arousal, which is a test later in the overall aptitude testing and training of a student. Tension is applying tension toward the method application and the student's ability to use their understanding of principles to overcome the tension. In combat, the opponent does not simply act as you wish them to act - they must either be forced through pain compliance to act in a compliant and expected manner, or their compliance must be attained through a separate means of application such as a targeted strike to the kidneys, disabling of a body part that renders them unable to defend themselves, chokes, or through a concussion or knock out.

In tension testing a student is facing a training partner who will not comply with the method being applied. The testing student must adapt to the tension and decide how to stop the tension, or move around the tension and accomplish their overall goal based on the strategy they have decided upon. If the strategy is to immobilize the partner and a joint lock is the tactic, then the partner must give tension to not allow this joint lock, and the testing student should use other means to force compliance with their application.

Tension testing should be performed on a progressive scale so as not to create an overabundance of negative feedback that will psychologically affect the willingness of the student to continue. Remember, the point is to assist the student in getting to their goal, not to prevent the student from doing so through insurmountable obstacles. An instructor must determine the level of tension needed. The instructor should be the only one who executes this (example may be to create an arm bar). Then the level of tension should be raised to adversely affect the ability of the testing student to accomplish their task. This is a gradual process where the students should be placed in various physical poses forcing each to work from that pose. For the following examples of tension level, an arm bar will be used as the goal of the student, while a joint lock and pain compliance is the tactic of the student.

0 - 25% - A compliant to semi-compliant training partner. In this testing, the training partner should stiffen the area that is the object of the student's goal. If, for example, the method used is an arm bar, the partner should stiffen their arms and shoulders, but leave the rest of their body relaxed and compliant. This

will allow the student to work against the arm itself and use the rest of the body to position the partner to allow them to achieve their goal through their tactic.

25 - 50% - A semi-compliant partner who will use their upper body to create tension, while leaving the lower back and legs relaxed.

50 - 75% - A semi to non-compliant partner who will create tension throughout their entire body but will not move from their initial stance and will not forcefully prevent the testing partner from accomplishing their goal.

75 - 100% - A fully non-compliant training partner who will forcefully use tension and movement to prevent the application of the method, preventing a student's tactics.

Once a student has shown the ability to overcome each phase three to four times consistently, they should be allowed to move to the next level of tension. If they fail once, it is ok...let them attempt again, as this may have been a perceptual or conceptual failure, or something as simple as nervousness. The student needs to adjust to the new training environment psychologically. If they fail twice, they should be moved down a level of tension percentage to continue working and moved back up. This will ensure feedback and learning.

Chapter 9: DPT Level Two: Stress Testing

Stress testing is often used in the martial art world as a means of determining if a technique will work in the real world. In Pramek, this is not a determining factor, as stress in Pramek is on the student psychologically to accomplish their tasks but is not a determining factor as to whether the technique or method will work. Anyone can wrestle someone to the ground and then begin a struggle to be victorious. In real life, wrestling someone to the ground and struggling opens the student up to a host of threats that they should not voluntarily open themselves up to.

For Pramek, stress testing is discovering the balance between the demands of the test and capacity of the student to accomplish their task. In doing so, the aptitude of the student to perform the task can be observed, as opposed to the actual method being applied. For these purposes, the stress on the psychology of the student, not the stress of combat is, being analyzed. These are different concepts. Stress on the student to perform their workload is different than the stress of combat. A student who is well versed in 20 techniques will attempt to find a way to achieve their task, versus the psychological stress of not being able to accomplish a task. Stress testing is the next level of tension testing, as the student is asked to perform the tasks repeatedly against varying levels of tension, creating a psychological stress on the student at their inability to accomplish their tests.

How to Perform a Stress Test

Stress testing is a quick process, as the student is given a goal and must decide their principles to employ through tactics, for this example, the arm bar. At which time stress testing begins, the student will be put through a repeated number of attempts at varying levels of tension. The period should be quick, at 30 seconds to a minute, and then the percentage of tension should be changed. This will stress the student, as they are unable to apply the same technique or method twice. The student should be moved repeatedly through levels of tension, with the instructor calling out the level of tension. One example may be calling '25%', 30 seconds elapse, '75%', 20 seconds elapse, '50%', 45 seconds elapse, '25%', 20 seconds elapse, '100%' 30 seconds elapse. This should continue for 5 minutes maximum. At this point, a stress evaluation must be done – write down in a log for the student their heart rate, respiratory rate, pupil dilation, and the verbal observations of the students. Around the two minute mark the student will shows signs of high levels of stress, as they cannot duplicate success, and you must assess and track this information as well.

Pramek CLM

DPT 5 Minute Stress Test

Time	Tension
0.30 min.	25% tension
1.00 min.	50% tension
1.45 min.	25% tension
2.30 min.	100% tension
3.00 min.	50% tension
3.25 min.	25% tension
4.00 min.	25% tension
4.20 min.	100% tension
4.45 min.	50% tension
5.00 min.	Stress Evaluation

Frustration in Stress Testing

Frustration can develop quickly at this testing stage and the student must be monitored to ensure they are obeying the rules of the game (efficiency versus effectiveness) and safety is a must as frustration and embarrassment often create injury. The student must learn to place their ego to the side and concentrate on learning.

Stress testing will show two particularly important training issues to be addressed. Procedural based learning students will quickly succumb to proper stress testing as their techniques become limited in their ability to perform the task. What works once will rarely work repeatedly with varying levels of tension. Their capacity for adaptation will be shown quickly at the limit of their skill set, and they become stressed by the work versus their ability to perform. Perceptually based students will succumb at a slower rate, as they have been given concepts and understand the theory but use their body to perform using simple machines to accomplish their work. It is a test of their ability to adapt the theory to their movement to create the application.

This testing level should not last longer than 5 minutes, as the negative feedback can affect the willingness of a student to continue. It should only be performed in a trusting, positive environment that will support the student, as opposed to using punishment, scorn, or belittling by a group at their inability to perform the test. The first time a student is stress tested, the student should not be communicated with. They are on their own with their work capacity. In subsequent training session, there should be communication from the teacher. The teacher must constantly be reminding the student to utilize their technique or method, constantly engage the student and remind them of, for example a lever, or a wheel and axle, or a screw, and ask the student to perform these tasks.

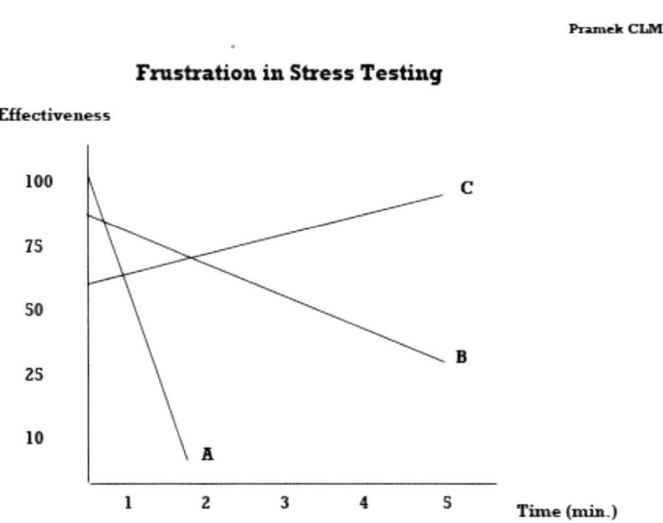

In the above chart, frustration can be seen between three students. Student A, who is a new student, student B who has been training for a short period of time and has been exposed to stress testing, and Student C, who has a large amount of experience gained in stress testing. Student A will quickly become ineffective through frustration, whereas Student B will take a longer amount of time, but will eventually succumb to frustration, thus becoming ineffective by the halfway mark. But Student Cr rises in effectiveness. This can be seen because unlike the other students, Student C will start slowly, not exhaust himself or herself, and will balance his or her experience versus the test in front of him or her. By pacing oneself in the stress testing, one can remain effective. Effectiveness is about work performed and whether it is making progress toward a goal, versus efficiency. When a student starts slow and uses the stress test as a learning tool, he or she can become more effective. Then, but tracing their progression on paper (heart rate, breathing, etc.) one can combine effectiveness with efficiency (lowering heart rate, lowering breathing rate), creating a stronger student who is less frustrated.

It is vital that the teacher can recognize frustration - this cannot be stressed, pardon the pun, enough. If the teacher is unable to recognize that the student is stressed to a level of being unable to properly function mentally, then this exercise will become useless. Cues should be identified to recognize that the level of stress is becoming unproductive for the student and learning has stopped.

There is a difference between being stressed and being stressed out. One is momentary - one is longer term. When the student moves from stress to being stressed out, they will be unable to interact properly within the exercise for a period after the testing phase. This, for junior instructors, is a trial and error method. It is best to err on the side of short-term stress than prolonged. No one should be forced into stress more than 2 minutes unless the student has shown the ability to pass successive stress tests and is ready for the next phase.

Stress your students, but do not let your students become 'stressed out!'

Chapter 10: DPT Level Three: Fatigue Testing

Once a student has performed admirably in the stress testing section of Pramek's aptitude tests, the student must enter the fatigue-testing phase. Fatigue is stress over a period. The goals must become more difficult, and at this point a variety of training partners must be used over a period. This will create different dynamics, as the student is constantly challenged by personality, body type, strength of tension, and their own physical limitations.

How to Perform Fatigue Testing

For this example, the arm bar for a takedown must be applied to the right arm for 2 minutes (four 30 second periods) in the form of the stress test. Then, at the end of two minutes another training partner comes in and the student must then work an arm bar against the left arm for two minutes under a stress test. After two minutes of testing, another partner is used, but the overall position changes (for example, both starting at a standing position and the student in an advantageous position holding the wrist and shoulder). The student must now perform the arm bar against a different position and body type. Then, after 2 minutes, another student is introduced, and so on. Fatigue testing should last no more than 12 minutes. In a 12 minute period, the student will have worked with a variety of body types, positions, and levels of tension. The instructors can also input further challenges, such as math testing, puzzles, memory exercises, etc. This will call on the student to use their brain for something more than physical problem solving – but actual problem solving. It will also force the student to be cognizant of their breathing, heart rate, and their ability to perform tasks outside of combat, such as using a radio, memorizing a license plate, firing a pistol, applying CPR. The experience from fatigue-testing is difficult to duplicate for a student in other testing methods. It challenges the mind, body, and spirit (willingness to continue) of the student.

DPT Fatigue Test

Initial Partner	Arm Bar
30 sec /30 sec	25% / 50%
30 sec /30 sec	100% 10%

New Partner	Position Change
30 sec /30 sec	75% / 25%
30 sec /30 sec	50% / 100%

Basic Math Test - 6 verbal / 6 written (under 30 seconds)

New Partner	Position Change
30 sec /30 sec	100% / 75%
30 sec /30 sec	25% / 25%

New Partner	Position Change
30 sec /30 sec	75% / 25%
30 sec /30 sec	100% / 25%

Puzzle Test - basic children's 15 piece jigsaw (under 30 seconds)

New Partner	Position Change
30 sec /30 sec	25% / 75%
30 sec /30 sec	50% / 25%

New Partner	Position Change
30 sec /30 sec	100% / 25%
30 sec /30 sec	50% / 25%

End	Fatigue Evaluation

Over time, we have found that visual acuity lessens, physical strength begins to dissipate, situational awareness will reduce, and the performance of the student will become erratic, frustrated, and disorganized and eventually the student will succumb to fatigue or quit.

The first time a student is fatigue tested, the student should not be communicated with. They are on their own with their work capacity. In subsequent training session, there should be communication from the teacher. Just as in stress testing, the teacher should be acting as a guide and an assistant, not only through ideas, but teaching the student to listen and communicate even in the most difficult of situations. Commonly, in this kind of training, the student's conditioning will be called into question, as blood flow and oxygen flow to the brain will be diminished and the student will become 'dumber' due to fatigue. This can be untrained through conditioning and experience, and the student after a period will be capable of two way communication.

Chapter 11: DPT Level Four: Arousal Testing

Arousal testing is a primary means of testing a reality-based style of martial art. At this training level the student should begin to be introduced to uncomfortable stimuli that arouse a response in the autonomic nervous system. Thus far, the student has performed tasks in a safe, simple environment where their stress is based upon their partner and fatigue that sets in after a period. In the arousal phase of testing, physical and psychological stimuli vastly different from that so far experienced must be used.

The goal of arousal testing is to begin teaching a student to operate under stimuli that make it difficult to perform work, increasing the load while diminishing the capacity through stimuli. It does not take a lot to arouse the autonomic nervous system of a student. There is no need for extreme bodily contact in the arousal phase, as the student will quickly be overcome by the workload versus their capacity to perform the work (stress) by external threatening stimuli. The goal of the testing is to create highly stressful, but controlled situations that challenge the student to utilize learned methods to accomplish work, while still maintaining a safe environment.

How to Perform Arousal Testing

Arousal testing is best described as stress testing or fatigue testing with third party involvement. With the above example, the student must now be given stimuli that will distract them. It is best to start a student in stress testing, and then introduce third party interference and added obstacles to the student workload.

Examples of third party interference and added challenges may be: forced dizziness (dizzy bat race), increased heart rate (wind sprints before testing), inability to use particular body parts to simulate injury, blind folding one eye, lack of oxygen through use of breathing exercises, extreme verbal challenges by the training partner, introduction of third parties who push or pull lightly on the testing student or use extreme verbal challenges, objects thrown at the student, a group converging on the student and surrounding them, unfamiliar locations such as a bathroom or stair well, etc.

Introduce these into the stress testing first. Perform stress testing as it is always performed but introduce the challenges like those listed above into the training. The student should show an ability to complete their tasks as they have previously while having these distractions and challenges. Once the student shows the ability to consistently pass stress testing with this, then move the student to fatigue testing. Generally, the first time a student is fatigue tested in the arousal state, the testing should go no longer than 5 – 6 minutes. These challenges create fatigue of their own.

Students are highly susceptible in this stage to psychological trauma. It is highly recommended that this be a controlled environment, where the student is told what to possibly expect beforehand without details that will hurt the process, as well as explained to that they will not be extremely physically harmed by third parties or objects thrown, etc. The student can become fatigued, embarrassed, or disheartened quickly in this training phase, as they become a victim to their emotional intelligence, conditioning, lack of exposure to this kind of stimuli, and their own autonomic nervous system. They will tend to match force on force, moving to gross motor skills to address third parties and defeating the purpose of the training. This is about controlling the physical and the psychological within the arousal state - not dropping everything and fighting someone who throws a ball too hard at the student's head.

Third party participants must be given strict guidelines on behavior expectations and understand their role. Should these guidelines be infringed upon, the violator should first be made to apologize, and then removed for a period from the training room to continue learning. After a period of time (usually after the student has completed their phase training, become a third party, and is ready to be the focus of testing again) the offender may be reintroduced. This can be used to heighten the student who was the victim of the violation but remember to control this.

This is high-level training the student is undergoing. This training should be done in short stints (4 minutes the first time) at first to acclimate the student to the rigors of real world combat, while stopping the exercise when the student has shown the stress level leads them to frustration and embarrassment. At any time, the student seems to be completely unable to operate, the test must be stopped, or brought back to the tension or stress phase and the obstacle worked through.

This testing is not only about the ability to accomplish tasks - it is also adjusting the student to hostile situations. Any student, over a period of scenario testing in the arousal state, will be able to focus, perform tasks, address third party threats and thrown objects. The point of the test is to build the student up to the ability to do so, not be able to apply an arm bar. Expect a sloppy student, so control the combat for injuries. Only advanced students will be able to focus through arousal, accomplish their goal, and address other stimuli.

Better training is a matter of prioritizing threats, which will be addressed in other manuals from Pramek. A student should prioritize and react to threats appropriately. Through tension, stress, and fatigue training the student will show an ability to perform tasks in their own time. This testing is no different, as it is an external stimulus to arouse the autonomic nervous system and emotional intelligence of the student and familiarize them with their own limitations. After a period, it will assist them in recognizing their limitations, work around them, and overcome those limitations, which are primarily psychological in nature as opposed to physical.

Chapter 12: DPT Level Five: Scenario Testing

When a student has shown the aptitude to pass all phases of testing, it is time to create scenario-based testing. This will take the student full circle as they feel the stress, tensions, fatigue, and arousal of a scenario. The scenario should be set up, and then the DPT phases worked through within the environment. If it's a situation at an ATM, set this up and then devise the scenario. After this is done, work through each phase. Remember - survival is not a race: we will all die one day. We are trying to create a student who will survive a situation, not show we are able to set up neat scenarios that are realistic.

Once the scenario is set up (as will be laid out below), work through the scenario full out (with protection) so the student can be immersed right from the beginning. At this time, there is no correct, incorrect, efficient, or inefficient - we are working to educate the student by throwing them into a selected scenario as chosen - letting them defend themselves within the scenario.

When completed, and the student has immersed themselves, it is time to work through the scenario using the DPT. If the student performs well in the scenario, then change up the scenario to the point the student cannot perform well and loses within the scenario. It is important to set goals such as escape, evasion, fighting the enemy, protecting a second person. The student, in general, must lose the first time. Even if it is being stabbed with a training knife, or they fall to the ground and get back up - at this point the student has been stabbed (even if they would survive) and fallen to the ground (even if they get back up). They may bleed out, they may be jumped, or suffer a cut from glass on the ground that creates a staph infection.

Why, you may ask, are we throwing a student into the scenario when we have been so careful in training procedures beforehand? Most students, outside of real life experience, will not go through a scenario. By exposing the student to the scenario, they will develop a cognitive understanding of the situation and learn immediately. If class is ending in 10 minutes, and the student goes through the scenario...and then walks down the street and ends up in the scenario in real life, the student will at least have exposure. It is better to teach something that is immediately accessible, even if it is only psychological experience, than to wait and the student fall into a real life situation and that training may have saved their life. Therefore, in Pramek we teach basic combatives first (knees, knife hand chops, eye gouges, ground evasion, etc.) before principle based work; so, the student has access to some basic combative skills.

Once you have worked through this, it is time that each phase of the DPT is trained as long as you want or as long as the student will be willing. If the student has an issue in the scenario that is repeated, use the processes within the DPT to train the student, study the challenge, and work through it to give them positive feedback.

Definition of a Scenario

First, we must determine what the scenario is.

Here are some simple guidelines on deciding on scenarios:

1. *Does the student have a job where the student confronts certain situations, such as security, a soldier, emergency responder, police, and law enforcement?*
2. *For civilians, do they have a situation they have been confronted with in the past that is creating an emotional block or difficulty they need to overcome? This situation should become the scenario to be set up.*
3. *What is the most statistically common crime situation in the area the student lives? If it is muggings, or knife attacks, carjacking, etc., then these should be the scenarios.*
4. *Is the student interested in particular scenarios? This will engage the student and heighten the realism.*

Setting up a Scenario

Once the scenario is chosen, every effort must be taken to create a realistic scenario. If it is a house, go to a house. If it is a parking lot, go to the parking lot. If it is a patrol, set up an area for a patrol. If it is at night, set up at night. Use realistic props, clothing, and environment. It must duplicate, in general, the actual scenario. There is no point of acting like the weight bench is the side of the car. To put it bluntly, whichever student has the worst car should be the student you work the scenario with. We recommend damage waivers in this situation, but that is up to the teacher and students. You must create an environment that is an accurate portrayal.

The students should be involved in setting up the scenario. An active discussion should be held while setting up about available improvised weapons, choke points, exits, and any other environmental stimuli used. The student should discuss the clothing as it is selected, not only to pick the correct representation of clothing, but also to discuss how that clothing can be used. Our goal is not to have a room set up and the student be thrown into it after the initial immersion - the student should build their scenario, under supervision, to make sure it is objective and not weighted toward easy victory.

Always provide protective gear that will protect the student, but not give the student a level of confidence against impact. There is no reason to put so much padding on the student they do not feel impacts. General safety rules must be observed if a student has a weak knee; it must be paid attention to and the attacker should 'go easy' on this knee. An injured knee in training is a knee that isn't as effective in a fight. Use gear that will protect your students while giving them the maximum effect of the training, and the attack.

Remember - this is about education. The student construction of the scenario is valuable intelligence the student can use in the scenario, but also when they leave training class. Remember, the student may be faced with the scenario when they walk home from class. Even if they never participate due to class time, the ability to identify a choke point for escape or defense may save their life.

The Scenario

Once the scenario environment is set up, it must be scripted for the initial run through. Script the scenario in general terms with the students as a whole. Then, separately give each participant a role and discuss the role in private with the actors. The defender should not know the goals, methods, tactics, and strategy of the attacker. It is vital this occurs to induce a level of duress in the students, so their nervous system activates. While they may know their environment, they don't know their attacker and this will create anticipation, which will then engage the nervous system of the student.

Prior to scenario activation, there must be a general agreement about level of speed and force. Optimally, this will be a full out scenario driven fight, but after the initial immersion, if the student needs certain exceptions to learn, and then give them these exceptions willingly to protect the learning environment.

When it is time - act it out with full aggression, full sound, and full environment. Unless otherwise specified, under supervision allow this scenario to play out to its fullest the first time. Recording this event is important, with video or transcription, as it allows the students to observe their own actions. This video should be given to the student and a copy kept by the teacher. We recommend some kind of non-disclosure for this situation to protect a student and school's reputation. After the scenario, a full debrief should be given. This debrief should include the minimum following typed or written information:

- Name and length of time of the scenario
- A paragraph written by the person attacked about the scenario, observations, and recommendations.
- A paragraph written by the attacker about the scenario, observations and recommendations is necessary.
- A recommendation about how to better function within the scenario by you, the teacher, should be completed.

The scenario process is a learning process, not a full out fight to see who survives. A debrief will allow you to track the student progress and they be able to track themselves. Other students should not be allowed to observe the scenario the first time a student is immersed, nor the first time they scenario train post-immersion. This will stop any fears of embarrassment if the student loses. Group learning is important, but a student who can learn from this highly dynamic environment is more important. We recommend scenario training be limited to certain numbers of students, on different training occasions. If you have 10 students, you should work to have 3 - 4 each night. Scenario based training is a delicate subject, and Pramek will be releasing a separate manual and video to instruct the subject matter in the future.

Chapter 13: The Two Paths

Within CLM, the student develops through the EPL learning stages and the DPT testing phases. Both paths can lead to conceptualization - they are not mutually exclusive. Though they work extremely well in coordination, one can utilize each separate from the other to reach a stage of conceptualization. In this phase, one can never directly test their knowledge and still comprehend what they are doing and why. For example, an EPL based student may take a certain defensive method and work it through to understand their goals better, why they are not achieving their goal, and how to become better at this defensive technique. Then, they may go back to their sports training and never enter the DPT…they may just need EPL for that instance to conceptualize what is happening and gain a deeper understanding of the obstacles or difficulties they face.

On the other hand, a student may test their technique within the DPT, carrying through each individual phase to reach the scenario phase to understand the basic concepts of difficulties they are having within the application. A police officer may wish to challenge what he or she is taught in the police academy and utilize the DPT to thoroughly 'vet' the techniques they have learned before going into the street. This allows them to understand the basic concepts behind what they have already been taught, but in real world application.

This process of searching the two paths is encouraged and when time is of the essence for training, both are sufficient to quickly train a student through exposure and to build confidence, while still testing them thoroughly if they already have a developed skill set. The two paths are always open to exploration but in general should be followed upon their training trajectory, toward an attainable end. Skipping straight to one stage or one phase may lead a student to be confused or lacking much needed skills. This leads to partial conceptualization and still can leave answers left unasked or unaddressed.

Full Conceptualization

Full conceptualization is when the two paths are engaged in a progressive manner,

Providing a comprehensive exposure to the methods of EPL and then the DPT is necessary. In full conceptualization, a concept is understood in the learning process and then the understanding is imbedded in schema through experience found in testing. This process educates the students within the EPL, but then refines that understanding through the testing so that the concept is imbedded through experience in the psyche and neurology of the student. This is the best path to creating a most complete student.

Feedback in training

Without feedback, one has no sense of accomplishment…one would not learn ideas, patterns of association, and schema. Information related to what works and what does not work is governed by the neurological feedback we receive in our interactions with the world. Motor skills are refined using progressive tests like DPT and test the aptitude of the student.

The only phase that should not engaged within the first two levels of the EPL is scenario testing. The first two levels of EPL (attention weighting, imprinting) should not be used with high stress, high fatigue, high arousal, or any scenario based training. This is because weighting and imprinting are educational for the student as they respond to stimuli and work toward their goal and their primary feedback is success or failure under safe, optimal training scenarios. Only in the differentiation and unitization stage should feedback training be used so as not to disrupt the perceptual learning of the student as they achieve goals.

The goal of testing is not to fail a student but to give the student feedback, both internally through the student's aptitude and externally through the instructor and group. This feedback is integral to the advancement of a student. Training can be configured for specific purposes in the EPL and DPT. A front line soldier may need specific goals and to only work toward those goals consistently. Advanced joint locks used by a sportsman may not be a goal for a soldier, and thus the soldier is not trained in the EPL to achieve these goals. It is in testing the student we can ascertain their aptitude in achieving goals.

We must test the aptitude of the student based upon their ability, using certain tests to determine where they are physically and psychologically in their training, and then direct their training to 'pass' these tests. Being able to accomplish tasks may be a goal instead of 'passing' and becoming advanced and create a feedback loop through accomplishment of tasks. What use is a technique or method that never achieves the goal? It is within this that we find the goal as the reason for a martial art, not the methods or techniques to achieve it.

☐

Chapter 14: Monitor and Control

Teaching of the monitor and control state is an important component in creating an active, adaptive student. This draws upon the process of perceptual learning and on how these lessons learned are tested. The monitor and control process began prior to Pramek in the K-Sys organization. As K-Sys was an American attempt to describe the processes of the Kadochnikov System from Russia, monitor and control was a process that was used by K-Sys to fully realize something not being realized within the Kadochnikov System. Within that system, principles and theory were utilized, but they we still being expressed as techniques for the students to use. Monitor and control started as an early attempt to realize the perceptual learning method but was the result and not the process by which to get to this state.

Monitor and control is exactly what it sounds like. It is a matter of gathering vital information about the enemy and the environment in which combative interaction will take place, and then utilizing this information to control both. They are each a phase in their own right but intertwined to create a state in which the student is actively participating in combat and making conscious decisions based on information to control the combat.

Macro M&C

In the monitoring phase, the student must first 'size up' their enemy. This does not mean strictly physical size, but information about the enemy. Intelligence such as size, build, stance, tactics such as verbal interaction and deciphering true threats from implied threats, physical injury, or movement limitations, as well as general methods being employed by the enemy. An example may be that the enemy takes on a grappler's stance, giving certain verbal cues as to their methods and strategy. Often, a person, to intimidate another person, will give certain clues as to their tactics or methods.

Take the following statements and see what can be derived from them:

- *'Get out of my way or I'm going to knock you out'*
- *'Keep running your mouth and I'm going to kick your teeth in"*
- *'Don't make me put you on the ground'*
- *'Take me to your car or I'm gonna cut you'*

- *'Keep talking to my girlfriend and you're going to swallow your teeth'*
- *'Get on your knees and pray'*
- *'Give me all the money or you're gonna get shot'*
- *'My boy is gonna mess you up if you don't do what I say'*

In each verbal warning, clues can be found about the possible strategy, methods, tactics, as well as de-escalation methods that could be utilized. Obeying the verbal cues may deescalate the situation, as well as provide tactical advantages if the commands are followed and the interaction controlled. If information is gathered based on stance or assumed stance, body language, as well as physical clues within the enemy's movement then information can be gathered to form a strategy around. Many times, one can know exactly what to expect by the verbal exchange. People will frequently, being the victim of ego and self, promote their abilities within intimidation, giving the target a false sense of insecurity as to the skill level or willingness to engage in combat by the aggressor. One must apply a filter to these statements and examine the deeper meaning.

Within the monitoring phase, the students can gather such information and develop their own strategy, tactics, and methods to address the threat. Let's look again, but through the filter of the monitoring phase.

'Get out of my way or I'm going to knock you out'

De-escalation: getting out of the way; Tactic assumed: punch.

'Keep running your mouth and I'm going to kick your teeth in''

De-escalation: stop verbal exchange; Tactic assumed: kicker

'Don't make me put you on the ground'

De-escalation: none based on threat; Tactic assumed: grappler

'Take me to your car or I'm gonna cut you'

De-escalation: Take the aggressor to the car; Tactic assumed: stabbing

'Keep talking to my girlfriend and you're going to swallow your teeth'

De-escalation: Stop verbal exchange; Tactic assumed: striker

'Get on your knees and pray'

De-escalation: none based on threat; Tactic assumed: lethal due to finality of language

'Give me all the money or you're gonna get shot'

De-escalation: give enemy money; Tactic assumed: gun shot

'My boy is gonna mess you up if you don't do what I say'

De-escalation: comply on demand; Tactic assumed: multiple assailants

These verbal exchanges are not the limiting factor. The environment will give cues as to what weapons or methods may be used. A pool hall is different from an open room with couches. Both are different than a dark alleyway or parking garage. Monitoring the enemy and the environment, perhaps at a bar with a friend, gives vital information regarding what to expect and how to develop an initial plan of defense or attack.

The control phase, while intertwined with the gathering of information, is the phase after which information is gathered and deciphered, and then the information is used to control the situation. Control is active, not reactive. You do not reactively drive a car or operate heavy machinery. In the case of driving a car, the constant gathering of informational stimuli and deciphering it, or drawing reasonable assumptions on the next event is what gets us to work every day - and allows us to act away from a car coming into our lane. We see the car move toward the lane, and first look for a turn signal. The lack of turn signal will lead to a different response than a turn signal because one is controllable to an extent and predictable (someone changing lanes and does not see us) and uncontrollable (one is changing lanes rapidly to avoid a wreck or object in the road). Controlling this environment, in a car, may be by using the brake or accelerator, a horn, or defensive swerving to avoid the other vehicle. With this in mind, let's look at controlling the situation based on information gathered in the monitoring phase.

'Get out of my way or I'm going to knock you out'

Control: Move out of the way to an advantageous position and prepare to defend against a punch

'Keep running your mouth and I'm going to kick your teeth in"

Control: Use verbal methods to initiate an attack and prepare to defend against a kick or stomp

'Don't make me put you on the ground'

Control: Prepare to defend against a swing/dive combination or a leg attack which has the purpose of going to a grappling fight

'Take me to your car or I'm gonna cut you'

Control: Lead the aggressor to an area that is confined or offers advantages with exits and choke points and use these to escape or even the odds in the fight, while preparing for a knife attack

'Keep talking to my girlfriend and you're going to swallow your teeth'

Control: Change verbal interaction to illicit an attack, prepare for a general attack with an emphasis on strike defense

'Get on your knees and pray'

Control: Position to within a distance that will allow for an attack based on being in the kneeling position

'Give me all the money or you're gonna get shot'

Control: Use distraction with the money to affect a more advantageous defense against a firearm

'My boy is gonna mess you up if you don't do what I say'

Control: Comply with demands in a way that allows positioning both enemies to the front, preferably lined up close to each other to reduce the effectiveness of a multiple assailant attack

As discussed, most people are victims of their nervous system. They allow the system to act as the filter to what they should be accomplishing, instead of actively looking for clues as to what they will face using their conscious mind. Which is more effective in increasing the chances of survival: the control tactics and methods above, or winging it and hoping for the best? The primary issue within most martial arts and combat is that physical cues are observed once the altercation begins, when there is a wealth of information that is readily available which will increase the chance of survival within a situation.

Why is M&C referred to as a state? The primary reason is because it is a psycho-physiological state for the organism the mind is monitoring, and then communicating to the body how to control the environment. This may seem counter-intuitive, as it relies on the brain to make decisions and the body to carry them out physically, while procedural methods only ask the body to begin creating learned motor patterns for defensive or offensive purposes. What is being missed in this mindset is the notion to quickly end an altercation, to achieve the goal, instead of letting the motor patterns become the goal.

Noticing an improvised weapon during the monitoring phase and then setting up combat interaction to get to this weapon through control is an active state. 'Flow' in a martial art is many times is referred to as the holy grail, but as has been noted, flow is the neurology recreating chains of movements that have been ingrained through the associative phase into the autonomous phase. One need look no further than a student who has performed particular drills which they are able to 'flow' through, but the student will autonomously use methods that are inapplicable because they are held within the autonomous pattern.

An example is within many training methods and traditions that require complex movement developed by drills. Unfortunately for the student, their neurology is controlling them based on what they have learned in procedural based learning - so, in a Pavlovian manner - they will follow through the drill, even when this drill will leave unexpected openings or present techniques that are inapplicable.

M&C is different in that the student is consciously making decisions on what they will do, utilizing the principles, which are adaptive; to achieve their goal within the physical interaction once the altercation has moved from the psychological phase such as the statement above. This is what is referred to as micro M&C state

Micro M&C

The monitor and control state can be applied within combat, even amid physical combative interaction is a student has been properly trained within the EPL. Students must understand that their reason for fighting is survival, not to engage in prolonged combative interaction that reduces their chance of survival or increases their chance of being injured or killed. If a student does not understand this from the attention-weighting phase, they must be reined into this phase to learn about goals and goal setting.

Combat seems fast. To the untrained student, it is fast and uncontrollable. To an experienced fighter or student trained through EPL and DPT, combat is not as physically fast as it is mentally demanding, the processing of vital information that will help achieve where attention is weighted, or the goal. Within combative interaction, the M&C state is still possible. Micro M&C requires a student to look at the active, conscious decision making skill in Pramek to decide what to use and then utilize the method. Within combat, the student must draw upon their theoretical knowledge to achieve the goal. An example is the removal of equilibrium. As learned within EPL, stimuli will be presented that is important and unimportant in how it must be addressed. Wild flurries or strikes are vastly different than target jabs, hooks, upper cuts, knees, or procedurally based combinations. The student must monitor this and make the decision on what to address. If the student is guided by procedural based learning, they will engage in a sort of 'tit for tat' response, using their own techniques to address the strikes because doing so creates positive feedback psychologically, even if it makes no sense for the student to do so. Within the EPL process, the student does not engage in this, but looks at the strikes as stimuli that act as their own filter to the goal. These are the walls, which seem insurmountable, as opposed to attacking the drawbridge door, or starving out the enemy within the walls will work more efficiently. The student must monitor the stimuli, and then control the stimuli only so much as to achieve their primary or secondary goal.

Within micro M&C, the student must control the information to get to their goal and in the example of the removal of equilibrium this becomes a matter of controlling the center mass based on the information on where the center mass is. Moving the line of gravity outside of the load bearing area is much more manageable to control than addressing strikes and kicks, as well as the rest of the environment. The student must see the information, and having been trained to differentiate stimuli, control the line of gravity and the center mass.

EPL and M&C

This takes the training process within the EPL to another level as the student is taught to actively monitor the information they have and control it. It is difficult to train someone to flow - this is a neurological state. It much easier to use the testing phases and the DPT process to teach a student to control the information they are being given. If the attack is a kicker, then the stimuli is the kick, but the goal of equilibrium remains the same…the tactics and strategy change, not the principles. This goes for a grappler, striker, or knife-wielding opponent. The student must be brought back to the phases of training, and then have their ability to monitor and control tested through tension, stress, fatigue, etc. In doing so, the student can be trained on entering the M&C state, which is conscious in nature, versus a 'flow' state, which is unconscious in nature.

A teacher cannot forget these phases of learning and phases of testing because it gives a verifiable method of teaching that is structured. These methods of instruction allow a student to go back to a starting point and work from it. Eventually, as the student comes into the M&C state the drills will become more manageable and the student will become more successful. The goal, and the proccss will generate the positive feedback needed within training – one way is the use of technique or learned procedural methods that have only a trial and error, success and failure test...as opposed to EPL, which is progressive, structured, and manageable through documentation, group reviewing, etc.

While perceptual learning is the ultimate expression of the Pramek active equation of Theory + Movement = Application, monitor and control is an expression of perceptual learning because it takes all the phases of the EPL and makes them into one usable strategy within combat - to look at the stimuli and adapt to control the stimuli. Where something may not have seemed apparent to be controlled and utilized toward the goal in regular training, M&C can quickly assist in seeing the stimuli and controlling it using a principle.

Chapter 15: The CLM and the Traditional Martial Artist

As we have seen, many students come to a class already ensconced with procedural methods. Often the question is asked, 'how do we teach someone who has learned their entire life through PBL?' 'How does a procedural student learn conceptually?' This is done by teaching the student the concept behind what they are doing - be it tactical, mechanical, biomechanical, etc. We must look to the EPL and DPT system to educate them on this alternative method of training and assist them with the paradigm shift, which it will be, but allow them to determine the degree of shift they experience. Some students will want to use the EPL/DPT system exclusively; others will use it in targeted ways to enhance their PBL based techniques. The goal is learning in the end, and both ways, while different, can develop a better rounded fighter, soldier, martial artist, etc.

Sometimes it is important to develop these procedural or perceptual methods further in training, but sometimes it is necessary to alter and changing these methods. This is plasticity in training, as we recognize nothing is set in stone. Traditional martial artists will see elements of the EPL in training processes previously used; they just won't know it has a name and process. It is important to remember that within discussing training methods, a flexible approach must be adapted to the student. The questions must be asked 'how did the student previously learn?', 'how much has the student been retained', and 'how neurologically engrained are the techniques within the student', or perhaps 'can these techniques be refined, used, or do they need to be ignored for now?' Within these questions conceptual learning is a powerful tool.

The goal of conceptual learning is to break down the procedural methods into concepts, building them into perceptual methods. As stated previously with division, conceptual learning can teach a student the principles behind their procedural methods. A teacher of Pramek must understand the basics of the theory to educate other students on the theory - if they themselves do not understand the theory, they are worthless to the students of the system.

The goal of the overall CLM is to ultimately explain the concept behind what the student is doing and then allow the student to devise their own ways of achieving their goal. A traditional martial art student should be approached progressively in learning the EPL:

- *Education on teaching method in general;*
- *Discovery of difficulty that presents a training opportunity;*
- *Processing the difficulty through the EPL;*
- *Integration into overall purpose of traditional study;*

Education on teaching method in general

A teacher must first explain to a student the process by which they will be training. If student has not been educated on the actual method, they will spend more time trying to figure out what is going on than what they are supposed to be learning. This learning process can be rapid and create an effective student in a short period, or it can create a student who is confused for lack of the ability of the teacher to teacher. Explain the process and give them excerpts of the manual as they are trained in it so they can see what is happening. It is important not to provide them all the manual and your notes and anything else they ask for. Yes, it is a first response to a request…the teacher wants to be forthcoming and hold little back to show their expertise and showcase the CLM. But this may prevent effective student learning and from you being able to teach well. The student will attempt to get ahead of the teacher because of the drive to succeed, and the teacher will not be allowed to let the process play out for the maximum output of the student. Once a student has passed a level, they should be given the notes on the phase or stage, or excerpts of this manual to review and understand.

Discovery of difficulty that presents a training opportunity

Talk to the student about their strengths and what they feel is their strongest skill set, their great technique and what they are best at. Get a feel for your student and their weakness or strength. This does not have to be a 4th Dan in an art - it can be a woman with 1 year of cardio kickboxing who has good strikes and shin kicks. Let the student demonstrate. The teacher should develop a good grasp on the student's strengths first and only then discuss their difficulties and weaknesses. This list will usually be much longer than what the student is good at if the student is pressed because, in the face of a teacher most people are self-deprecating within the martial art training room with their teacher. Just remember – this is where the respect of the student is gained by skill in how to teach and how to put what is taught into action. If a teacher is unable to grasp the kicks of a 1 year cardio kickboxing student, the student may not respect the teacher. This is why a teacher must be well-rounded and under the principles of the mechanics and biomechanics utilized within martial arts.

Once you have learned about their weaknesses, tie a weakness back to their strength so that you will be able to create positive feedback within their training. The student may feel success in their own work - but if they do not, they will receive positive feedback initially through being able to accomplish a task. Once the student discloses their weaknesses, discover through conversation or through sparring how much of a weakness this is and how embarrassing this weakness can be. Students will come through who are incredibly powerful fighters but cannot front roll or perform a kick due to knee injuries and therefore only strike or use one kick. By discovering the level of weakness, and tying it to strength, you have set the student up to be able to process through the EPL effectively.

It is important not to select a process that the student feels they have a full grasp of or are completely proficient, nor a complicated motor pattern. Sometimes effective is efficient - if the student has been performing the same technique to proficiency then it is efficient enough at the time. When a procedural student is exposed to the EPL, it must be simple, so they familiarize with the process, become adaptive through the process, and then move to the next level or motor pattern complexity or tension. The goal of this exercise is to use the EPL in an area of the student's repertoire that they do not feel comfortable with or need assistance with. Picking a topic that is a weakness will assist the student further than fighting them in changing some they are good at. How often are people offended when told to correct their posture - when talking to someone about their headaches and backaches and how to alleviate them will do just as well and accomplish the same task. The teacher should be honored to have a relationship with a student who will ask those questions and work to assist the student in developing more strength, not picking apart strengths to show weaknesses. Pick a simple, but effective topic.

Processing through the EPL

The EPL is a progressive process, but this does not mean it is an open process where steps can be skipped. Too often it is easy to skip steps because of time constraints, or the student is bored, or it seems silly to follow the process. This is true of any area of study, be it martial arts or basket weaving. This manual has shown how to move through the EPL and then to the DPT - what it is has not discussed is the overall is these processes

Think of learning to play baseball. What if one first learned to run bases?

There is no reason for this - but in martial art, it is quite possible to teach how to learn to run bases before ever learning to hit the ball. One cannot learn to run bases unless one has learned to use hand-eye coordination to watch the ball; hit the ball. Running bases is an act, whereas how one gets to the point of being able to run to the base or to stop someone from doing so is an attribute that separates casual from amateur, amateur from semi-professional, and so on. When moving through the EPL, take each step to its fullest and make it a habit to never skip ahead until the teacher and the student feel the learning process is completed and ready for the next level of challenge. When one skips a level, it will become apparent in the next level.

Imagine taking a student in the attention weighting phase and then putting them next into scenario driven exercises on a street? Perceptually and procedurally, this is what is done even by switching from attention weighting to differentiation. The steps exist for a purpose for the student to move through at their own pace. There is no rush - even in the simplest of combative methods, unless the student is being sent out at the end of class to fight against the enemy, there is always time to work through the EPL.

It may turn out that blending procedural with perceptual works best and there is nothing that says this cannot be done within the EPL, especially when time is of the essence in training. Note this is not class time, but a time cycle in the learning process for the student. This about experience. A student who will study five times a week for 3 years is different than an officer who only gets 20 hours total of self-defense training and rarely ends up in an altercation. If time cycle is an issue, then maximize time to get the most effective results for the task at hand, and then hone them to become efficient. Your students' survival is more important than their level of bioenergy. This is all too often forgotten but soon remembered by the experience of an unprepared student. As has been stated, a strike to the eyes or throat is extremely effective and can open a route to more perceptual tasks, like a principle or a general tactic. Efficiency can become effectiveness, it's just a matter of in what topic and how long you must teach it.

Integration into overall purpose of traditional study

Once the student has shown proficiency, then it must be integrated into the overall skill set the student already has. This is an individual act, as the student has been presented with their self-admitted obstacle, taught through the EPL and DPT to overcome the obstacle. But, at the end, the student must integrate this newly learned method into the overall purpose of their traditional study.

This may mean a number of options the student will work through and adjust to and this is not a rushed process. The goal of the EPL is to assist the student to develop goal achieving methods, and the DPT hones these skills fully. A student must then look at what they have learned and the integration methods. Common integration may mean adjustment of their overall strategy for their purpose. A sport fighter has an entirely different chain of integration than a law enforcement officer. A LEO should come into the situation knowing the boundaries of what they can and cannot do, judge it against their department guidelines, and then ensure that the integration is within the boundaries. A sport fighter must look at their overall game plan, confer with their coaches and trainers, and then test it within their overall plan to see how it will work within time limits or rule limitations. Do not expect the integration to happen overnight. Be it 6 days or 6 weeks, the goal of the EPL is to overcome the obstacle, but the student must make the decision on how to integrate it.

For many, this will be a procedural adjustment, as they are conditioned to work within procedural training guidelines. This is okay and must be encouraged. A reality based fighter who has a hard time with the clinch and is taught to overcome this using these methods will still have to adjust the procedures they have learned to utilize the EPL learned methods. The EPL learned method may evolve over time into a procedural technique. This is up to the student.

The most common integration is to use the EPL to test the most common techniques and the transition to the new skill set and methods. The goal may have to become just this integration and the DPT utilized to test the integration method. It must be remembered that this is an overarching training methodology that is not just about a better way to throw - it can be applied to testing someone's overall skills within combat. To make the EPL and DPT only about technique is to rob it over its methodology of identifying obstacles, progressively adapting to the obstacle, and then testing this adaptation. A good teacher of these methods should be able to make the goal the integration and not just the method and then use this process to hone the skill set within the current skills the student already has.

The ultimate goal of the EPL is to teach the student to teach themselves, and thus others. Eventually the student can EPL themselves without you once they know the method. This process is about freedom and the student will be able to at the end to look at their current methods and improve them; conceptualize a method they have seen and duplicate it in their own way; teach others to be better students and teachers. One should never withhold information in this method, as it will stunt the process. One must be looked at as a conduit to learning, and use the EPL and DPT in application, efficiently in training time, so the student comes back to train because they want. They come back because they feel the need to be guided by a good teacher; not because they don't know what to do because a skill was skipped or never taught to prolong the teacher student relationship for financial or otherwise gain.

Chapter 16: On Drills

Drills are an important part of martial art training. Beyond the concepts of this manual, drills provide a sense of immediate feedback in their motor functions that is not only positive in feedback, but a keen insight into the student and their motor functions. The nature of drills is one that is as old as martial art itself as a student works through procedural motor patterns with another student. Drills can range from flashy in demonstration often seen in many martial arts like Tae Kwon Do, to applicable in function like seen in Wing Chun.

The obstacle that presents itself in drills from the perceptual and neurological mindset in training is that drills can present false positives, where a student perform motor function that have worked into associative phases...but these functions may leave openings in their overall tactics and strategy that a rudimentary enemy may take advantage of. This can be found easily in many drills by performing a 'push away', as two students engage in a drills, but one student may push away, or disengage from the drills and the other student will carry out motor functions to complete the drills. The age old tale of policemen handing the firearm they have disarmed back to the subject they disarmed is not only a story, but a learning tool. Drills drive beyond procedural based learning in the replication of techniques to combinations of techniques that imbed deep into the neurology of a student.

Students who are exposed to long term drilling will develop complex neurological pathways that can lead to completing drills when completing the drills, in an actual confrontation, may lead them to disadvantage. This is primarily because students taught drills are started in the associative phase and will train through repetition to larger, more complex motor patterns of movement. These large, complex motor patterns start to hold more sway, through positive feedback, than the question of whether the drill itself is applicable. Simply put, the goal, becomes completing the drills mechanics and movement patterns. This is opposed to the goal of the drills when it was originally developed: an adaptive skill for basic attacks and defenses to end a fight or to gain mechanical advantage over the enemy. This is what is termed in Pramek as the 'kung fu fighting principle', the student will engage in the drill and work toward the drill's end, instead of seeing a goal and working toward it, which may be an eye gouge and throw.

This is done not only through the carrying on of tradition through application of katas or exercises. Many drills are adapted from what is commonly seen as means of attack by most opponents. Ancestors of certain fighting styles adapted their style to the sociological norms of the day...counting on the enemy in their geographical area to be trained based on what others were trained on. These enemies were often coming from similar schools, from teachers who might have left the school to develop their own path - but still holding the general motor patterns, strategies and tactics from the base school. We often hear of the enemies who were different in method and philosophy, but in general were taught in the same geographical areas, thus leading to a limited number of teachers. These teachers were taught by the same fore-bearers of the knowledge. One fought using trained drills because the enemy was closely trained and would most likely respond predictably.

This is vastly different from the martial environment of today, where school expansion has been aided by the intermingling of cultures. Strikers may end up with knife fighters, and kickers may face catch wrestlers due to the proliferation of MMA schools in modern society where commerce has created an environment leading to 20 different schools in a 10 miles geographical radius. Students must be able to apply principles to situations, as opposed to techniques which were developed based on training within a school, instead of training in a world filled with various fighting methods and styles. While MMA teaches some of these methods, it is still sport based. Convergent evolution teaches that what is most effective in a sport environment is not reflective of the reality based world filled with people who have trained in various schools, reaching partially associative methods of attack and are thus more inclined to use these methods in an engagement. Not to mention, drunk, high, or starving. We, as modern humans, do not live in feudal societies, but in cultures where any immigrant or son of an immigrant will garner students by what they teach. The pool of available styles to train against, and likelihood of a student facing an enemy who will not respond to drill trained techniques leads to the end assumption that principle based learning methods may have a statistical edge in success over procedural based methods that are not adaptive outside of their training classroom.

Some drill training is necessary in teaching a student motor skill and how to use them...drills can teach coordination, combinations, fine motor usage. The danger of deep drill training is that it leads a student down a path that is not physical, but psychological in nature. The psychology of assumption...assuming the outcome of an enemy's purpose and goal, versus the reality of nervous feedback and what people in actuality do: fight to survive. The willingness to survive is a greater instinct than most techniques, as a student who has 'choked,' or approached the end of their technique based skill level will revert to more basic hand to hand combat methods more commonly found in untrained, ANS-based fighters. When this happens, circumstantial adaptations will occur that are unexpected, deviating from the assumed path of trained fighting to an unpredictable method of visceral combat that even the most trained fighters will fall back to neurologically. A student may be faced with an enemy using methods they do not know; or the student may lack the cognitive ability, in the short period of combat, to comprehend and form a workable solution to overcome. In turn, the student may choke or hesitate because of the extreme lack of familiarity.

Students must differentiate between exercise and goal. A drill is an exercise. If the goal is a complex drill, then the goal is a drill - that is not a goal of survival. In true combatives, the primary goal of survival is always paramount - all other goals are secondary, thus sprinting away may be the best survival method one can learn. If the goal is a drill, and perfection of the drill becomes the goal....it will be repeated, and thus neurologically embedded until it is the nature of movement, effective or not.

This is not the goal on the street or on the battlefield. Complex drills do not matter on the battlefield, as rarely do interactions of the strikes go beyond two to three punches or kicks before there is disengagement or the nature of the engagement changes. Thus, simple drills are acceptable, such as training a student to palm strike quickly and then transition to a knee, as opposed to a palm strike to a knife hand strike to an upper cut to a knee to a kick to a head butt. How often does this actually work outside of training? We submit that through experience - it happens rarely. The palm strike to the face and a knee is much more attainable and achieves a goal, as opposed to the complex drill which accomplishes the drill and leaves too many openings.

Adaptive, perceptual based learning holds an advantage here as it is goal based and not interactively based. In goal based training, the student picks a goal and works toward it - as opposed to drill based training where the goal inevitably becomes the completion of the drill. Within adaptive training found in the EPL, the student learns to adapt not to the technique they see, but the stimuli presented meant to distract them from their primary goal. An advanced student may present stimuli for an enemy to react to with technique, hastening the ability to achieve the decided upon goal.

Adaptive training within the EPL training phases and testing phases allows the student to develop their own responses based upon principle, as opposed to procedurally learn technique which is governed by the ability of the student to meet the technique with another techniques. This is commonly why procedural based methods are engage-disengage methods, as the student reaches the limit of the autonomous skill, transfers to associative, then pulls out to gain a cognitive understanding of the situations at hand and then uses technique to address the technique. More than likely, a bigger and stronger trained student who is overmatched in associative and autonomous skill will eventually revert to overcoming an opponent through size and speed...their natural state, as though never having been trained in martial art. It is within this the nature of sport fighting can be found, as the students train to a limited number of techniques (ex. single leg pick up), strategies (ex. drive the opponent to the cage wall) and tactics (gain mechanical advantage in the clinch through having arms over the opponents arms). This can be drilled deeply, as it is the nature of the sport interaction and the confines of the ring and the rules dictate this is an effective means of fighting.

This rarely happens within true street confrontations, as the enemy is using unexpected methods of attack and defense. Here lies the fallacy of in-depth drill training as the student gains positive feedback through their completion of the drill exercise, while paying little mind to the adaptations a true enemy will employ in the 'split second.' When one expects the enemy to do something, unless it is based on good physiological evidence such as a true kick to the groin that meets the testes, the student will be forced into an adaptive scenario where they must overcome the enemy. Combine this with the adrenaline and the student may revert to animalistic methods instead of training technique.

Stopping the Flow: Drill Dos and Do Nots

Sometimes, when a student continues a drill without a reason, we find that 'flow' isn't the optimal state, but can be actually be a considerable weakness when used against an observant, trained enemy. But this should not push one to throw the proverbial baby out with the bath water. When used properly drills can be a powerful training tool to use within the CLM. If used within the CLM, parameters must be set - there is positive and negative feedback associated with drills and this feedback must be monitored closely.

Drill Do's

1. Do let students create their own basic drills. Feedback within martial art training is important, especially within the EPL/DPT system where the immediate feedback of a technique is not readily existent. Students can develop limited drills which will problem solve and act as feedback.

2. Do use basic targeted drills. Within the EPL/DPT system problem spots where basic drill can assist in training will occur. An example may be a 1 - 2 - 4 combinations and a student having a difficult time. Developing servomotors (hand-eye coordination) to see the initial movements, cues, 'tells', and body mechanics can assist in learning.

3. Do use drills to get over past difficulties. If a student has an emotional attachment to a past experience which is causing a large obstacle in training, a drill may assist in getting past this if the student is unable to emotionally handle a scenario.

4. Do develop drill for life saving methods. Firearms users, paramedics, firefighters, law enforcement, soldiers, etc., must have drills developed for job related motor skill patterns. Allow them to do so, if it falls within the boundaries of goals and the EPL/DPT process. A general rule is - if it does not stand up to the DPT, it should no tube drilled. An EMT picking up a gurney or soldier pulling his pistol in a drilled manner will stand up to the DPT. A complex takedown drill for a police officer most likely will not.

5. Do let students unwind the dogma of known drills. There are no sacred cows. Nothing will teach another student not to drill like a student disengaging and striking them unexpectedly mid drill. No one is ever wrong in doing so -

nor are they right, they are learning. Do allow students to alter and corrupt the dogma of drills.

Drill Do Not's

1. Do not let complex drills occur. If a student must stop multiple times to remember a drill, it's most likely too complex. There are always exceptions, but this is the general rule. Complexity leads to focus on the drill, not the goal.

2. Do not allow students to perform complex drills, yet not correct them. Remember - every movement must have a purpose. If the purpose is to recognize the goal and not the drill, even allowing a drill to go on for long can distract the student psychologically as they think about the drill. The student should look at movement and its consequences, not drills and their outcomes.

3. Wrestling is a drill. Many times, students will come to a standstill and begin wrestling and grappling. This occurs because they know each other's tricks and will keep blocking until no one can gain advantage. Always be willing to alter this by blindfolding, tying hands behind backs or around necks, tying feet together. There is always a lesson to be learned, but unless a grappling goal is the objective (such as learning to quickly stand back up or vitally strike from the ground), do not generally allow grappling. You can turn grappling into a lesson if it occurs, but make sure it has a goal, such a breathing, shrimping, joint lock transitions.

4. Do not use a drill on a student to 'teach a lesson'. Many times when students do not understand a concept, a teacher will force them into a disadvantaged drill to teach them a lesson...a trial by fire. This will only develop negative patterns of association, negative schema, and faulty emotional intelligence. Never 'teach a student a lesson', always instruct a student on a better way to perform tasks. When you feel the need to teach a lesson, either you or the student should leave the training area. Calm pressure on the psychology beats erratic physical stress every time in most drills. Make the student work through problems – do not create problems for the student to overcome on top of their goal.

5. If it won't work three times with full tension, it should not be used. Often time's drills are used because they work at slow speeds and are creating a

positive feedback that is addictive to the student. If a student is repeating the same method repeatedly, first switch partners. If they continue, switch tension levels. Test the repetition. If they can not perform at 75% - 100% tension, they will not move forward in the DPT. Therefore, it should be altered or no longer used.

The most important thing to remember as a teacher is that you are there to facilitate learning survival, not to facilitate someone feeling good about something that may get them killed. Often people are repeating the same method because it's all they can do, thus it's their only option. By stepping in, stopping this individual drill, and giving them new methods - you will not only create a student who possesses a greater sense of accomplishment; you may create a student who survives using it when they may have used something that didn't work.

When to Drill train: Training to the 'Common Denominator'

Drill training can be effective for what in Pramek is called the 'common denominator.' The common denominator should be looked at as the most likely scenario a student will face in real life. We have looked at scenario based training without the use of the term - it is important understand the term within the Pramek context.

In Pramek, we look for general movement patterns to gain advanced warning as to what the enemy will do or commit to. This is seen in the use of information to escalate and deescalate situations as has been described. The scenario's faced by a police officer in an area of operation or patrol will usually give them the common denominator within which to train against. A civilian who lives in an area where multiple assailants or knife attacks are common crimes will use this as their base line as to where to train for reality. Within this, drill training can be effective.

Individual Drill Training

Once a common denominator has been identified, for example, knife attacks while mugging, the student can mold their training around this for scenarios as well as in general training within the CLM. This allows the student to look at the movement patterns used within the attacks, as well as cues as to how attacks will begin. The drill does not have to be rote technique and patterns, but can also be drills with which the student can identify stimuli and cues, can discern behavior, and drill to look for specific stimuli such as a knife being held low or held in a particular way. With this common denominator, the student can utilize their most effective methods and principles within the EPL, those that they feel most confident with, to address situations and create drills from this. This allows the student to drill and train against known threats while avoiding the traps of 'kung fu fighting' engagements where the limits of the techniques and technique patterns leave a student relying on their animalistic fighting skills because they are left without options.

With procedural based learning, there is no issue with the student creating drills for initial movements that are general in nature to prepare for attack, or to develop one to two steps beyond the initial movements to get to their principle application. For example, a wedge is a principle commonly used within Pramek training. The student can drill to apply the wedge to begin their offense or defense, and then from this work within the EPL phases to address combat. This can become quick, prepared responses to the common denominator that the student programs neurologically, while not putting themselves as risk of leaving openings in their applications where an enemy can take advantage. For example, the wedge to a knife hand chop or eye gouge is combining principles within the procedural and perceptual realm. Sometimes it quicker to teach gross motor skills through repetition to create a set of prepared responses to the common denominator.

Nothing in this manual is written in stone - sometimes it is easier to teach a police officer certain motor movements that they can always access and then move from in the EPL to achieve their goal. What must be avoided is the traps of drilling that create neurological sets of movement that are inapplicable by the third technique leaving the student open or resetting during combat, which can be dangerous.

Group Drill Training

Group drill training is common amongst teams who function together repeatedly in risk filled environments. It should be encouraged for these groups to foster teamwork and operate with the ability to know how their partner will function in situations. No one should guess about their partner, even if they have rarely worked together. Too often, drills are so specific that in the field, when the drilled methods go wrong, like in law enforcement, brute force instead of principle application becomes the force used. This must be obviously avoided.

One positive way to use drills is to teach 'second man in' and 'third man in' scenarios where the second or third man looks for specific goals, as opposed to engaging in the scenario itself. This is the macro sense of monitor and control, as the 'man in' monitors the scenario instead of acting in a situation in a manner that may be detrimental to their partner or other personnel. Often, when the nervous system takes over, the optional man will jump into the fight, instead of working toward a goal to achieve a desired result. This must be discouraged.

One drill commonly used in Pramek alleviates this and teaches individuals to work as a team, instead of individuals working to communicate while fighting and enemy in hand to hand combat. This drill is Pramek's 'second man in' drill. First, a goal must be set beforehand. For law enforcement it may be the containment of the subject and the use of pain compliance to control the subject be it joint locks or use of a taker. In military this may be looking to get a shot with a firearm on the enemy that will render him hapless, or will kill him while not injuring the partner. In this drills, the primary student engages the target in combat. When the combat becomes a standstill, the second man in attack a target on the body of the enemy, for example a leg, or taking hold of clothing, and then the partners will work toward their agreed upon goal. It is vital that this be the target and the goal of the second man in. He must attack the one target he has picked up and agreed upon ('If I'm in a fight, attack the left leg of the target every single time') so that the primary knows what the secondary will do, and then work based on the opening presented. This drill is effective and achieves optimal goal.

This process can be trained within the EPL and then tested in the DPT to ensure effectiveness. Sometimes, it may not work. If it does not work consistently, then another target should be selected. A target may be a general area instead of one body part. This will give the students feedback and allow them to learn. In Pramek, it is often said, 'If you have 10 targets, and I have 1, I will most likely get to my 1 while you are going for 10.' This is the goal of group drilling - to consistently achieve the goal in a targeted manner. Law enforcement, private security, and military personnel often do this in real life but rarely train it. By using the EPL and DPT, they can consistently train to achieve their goal and know in the field exactly what needs to be done to achieve it.

Chapter 17: Goal Setting

Teachers are often asked: 'how does one select a focus for the EPL or for Testing?' This is a question with an individual answer, as each must decide their own goal within utilizing the method. However the method is being applied, in life, in business, in combat the answer is found within the particular focus of the user. In combat, this is a two-fold answer to a seemingly, open question.

How does one select a goal, and is it the correct goal in combat?

Who is the user and what is the strategy?

One way to break this down is to look at the overall strategy being employed. Is the strategy related to a civilian, a police officer? Who is setting the goal? Within this question, many answers can be found. For a sportsman and a soldier will have vastly different goals in the end. Within the EPL, the attention weighting phase must be placed on the goal and sometimes the goal as has been stated is the strategy being employed. Before looking to tactics and methods, this must be answered.

Secondly, narrowing options, but having as many options to train through as possible.

People can only choose the answers available to them that are apparent while other options may be a better path to the goal. In combat, options can be useful and can be detrimental. If the student has one tool for ten jobs, then this is easy - they utilize that tool and that utilization is their goal. In reality the goal is dictated by the strategy and the tactics employed to get to applying methods. If strategy is removal of equilibrium, then the tacit must create a method to do so.

Having more answers to choose from is the goal of the EPL. Techniques can become limiting in their usage, which is why Pramek relies upon principles and their application. If a student only has 5 techniques, they are severely limited in their options. Using the EPL, other options can be found in the learning phases, as well as in the testing phases. Some options a student has never seen may be the best for them - only through the EPL can this be found.

A student must always been willing to ask themselves: 'Is what I'm doing productive?'

Just because a focus of attention weighting seems to be interesting doesn't mean it is applicable. Often, one can waste an inordinate amount of time weighting attention on topics that don't merit the attention. For example, what should commonly be unrealistic should not be given attention. A student may spend 5 years weighting attention on the mechanics of a one strike knockout, chi, or a back flip kick to the enemy's head...all of this is activity, but is this a productive allocation of time?

Students should categorize their attention weighting based, and in turn EPL, on the near term, medium term, and long term goals. The near term should be immediate survival of the organism; the medium term should be refined efficient methods; and the long term should be incorporating quality of life into these goals. It is possible to develop explosive strength in a push while learning to stand up in a way that is mechanically proper and does not cause long term lower back problems? It is, for example, in Pramek's 'The Pulse.' This is an example of production, versus simple action. One is long lasting in it's affects, and one is short term, leaving the student searching for more information.

A general rule of productivity is if it takes more than 5 attempts to receive one positive feedback response (accomplishment), the effort is probably being wasted. If a lot of work and time are going into the study for little to no effective output, the student will know because it will either be unrealistic in application (tested in the DPT); or the feedback cycle will be drawn out and the student will not feel accomplishment (EPL). Other rules are: have at least two days off of training a week; track progress on video or paper to see results and see if the study is productive; do not study one topic for more than 40 minutes without a break to feel the limits of attention spans; do not train hard when injured (if it's pain rather than discomfort; do not do it).

Whenever a student approached a goal or focus, they should ask themselves in every action: what is the efficiency versus effectiveness ratio?

The primary purpose of survival is to put the minimum amount of force into a problem while receiving the maximum amount of output, or answer. The ratio between these two concepts is considered to be efficiency. An optimal focus of attention weighting would be a general method of controlling the legs of a person, making them fall, while taking the minimum amount of damage and using the least energy to do so. This is efficient - as it addresses the enemy while protecting the self and leaving energy to spare for other events such as running, sprinting, carrying another person. As such, efficiency should always be considered in the medium to long term goals of survival. Often, in the near term goals of survival, surviving physically against and enemy is the primary goal - this may mean using more effective means rather than efficient. An example of this would be using the maximum amount of force to impact the nose in a palm strike and following up with an attack to the legs; versus letting someone grab at the shoulders and tripping them as they do. One requires significantly less force input, but requires a higher degree of experience, motor skill, and servomatic action. As such, in the near term, effectiveness will create efficiency - over the long term, the focus of taking little damage, using as little energy as possible, while inflicting the most advantageous injury is most efficient.

☐

Chapter 18: Realistic Training: 'Preventing the Choke'

Think for a moment of a professional athlete, who has practiced for hours on end. The same movement over and over, thousands of repetition against varying stimuli. They have honed their movements to the finest of points and are considered the best in their game, which is why they are professional and elevated among the population. Anyone can throw a baseball, but only a few people can do it professionally.

This professional athlete, after thousands of repetitions stimuli, will often 'choke.'

It must be remembered that we draw an association between the motor skill or pattern we are practicing and the environment around that practice. Whether procedural based learning or perceptual learning, the environment that the training takes place in must match the environment in which the student is expect to use the skills in the presence of distracting stimuli? Let's take for example, student A and B. This is purely a thought exercise to demonstrate a reason why a student may choke in a fight, and the numbers used are purely for the thought exercise.

Student A has trained in an MMA gym for 18 years and is working from a neurological base of 70 techniques, 40 in the associative and 30 in the autonomic phase. He is a consistent point fighter for sparring, and lives a life in a safe neighborhood in a part of town where crime is general nonexistent and thus has had rare occasion outside of competition in which to practice his skills.

Student B has been training in a reality based gym for 5 years and is neurologically working from a base of 40 techniques, with 20 in associative phase, and 15 in the autonomic phase. Student B lives in a 'bad side' of town, where he has been the victim of assault and robbery, and thus works hard to refine a limited number of skills.

As we have seen in previous sections of this manual, the higher number of repetitive movements that are well-learned and well-practiced give way to neuro-pathways which generate automatic responses. This should generally lead to these skills being highly resistant to deteriorating under pressure.

But what kind of pressure?

A fist fight or a survival type of fight is the Super Bowl of survival for a human. Every pressure that can exist comes into play in a true reality based altercation. The question becomes: how many amateur football players can perform at peak levels required by the Super Bowl if they are physically capable of doing so. The number of stimuli becomes overwhelming, and eventually lead to the brain not being able to automatically fire, as it is overwhelmed by the sure amount of stimulus.

Referred to by many as 'analysis of paralysis,' this is when the student has so much affecting his neurology that well honed, time worn autonomic motor skills deteriorate into rough, basic sketches of their under-stimulated selves, or they are not reproducible. This is why training for the environment through stimuli is a vital part of training in combatives, be it sport or reality based.

In training a sport fighter, it is vital to artificially reproduce the scenario they will be faced with. The fighter must be taught to listen to their coach, or perform in a disabled state that would reflect damage they might take in the sport fight. Doing so begins to train the fighter's neurology to accept such stimuli. Loud noises, like a blaring speaker system of crowd noises that make the coach's commands barely audible is one stimuli that can be used. By conditioning through training the fighter to expect such situations, the good coach will lower the chances of the fighter becoming overwhelmed in such situations.

Recently, in Atlanta, a student of another art that uses our gyms trained for 6 months for a specific MMA fight. He had boxed and has trained in grappling, as well as proper conditioning work by a qualified instructor. Going into the fight, he knew the basic rules of the fight and was prepared for what his opponent would use against him. He was prepared in the physical sense.

He was not prepared for the level of over-stimulation that he would be faced with.

He 'choked' in the first round. He was overwhelmed by the crowd, could not hear his coach, and took mechanical damage early in the first round while adjusting to his environment. While physically he was trained appropriately for the fight, he was neurologically unprepared for the fight. He was defeated in the first round and stated later that he 'choked' but did not know why.

As a Pramek student, we understand why he choked and why he was disadvantaged against an opponent who had one more fight than he did in the amateur MMA league. His opponent was conditioned to accept the stimuli because he had fought in a public fight before, and therefore was able to access more of his autonomous techniques.

The same holds true for training for real survival fighting. In training, we must duplicate, safely, the psychological environment so that a student is able to not become over stimulated in combat. Using loud voices, threatening mannerisms, high levels of forced related to the attempt at physical assault can assist in conditioning a student's neurology more than any amount of protective gear. Far too often, a reality based trained fighter is prepared mentally and physically for a fight, but once the scenario begins, they become internally and externally over stimulated. This leads their neuro-pathways to revert to the technique that have been given the most repetition in motor learning. As we have discussed, these are our primordial, base instincts to fight like an animal. Once the student's autonomic nervous system begins to operate and take control from the central nervous system, the student's heart rate quickly rises, the body fights to oxygenate blood for the muscles, the visual focus narrows, they have auditory exclusion, leading to gross motor skills because these skills are the most used in repetition.

This is why we usually state that without proper neurological training, the student must have a number of real world fights before the techniques learned for real combat are neurologically embedded into pathways that are accessible in combat, leading to more autonomous techniques that are readily available in combat.

For Pramek, the issue still becomes the method of procedural based learning being used. As we have seen, there are some advantages to procedural based learning, moving from cognitive to associative to autonomous phases for embedding techniques neurologically. Very basic techniques can be taught through this method and most people are familiar with this kind of learning, so it is not a leap for them psychologically to learn in such a method.

As we have seen, Pramek employs learning concepts to train using a procedural based learning path. Unfortunately, for example, a soldier needing to learn quickly, or a high risk corporate executive who needs to learn basic self-defense are slaves to time and movement repetition in procedural based learning methods employed my martial arts. It also leads to a high level of students quitting classes out of frustration, as well as a low level of long term mastery that allows a student to 'flow', which is fighting by accident. The 'it just happened' method of fighting. While this can happen, and is not bad or good, it is not an optimal state to fight in when seconds count and decisions must be made.

This does not mean training in a parking lot every night. The student must be placed into stressful situations with particular cues and stimuli, be it a dark alley for simulated attack or artificially replicating a high heart rate and shallow breathing (which run contradictory to each and lead to exhaustion) by forcing the student to do wind sprints up and down hills, then the student working against an opponent.

Lastly, techniques will generally operate regardless of environment, but not regardless of the user. If the user is not ready psychologically, physically, etc., the chances of actually utilizing the technique drop along the timeline of engagement. This is why highly overweight people learning an art of high kicks, whilst enjoyable for their own personal pleasure and fitness, should not be taught kicking for combatives. They may be unable to replicate results in the field, or their psychologically doubts about their height of kick or lack of abilities due to weigh or size will force them to develop unneeded action filter. They will be learning techniques they internally doubt they can use, causing the 'choke' when the time comes. More than likely, they will fight like an animal.

Instead, it is best to take students and put them within courses of study which they are physically designed to use from the beginning if able. If they are not able, a teacher must guide them to utilize the martial art skills they are learning as best they can within their physical ability and become familiar with the techniques they can use. Then the teacher must combine these with the natural methods their physical nature gives them the fullest advantage within. This will bolster confidence and create a better fighter. A large fighter with one or two kicks and an efficient overwhelming method will succeed more often than a large fighter who only uses kicks and then must revert to their animalistic, nervous system nature. For this student, they will receive their positive feedback while learning methods they feel comfortable repeating or conceptualizing and adapting. This will work to reduce the chance of a stall or choke in a real like situation.

The EPL is designed not to prevent the choke. It is a familiarization process that is then tested by the DPT. No martial art is complete without testing...one must endeavor to test skills in a way that benefits their student. But, more importantly, no martial art is complete without the teacher and student relationship...and the trust developed that can lead through the choke at the moment that trust, and guidance is needed most.

Early Pramek concept art

Matt with Dave Dempsey (far left) and other students

Teaching a seminar, notice the notes on the paper on the walls, a common occurrence in a Pramek seminar

With great students

Matt with Leigh Culver, an early K-Sy and then Pramek mentor

An early seminar in Florida

Matt with good friend and contributor, Aaron Cowan, the first time they met

Matt in Russia

PART 3:

THE TEACHER

AND

THE STUDENT

PART 3 Introduction

Pramek's Conceptual Learning Method (CLM) is challenging to write. This manual more so than others in the CLM series, as the other manuals are very specific and scientific in nature, is based on experience more than theory…my experience as a teacher and Pramek's experience as a system in development.

This difficulty is grounded in concepts beyond teaching someone martial art and testing their skills … with this manual we look at the teacher and the student.

You and I.

And, in looking at the teacher, we must also look at the student. They do not exist without each other, as the first chapter states. For me, the question becomes not how to teach someone, but the relationship between the two individuals and how to make the most of it. Some people we will learn from a teacher for 4 months, others for 40 years. This relationship is a delicate subject and a challenging one to define. Perhaps some readers will feel a pinch in their gut, an internal recognition, when they read what follows.

They will realize they have a role…they have pupils and not students; they are instructors, not teachers. When one realizes their role, they become better able to relate to the other in the current state of the relationship. They interact in the present, with the information presented, and even to the presentation. When one truly realizes their role, they can accept the past as the past, their experience as simply that…not a determiner of the future.

When we accept which role we are in, we can truly learn as a teacher and student….from others and from ourselves.

The goal of the CLM is not to punch someone in the nose, but to educate the trainer who is teaching how to punch someone in the nose. Adaptive Combatives exists to teach survival. The CLM exists to teach how to teach combatives but more importantly, any pursuit - be it fitness or health and movement. In these manuals, we focus on martial art, but the CLM is not limited to that pursuit. Most martial artists learn how to teach other by watching their teacher and (more or less accurately) following suit. But, as noted in the Efficient Perceptual Learning manual of this series, mimicry can be dangerous when someone mimics and copies bad behavior. When one teaches mimicry, they do not truly teach - they create a copy.

Copies are clones…clones are not evolution.

The goal of the Conceptual Learning Method is to prevent this from occurring.
.

In Pramek's Adaptive Combatives, we see the physical manifestation of the CLM … the combatives, the movement, and the theory written on the dry-erase board. At our seminars people often say to me, "You know just when I'm about to quit" or "I learned more about teaching today than I learned about throws, but now I know more about throws because I know how to teach them." It's a fine line I've walked for years, but after studying teaching, in the end I simply had to look at my worst student … the student who causes more problems, makes my life difficult, the student who acts out and clams up, and will in an instant take class into a direction that it shouldn't go and scare students off. My worst student has always been me.

This manual is most likely unlike any you have read before…we go to places where we don't like to go. We look at topics we don't like to look at. The reality of man's experience, in my mind, understands the past to make decision on the future. We can't look at our schools and our students, even our systems, without looking at the deeper question of, 'Why am I the way I am and why do I teach the way I teach?'

I share with you something I have shared with very few. In 2001, there was great concern in the A. A. Kadochnikov School that other Russian styles would become so dominant in America they would write Mr. Kadochnikov's work out of the American RMA experience … and to be candid, this happened until our first group of Westerner's went to Krasnodar and came back to teach. My main teacher was a man named Victor. A former soldier, Victor was an educator by trade. Victor, pardon the pun, 'wrote the book' on how to teach Kadochnikov System…literally. He wrote the manuals on how the system was to be taught for the patent that the system was granted. Our time was limited and there was a sense of urgency that my time with Victor was not so much on how to use the Kadochnikov system, but how to teach it so it would be spread in the West. Many remark on how differently I taught the Russian style in comparison to my contemporaries in the various styles of the Russian martial art family. It's because I was taught a system few had learned by a teacher they had never heard of … someone I consider the best teacher to have graced Russian martial art.

In my mind, Victor taught me how to fight using the Kadochnikov System by first showing me how to teach it.

As far removed as Pramek is from the Kadochnikov System today, the CLM is my contribution to toward paying the most important lesson I learned from that system forward: how to teach. We can't teach the EPL or DPT methods without first teaching someone how their students learn, how their students experience instruction, the words to use to communicate, or even why students come to class and why some burn out. In the trial and error process that we all face there are more important lessons than showing a sweep or a front guillotine … we learn social interaction lessons. In every class we have faced as a student we have learned how to teach.

I've often said that you can see every teacher a student has ever had just by letting the student be in control of a class for an hour. In that one hour, the education and the true level of mastery and knowledge that person has attained are revealed. Every time they have been hit by a teacher, threatened, taught theory, shown tricks, not had a concept explained … all these are exposed when they are given perceived authority.

My question to you is: Who does your student see when you teach for an hour?

All these years later, if my students see Victor…his lessons to me, how he taught me to look at my own path, to see what I couldn't see a few minutes prior, and to look at the world differently each time I have a student or enemy…if my students still see this, then I am on the right path.

Only you look in your own mirror…If you are ok with what you see, then you are ready to progress in your training. But if you don't like what you see, it's time to revisit the past and find out why you aren't ok with it.

This manual was more than two years in writing because I struggled with every section and every word, and with the help of Stan Fineman, an amazing editor, I was able to take what I learned looking in my mirror and reflect its lessons back into written word. I owe a great thanks to Stan, and an equal thanks to every student I have had since 1998.

In this manual I hope we can look into the mirror and see both faces, the 'ok' and the 'not ok'…and figure out together how to fix both faces we always see. But never judge ourselves…that is the greatest danger in becoming a good teacher.

Understanding ourselves and our students: yes, but judging rarely

Pay it forward,

Matt Powell

Founder, Pramek.

Chapter 19: A Prisoner's Dilemma

Before there is a CLM – there must be a teacher and a student.

Master and slave, instructor and pupil, sensei and gakusei.

There must be knowledge.

There must be experience.

There must be a relationship.

And when such a relationship is formed it is powerful in that it has changed lives and fortunes. The relationship between these two individuals is as old as man's survival, as the Neanderthal taught those around him how he survived against a beast … and shows another who he likes best something that he didn't show the others. Better to share a secret with a friend, as those with the most secrets to share grow older, gaining more secrets, and more students to share the secrets with.

Unfortunately, the relationship between the two roles, teacher and the student, while initially necessarily symbiotic, can turn parasitic and become a draining force for both parties. Without one role there is no means of progressing as the other, as they challenge each other's patience, knowledge, and spirit. But, in today's modern world, this relationship is vastly different than the past.

Classes must be filled, dollars must be made, reputations upheld. In most areas of the world, commercialism has replaced the almost feudal reasoning behind the teacher-student relationship. This relationship has disappeared and is replaced with a monetary business, as opposed to a business rooted into the furthering of an art for the art's sake. The student can find many masters – there may be 10 in town, but there are 10,000 online. And these 'masters' constantly compete for the dollars and attention of the student. In our interconnected world, someone with no skill but a great website can garner more students than a school open for 30 years in a big city. A student is never a student for long it seems, as martial art forums, the internet, videos, seminars … it would seem all of these outlets for learning can almost lead to a form of martial art attention deficit disorder.

Some students become teachers too early, and systems get reduced down to a level of realism and theoretical soundness that they become laughable. We look around and see less high level-practitioners and more athletes with an associative grasp of martial art information. Like any other area of daily life, distraction can reign supreme and students can't seem to stay in one school too long. The need for recognition as a teacher in their own right outweighs the humility hopefully taught within the martial study and a certificate takes precedence over experience. And if a popular fighter or teacher comes along, whole schools can change in the course of a few months.

The teacher is not only bombarded with this world of short attention spans and the need for the flashiest style, but the world in which information is available. In the past, magazines and journals carried martial philosophy across continents, and the yearly meet-ups and conferences were where people can get together and train, be tested for belts, learn from masters.

Today, a well-learned instructor with 20 years experience can be supplanted by a 6-year student, if the martial art is popular enough. Bills increase, prices go up, and schools once manageable see the need to raise prices because the business requires it ... and if there is a cheaper school down the road, or in most cases an available study online, the student will disappear and leave the school instructor without that needed money to keep the lights on. Even down to personality, there are many reasons why schools close their doors. And thus, instructors begin to make videos for online showcasing their talents ... some to keep the lights on because the niche for their art in their town is so small they must go online. Others do it because they can't get students due to their schedule, and many because they simply aren't that good or are horrible teachers in person, but with video editing they can be. It is often popular for teachers to blame the student for the lack of a school's success – while the teacher admires his stick and forgets where he put his carrot.

The good instructors suffer, the students suffer, and the bad instructors are created ten-fold.

Often the teacher and student live in the same house, eat the same food, and face each other daily because the student and the teacher are the same person. This conflict between the two can quickly overwhelm a student who is practicing by themselves and learning via video instruction.

In these video-only learning methods rarely do video instruction students become advanced at anything beyond duplicating what they see on video. The teacher-student relationship within combatives and martial art is so vital that without it, the student cannot advance to higher levels. They must have someone to adjust them, correct them, challenge them, and test them. But for someone in Topeka, who wants to learn from someone in Atlanta, this becomes difficult at best, impossible at worst, and the teacher and the student suffer as the teacher spends time making videos for one student while ignoring ten others, and the student eventually does what students do: drifts.

The study of this relationship is integral to the use of the CLM methodology. The CLM does not exist in a vacuum; the CLM requires a participant, not a spectator, in both roles. It requires someone to teach and someone to learn, and often requires them to switch roles for the betterment of both relationships, in today's world, must be discussed. The classroom at the school with students and the classroom in the basement or living room with solo trainers or friends must be analyzed.

To write a manual geared toward students who are studying solely by video would be a folly as they are not truly students ... they are spectators who would love to participate. There is nothing wrong with this as it's the nature of technology. They are people watching videos, duplicating movements, and then showing up at seminars when they can. At this point, and only this point, do they become students – they become willing participants. This is not negative or positive; it is simply the state of the relationship. These students make up a very large segment of the training population – some supplementing their learning by remote training, and some training only this way and only occasionally seeing their teacher in person. Most likely, they have a training partner or two, there is no true instructor or teacher, and while this relationship can be positive, it can be very negative if both individuals do not work with an actual instructor.

The classroom in the school is no different – a teacher can make or break a student quickly. It doesn't require much to turn a promising student into a scared, intimidated, or bitter former student. Sometimes one class, one word, one interaction can accomplish any of the three. Most martial art teachers have one common problem they face: no one ever taught them how to teach. Surely they can demonstrate but no one has ever told them what certain behavioral cues mean beyond what their teacher said. They rarely know why people say certain phrases or act certain ways that are important ways of telling if a student is learning, or identifying these cues and phrases can stop bad behavior.

And most students ... no one teaches them to be a student. They are taught to be a martial artist. But, if they do not know how to learn ... how to communicate ... how to interact and how look at the world to develop experience ... they will quickly fail.

Within the Pramek CLM one could say, "Teach the teacher, study the student."

Anyone can learn to punch someone or fire a rifle – but how they are taught, and how they will teach others is what truly makes martial art a system of evolution and anthropology. If properly taught, not just in technique or method, if their psychology is taught – they will teach as if they are a student, because this is what they are in actuality.

The Children of Bad Teachers

The adage "there is no bad student, only a bad teacher" rings true in every area of learning combatives and martial art. From a classroom to the field, if the teacher is incapable of instructing in a manner that engages the student and keeps their interest while educating them, then the teacher is ineffective. Ineffective teachers lose students and over time kill systems and styles. The best of styles can be killed quickly by an ineffective teacher, ending years, even centuries of lineage in the process. This should concern any system or style, and any teacher who is raising facilitators up through the ranks of study.

A teacher must be able to teach in a coherent manner that keeps students' attention. Looking at schools and teachers throughout the world the problems that stand out repeatedly are: students simply get bored with a teacher and leave, or the student simply doesn't understand the teacher and, lastly, if the teacher does not deliver on promised knowledge, this can quickly turn a student off. It is rarely a matter of skill –it is a matter of conveying how to acquire that skill that is the first obstacle to being a great teacher.

Motivation can be an important factor in determining the long term success of a student. One must fail and fail again; finding all of the ways not to do things in order to get to a methodology that works for the system being taught, and the various students who will be studying said system, especially Pramek. The teacher must assist in guiding this process. While fun and interesting, Pramek's Adaptive Combatives, for example, can become difficult for a student due to its theoretical nature. Without conveying this theory properly, a teacher can quickly turn off a student, if that student does not comprehend the material being conveyed to them. After years of research into various teaching methods, theories, pedagogies, I've developed Pramek learning tools, such as the CLM, at the disposal of an instructor to convey knowledge to the student in an interesting way, while getting the most interaction and retention in the student mentally, physically, and neurologically.

In Pramek, we are our own teacher first.

You are your teacher.

But, if you are unable to teach yourself, naturally, you are unable to teach others.

We must remember that the adage we began with – that a bad student is the product of a bad teacher – still rings true. If you, as a student on a course of self-study, become overwhelmed or are unable to retain information you are studying – you have crossed the threshold of student to teacher. When we remember that a student is a reflection of their teacher, we can see the vital nature of creating realistic, innovative methods of teaching a student together with the teacher about their roles, and about the methods they are training in. This will create an open-minded student, who continues training under the guidance of, and eventually alongside their teacher. This is the ultimate goal of Pramek … the development of students who are able to educate other martial artists on the principles behind their methods and techniques, but also on the methods within Pramek.

If students are the children of bad teachers, a teacher must ask, "What kind of child am I raising?" This concept extends to the martial arts in the behavior and abilities of our students. Is a teacher creating bullies or meek students? Bodybuilders or lean athletes? Or those who are confrontational or those who are more reasoned in their interactions? How do the children of a system treat other teachers, other students, other systems? Are these children abused? We should look to our own students and those of others to gauge what are the interactions and classes are creating.

Fade out vs. burn out

When we begin to study a martial art or combatives method we begin to change our world view as a student. Over time, that world becomes that of a teacher as what was once a student progresses. This process can lead to a student leaving their studies or finding new ones. It is important to remember that there is no combative style if there are no students. So, we should first look at how to retain students, so they can train in a style or system. With boredom, repeated misunderstanding, consistent lack of student management, and issues in their personal life happen, etc., over time students will begin to burn out.

Fading is much worse for a student than burning out. Burning out is quick and usually results from one or two failures in comprehension, leading the student to simply stop coming to class. It causes a momentary 'buzz' in the school, which is quickly replaced by the next bit of gossip or challenge provided by a teacher (note to teachers: a challenge that is physical and mental will quickly quell gossip about students leaving). A fading student presents a very difficult problem for an instructor or teacher. There is a difference in a student who fades while staying in class over a period of time due to a contract, and a student who is fading because they simply do not understand the material.

A student who is fading due to having signed a contract will generally bring down morale in the class and slow the class down, but in general will do the bare minimum to just get through the class, or may begin talking about the other style or teacher he has found. In this case, Pramek recommends the student simply be given the option to have their contract paid out pro rata, or be given an out. What would be worse ... losing one student's payments, or two students, one injured by the fading student and one so frustrated by the environmental disruption due to the fading student that they also begin to fade? A good teacher should be able to see this situation developing by having a quality relationship and understanding the financial situation a student is in, or if that student is simply wanting to leave and the reasons why. If a teacher cannot sort out and overcome these reasons, then it is best to sever ties. Sometimes things just don't work out and this is all right and should not be personalized ... it should be welcomed in these instances.

A student who is fading due to an inability to understand material can become a dangerous student – as they become more apt to act out their frustrations in contact with other students and this can lead to injuries and fights. For the sake of the other students, a teacher must be able to recognize a fading student and intercede before the student's psychological frustration manifests in a physical manner. Smaller class sizes for new students are important so that a teacher can work with each student, recognize how they learn, and work with the individuals and the group to create a positive group experience. Thinking outside the martial art classroom box is vital to the successful transformation from fading student to shining star.

Teacher vs. Instructor: What are you?

Before being able to teach a martial art, a person must first decide what kind of conveyor of knowledge they want to be. Not so much regarding the methods they will use, but regarding the mindset they will need to have in conveying knowledge to others. When teaching another, one becomes a facilitator of knowledge the other person does not have, or they have and do not fully comprehend. While this manual will cover how people learn and how to teach them, it cannot deal with the personality of the person who will be using the material for instructional purposes. So, the question must be asked, and you the reader must answer – What are you? Are you a teacher or an instructor?

As we will discover, there is a different between the two.

Within Pramek it is often said that there is no good, no bad, just efficient or inefficient. When it comes to instructorship, for the most part, there is little good or bad, just efficient ways to teach and inefficient ways to teach. Beating someone over the head with their hands down with a bat may facilitate information about concussions, but it will not instruct or teach them how to block or deflect – therefore, this is an inefficient way of teaching.

Is it good or bad? Right or wrong? Those are relative terms – the student has learned something bad physically, but is it not good to learn not to get hurt and this scenario, though extreme, the ultimate of teachers? This is why we shy away from good or bad and search for terms that are more objective and can be backed up by general theories ... thus, efficient or inefficient. The EPL teaches us to ask, 'What is the goal?'

The first question one must ask when they step into the training area and begin to transfer that knowledge is not what belt they themselves have, but will they be a teacher or an instructor? How will they transfer knowledge others – what drills, what tones of voice, what will they correct and how? These are the questions that must be asked because they will determine how interactions with students progress, and whether the facilitator teaches or instructs.

Looking at the Webster's Dictionary definition of the two words, we find the nuances:

Instruct: to provide with authoritative information or advice;

And,

Teach: to make known by precept, example, or experience

While it may seem simple, and in the higher mind people will read this and say, "Of course, I 'teach', I want to make known by precept, example, or experience" often they are not, do not, or should not. An instructor who is always hard will create hard students – students who will fight through pain and will work to accomplish tasks. But, this can create students who will be injured more often, and at an advanced age will feel the effects of the hard training. Instructors will hold steady discipline through authority in the class, and while this approach can have some negative effects, it can guide a class on a path to learn quickly and prevent injury by closely monitoring and not allowing activities to go on without the authority blessing such an activity. Think of a military drill instructor when you think of the instructor: a close eye for detail, a harsh or authoritative tone, and a persona that allows very little questioning within the training room.

A teacher is generally the opposite, and will guide students and allow for more creativity within the training room. Over time, the teacher will endeavor to slow classes down, take more time with technical aspects, and there will be fewer injuries as the classroom is more relaxed in nature. Teachers can have discipline problems within their classes if they have students who require constant monitoring or interaction to curb dangerous behavior. Teachers are often more advanced in age and experience, versus instructors who tend to be of middle experiences and shorter in years. Yet, being a teacher is not always the most effective path for students, as this can create students who are in the training room more for health or camaraderie, as opposed to actual martial art and combatives.

Ultimately, within Pramek, the goal is first to become an instructor, who can lead classes, and work toward becoming a teacher, who can create classes and is the most senior level. A teacher is not born – though individuals may have certain gifts that would make them a natural leader or teacher. Becoming a teacher who uses creativity and adaptation in their application, uses personal skills that encourage students to act out of loyalty rather than fear; flexibility in their teaching style to incorporate all kinds of students and learning types ... these are primarily learned skills.

Most importantly, a Pramek teacher must know when to guide students in exploration, but have the discipline to keep control and prevent injuries to both bodies and egos. The best teachers are able to work between the two and push their students to achieve more than they came into class with – and to walk away uninjured yet tested, wanting to come back to be pushed past a limit again.

A teacher must always be willing to wear both hats ... the instructor and the teacher. There is no room for horseplay that can injure another, bullying, or unneeded aggression in combatives training. As the EPL and DPT teach, combatives is control. In Close Protection and Executive Protection the instructor likes skills of control and discipline, and the ability to apply both can lead to professionals who rarely deal with physical situations. But, it is their training and creativity under stress that creates a problem solver. The teacher in the professional comes out, as they guide their team via command and example, and encourage thinking that achieves the goal within the confines of the mission. Teaching Pramek or martial art is no different ... a teacher must be able to wear both hats.

Chapter 20: Words Have Meaning

A new student faces numerous fears in their first classes in martial arts. We, as teachers, must recognize these fears and work to overcome them. First, one must understand the emotional nature of terminology in training students. Words have meaning beyond their sounds. Words, terms, and phrases have a profound effect on your student and you must take great care in their use. What the teacher or instructor says can touch upon every experience every student has had, martial art and otherwise, their entire life. We hear this often, but it is rarely put into practice within the training environment.

It is well known that criminals will often tell a victim exactly what they will do in order to engage the subconscious of the victim, creating a delay in their reaction as the person processes the threat, and thus gaining psychologically control over them. A teacher is no different in their effect on the student. Here we do not discuss abuse, but even the most simply of terms and phrases can affect the student and what performance, knowledge retention, and activity the student puts forth in class. In a Pramek class, we look to theory before all else, as we recognize that while applications are governed by the individual and will change from person to person, theory is absolute. Theory in martial art makes learning a process that can be replicated over time but also easily understood.

Within a CLM-driven class, the first thing we must teach students is to remove their emotional ties to concepts, and instead view martial art at its true core: science. Words such as 'submit', 'choke out', 'beat down', 'ground and pound', 'bitch slap', etc., can have a negative impact on the student. We do not wish to seem politically correct in discouraging the use of certain terminology. Our goal is not to worry if we are politically correct or not – our goal is to create a student who is without psychological fear, who makes very few emotional attachments to words or phrases.

When a student hears a word or phrase that is common, they will automatically draw an association between an experience in their life or a cognitive viewing of the phrase, e.g., a sports match, and the phrase. An example would be the word 'ground and pound', because it is common in fight lexicon and with the general public and most of the time has a very 'macho' meaning. A teacher may use it extensively in class not realizing that a student has been the victim of this tactic at another school at another time, under a less than observant or instructive class leader, and the student has an immediate psychological obstacle to overcome, given the use of the terminology. Unknowingly, the instructor has reinforced a psychologically profile of a student who will a) be afraid of being in the guard; b) will more likely to tie up the arms of a student in positional dominance; c) will be less than enthusiastic about ground work and will not be a good learning partner because of this unwillingness to go to the ground.

All of this happens every day, in martial art schools across America, unknowingly creating students with a fearful psychology. In Pramek, and through the CLM, our goal is to create a problem-solving fighter who has no fears, sees through no filters, and is a willing, prepared participant in the fight before them. This is the ultimate goal for self-defense training, especially with women, yet teachers will unknowingly engage the filters the student has and put up roadblocks in training. This is why words, which are an essential part of communication, are vital to ensuring the student is educated properly at the beginning. In some Pramek programs harsh words are used in order to replicate realistic scenarios and desensitize a student to hard aggressive language. But, this does not occur until a student has been properly trained to accept such harsh, realistic words so they draw no associations in their emotional intelligence.

Many would consider it to be weak, or politically correct to discourage the use of such words. But, let us contrast that with a more technical example of terminology.

'Malfunction' vs. 'break'… thoughts on language.

Does 'break' truly reflect the nature of injury in the arm?

How many times in a martial art school has it been said, 'When your opponent is in this lock, break his arm.' When looking at life, how many people does one meet on a regular basis with broken bones? It is, in fact, rare. For example, of the 300+ million people in the US, research shows approximately 6 million individuals break a bone per year.

Sprains, injuries to joints/ligaments/tendon are more common. The body rarely "breaks". The amount of force required to break a bone is tremendous. The body functions properly, malfunctions, or enters a state of hyper-function leading to injury. This goes to the core of the teaching system, as it differentiates between a martial art that is explanatory in nature or simply demonstrative with students copying and replicating movements and applications they do not fully understand. In advanced martial arts and combatives, like Pramek's Adaptive Combatives, the actual physiology of the arm is taught. It is not a technique; it is a theory of physiology, combined with physical action that creates an application, which in this case is a malfunction of a joint. Recognition of the difference between the information with demonstration, and demonstration without information, guarantees an instructor has taken the time to fully understand the subject matter, looked deeper, and established himself or herself as a reference point for knowledge for the student.

When an instructor removes the word 'break' from their general vocabulary and uses terms that more properly reflect the actually damage done to the body, the students who have broken a bone have that emotional tie removed. They are educated on why they might have broken or fractured a bone or injured a joint in the past. They learn from their own injuries. A teacher will often be surprised by the amount of knowledge held by a student with a surgically repaired ACL. This student's experience, and knowledge, can enrich the learning in the classroom. This is an example of the group acting as a teacher, as a student can teach the group about injury and damage. If encouraged, much can be learned by actual experience with damage to the body described by students who have experienced it.

The usage of a word like 'malfunction' can more accurately describe what is occurring and is explainable in terms of demonstration, showing the functioning of a joint and the malfunctioning of a joint. Students are more easily educated, can take notes, and can pass this knowledge on to another because it is theory, as opposed to a technique. Explaining in theory using mechanics or physics what is occurring to the body will allow the student to experiment and understand why they are using the application they are using. It can also prevent injury in training, as students understand what is happening. They can push to the limit, and find the limits of pain versus injury, staying safe because they have the proper theory.

This is not political correctness, or trying to appease someone's sensibilities. It is removing the emotional nature of training and seeing martial art in its very fundamentals: physics, mechanics, biomechanics, physiology, psychology, etc. The goal must be to quickly get past any physical or psychological obstacles, or "hang ups" a student has and move to teaching the student. Paying particular attention to psychology is vital and moving the language of a class to reflect a neutral learning environment within Pramek is key as we move toward explanatory rather than demonstrative learning models in teaching the system.

Psychological wounds, while not readily apparent, can become a student's greatest foe in training. With time and training, and paying special attention to the student's reaction to concepts delivered in phraseology, these scars from previous personal battles can be found and dealt with much more quickly.

Our Learning Obstacles

Martial art and combative studies, unlike learning social studies or a foreign language, can cause a student physical and psychological injury if care is not taken. Understanding the fears of a student can be the most important job of a teacher. A teacher exists for very real purposes in the realm of fighting, as they seek to change that which nature has given us: the ability to fight from evolution. We are all born generally the same – and while some may be genetically predisposed to larger muscles, or dense bones, we are all born without combative skill but with which nature has given us ... teeth, claws, strength, speed.

It is education that directs that skill and our natural weapons, and it is a teacher who conveys this knowledge. But even then, a teacher is not necessarily needed to learn fighting. With a book on physiology and anatomy, one can find the weaknesses of the human body. Our natural targets, such as the eyes and groin; or learned targets like joints and ganglia. With this knowledge from a book a person merely needs to use their natural fighting methods in combination with that knowledge to fight effectively against an untrained opponent.

An untrained opponent when utilizing our muscles and strength, our adrenaline is a situation which is common and left to chance.

But what of the trained opponent ... the street or battle experienced enemy?

What of the lessons and discipline learned through combative training, like studying martial art?

These lessons are not learned through our animal-like skill set as fighters and a book on physiology. These lessons are taught, passed down generation to generation by the survivors, who teach what they have learned works to the next generation. Our ancestors learned what worked and what did not as one generation's sling evolved into another's long bow, and each generation taught the basic methods to each other. Over thousands of years this has led to commercialization in video and manuals, like this one, in the form of study where family and village training were once the primary means of knowledge transfer.

Jiu jitsu taught in a school and Sambo taught in a village playground have become carnival mirror-filled schools with numerous arts taught in one physical space. They are blended with other arts and changed, sometimes radically, from their roots. As schools work to generate money, more and more it seems students take advantage of discounts and more and more instructors are created to service this flow of students. In many circles it is believed this has led to a large number of unqualified teachers instructing people on something beyond fitness or language, but a study that reaches our very neurology, as we have seen in the EPL. Most uncomfortably to those who have been teaching for long periods and have spent their lives dedicated to martial art ... this teaching, once full-time in schools and academies, is being done in a minimal amount of time, an hour blocks a week, in a way that is best for mass reproduction.

Chapter 21: The fears of a student

Instructors educated within this churn-and-burn, fast-paced level of instruction geared toward creating a teacher who can fill a class time can pose a very great hazard to students and their future teachers. These mass market martial artists and schools can quickly cause physical and psychological damage that lasts long periods of time. It is generally best to assume that unless someone has never been taught a martial art, they more than likely will come to class suffering from at least one or two physical or psychological conditions. Accept this, as a teacher, as something beyond your control. Once it is accepted that this will probably be the base state to operate and teach from, a teacher must be able to notice and analyze cues which will identify some of these physical and psychological obstacles.

We must understand not what the fear is first, that will come in time through communication. We must first learn to identify that there is a fear, a remembrance of a previously negative experience that creates a physical or psychological inability to perform a task. When a student has a fear, they see the world differently than another student who does not have that same fear.

Negative interactions in the past create a present filter, and each experience is viewed through this filtering process. There are countless books about fear, as well as emotional intelligence, but for the purposes of this manual we should look at the filtering process in brief to understand how to become a better instructor, who can work with the filter to create a functional outcome for the student, and a teacher, who can remove the filter.

In a perfect world, no one would need glasses or sunglasses. Our eyes would focus perfectly; UV rays would not create long term damage to the eye. No one would have astigmatism and everyone would have 20/20 vision. Unfortunately, that is not the world we live in, where the exact opposite is true. We view the world through a filter, a lens. That lens may protect the eye from sparks in a shop, or may bring objects into focus to gain better vision, or shield the eye from sunlight. In living, experiential filters are like wearing sunglasses. We view the world not as it is, but through our experience. For some people, this is a minimal process, especially for easy tasks. But, in martial art and combatives, these filters can be like wearing dark sunglasses smeared with Vaseline. They can be blinding, prevent effective training from taking place, or they can be deadly in the face of real combat when one fights, flights, or freezes when they shouldn't.

We have a filtering process where we see the event, we draw a correlation to a previous event that was similar, we draw an assumption on how the event will transpire, and we act accordingly. In the EPL we discuss how the mind draws assumptions constantly - we live in the unconscious mind, constantly performing tasks, such as typing, until something happens that brings the conscious mind to the forefront and we actively engage our environment making active decisions, like the unitization and conceptualization phase in the EPL. A student who has had a high number of negative experiences with a subject, for example, martial art which combines psychological trauma with physical trauma, will have a more complex process of filtering information than a student without. This can be positive, as the student can see through the eye of their experience and solve problems quickly…or it can be negative.

For the teacher, the goal must be remove these filters. Have them cast off and replaced with new, clear lenses…and eventually no lenses at all. So, while this manual could go into depth in topics like emotional intelligence and the filtering process, it is more important to recognize what it is and then work to correct it, replace it, or remove it.

There are three general fears in martial arts and combative training that will lead to a heightened state of discomfort in a student. They are:

1. The fear of physical interaction, and the fear of being physically interacted with;

2. The fear of injury, and the fear of injuring others;

3. The fear of embarrassment, the fear of embarrassing others.

These fears are simply obstacles to learning, and nothing more. They are psychological in nature. None of these fears should manifest for a prolonged period of time in a Pramek or CLM-driven class without being addressed due to the training class being controlled and structured.

Let's look at how these fears are expressed by students in statements:

1. 'I don't feel comfortable hitting him; I don't want to get hit.'

2. 'I've got a bad knee; I don't want to injure his bad knee'

3. 'I don't know why, but I'm not getting it; everyone else is getting it but me.'

Statement two is an expression of a different FP. For every psychological ailment, there is a physical manifestation, and vice versa. An injury can cause long-term psychological issues that affect varying parts of the human machine. In this example the physical injury affects the psychological willingness of the student to train for fear they will reinjure their knee. In Pramek, some of the first lessons learned are not about fighting, but about movement and range of motion. The lessons of injury rehabilitation, understanding the nature of the injury and then, through range of motion exercises, healing or creating movement that adjusts to the ailment, so that the student discovers greater range of motion in the joint. This builds confidence in the student as they realize they can move without injury. At this point, the student is introduced to combative training exercises that are controlled, and allow them to utilize this injured body part and, in time, through rehabilitation, regain maximum range of motion in movement, and develop tensile strength, which will protect the injury.

In our lifetimes, we face two threats to our survival: short term and long term. Short term is the immediate fight or injury that can kill us or maim us quickly. We train for such threats and work to train ourselves to avoid injury, to win fights, or to fall effectively. But, as our age advances, our long term threat becomes the body itself, or more accurately, aging inefficiently. Long term is quality of life. In the end, through convergent evolution and aging, all masters generally look the same because their range of motion is the same as the body degenerates. Mastery is not a matter of techniques, but range of motion…the one with the greater range of motion has

What kind of survival is a life of constant injury aggravation, health problems, pain medications, and any other number of discomforts associated with the aging process? It is survival as long as one breaths and the heart and brain are oxygenated - but is it a life that lives up to its full potential? Injury to the knee at 18 can exaggerate over time to a knee that cannot bend at 70…and a grandparent that cannot pick up their grandchild and lessens their quality of life.

Think for a moment, looking at this injury through the prism of the filtering process about the long- term effects of this injury. As described in the EPL, martial art should be first and foremost about freeing the student from fear of combatives, and its possible physical and psychological outcomes, be it victory or injury. The CLM is about freedom ... freedom from past experience, and freedom to engage in new activities to create a positive experience.

Were this student not to receive proper instruction in a range of motion exercises, to train in a controlled environment where they explore their range of motion, the student may develop long-term health problems. The student might stop exercising and find more psychological comfort in the couch and television than in fitness and in good health practices. Over time, the person may become overweight and slow, developing various health problems. Or they will develop movement habits that will compensate for such an injury long term and unduly stress the other parts of their human system. In the end, the quality of life of the student will decrease, and their happiness reduces. If they never confront a deadly serious physical situation against an opponent, they will have succumbed to the enemy within – the enemy that is injury and pain – and become complacent so as not to aggravate this enemy. Is it not the goal of martial art to increase the chances of survival of a student, and thus address these issues as described in the EPL? More importantly, should it not be the goal of martial art to ensure these injuries do not happen and manifest? The uninjured knee or arm may be the one thing the student needs when an enemy comes to call.

With this in mind, we see the vital importance of listening to objection two and setting the student on the path of freeing themselves from physical and psychological pain. Taking an extra few minutes to teach movement exercises that can assist this student, and using the training methods within this manual, will ultimately ensure the student maximizes his or her learning time in a class.

Objection 3 or, the fear of embarrassment or of embarrassing others is a powerful motivator in the learning process of the CLM. A student, who is afraid of being embarrassed, will automatically become a student who will not learn. There are no in-betweens – when someone is afraid of embarrassing themselves, they will not ask the proper questions needed for learning. Communication is broken, and the teacher and student relationship that is built on the comfort of not knowing every answer but trusting the process of learning is broken. Conversely, a person who is afraid of embarrassing another person will not become a great student as they will never properly assist in the development of another student.

Objection 3 is driven not only by conscious thought, but by the martial arts training environment. Think back to your first time working with a martial art, or in an unfamiliar class, it is easy to remember the tendency to be quiet and not ask questions. No one wants to seem like they don't understand. While this manual could expound on the reasons behind this, it is so common for most martial artists that a simple memory of the situation can assist in making sure the training environment does not create an environment absent of questions. It is the role of the teacher to solicit questions constantly in training and to see where questions need to be asked. One of the primary reasons for the use of theory in Pramek is to ensure that nothing is 'sacred', but everything is open for discovery and to questioning.

By having a principle that can be drawn, drawn on, and explained, the question of a lack of knowledge in training is removed from the matrix of 'teacher-student' relationship, and instead put out for the class to question through their use of movement and application. Within this environment, it is easy to solicit questions from students by asking them about the principle, instead of the technique. 'Where are you applying the wedge?' 'Why do you think the wedge is not working? Can you see other ways you can apply the wedge?' This encourages the student to interact with the subject matter instead of letting the subject matter overwhelm them.

Beyond the fear of questioning is the 'machismo' that often accompanies martial arts training. Think back, as a student or teacher, on the number of injuries that could have been prevented in classes – how often was this because someone simply would not signal they were done working, feeling pain in a hold they could not mechanically escape, or someone didn't want to make their training partner 'look bad.'

Conversely, a student afraid to embarrass their partner may not fully learn what they are doing because they will not effectively place holds on or strike their training partner. Few want to be called out for being too rough, and no one wants to be called out for not working hard enough. The best way to prevent this is to not have a training environment that will be conducive to these kinds of scenarios. The danger of feeling or anticipating embarrassment goes beyond a student who will not ask questions – it can lead to the worst case – that of preventing a student's ability to survive and can become counter-productive to training in general.

A Role Model

While the CLM addresses how to train and work in a progressive method, it is up to the teacher to see the danger of a training room where ego is encouraged outside of friendly competition. If a student is afraid of being singled out, or working too hard against their partner for fear of being singled out for being 'too aggressive' then training is ineffective. Communication is not open in this environment. Instead, the teacher must work to ensure training partners are evenly matched and that goals for training are set forth in easy-to-understand terms. After making sure these factors are understood, students should then be allowed to work and the instructor acts to constantly encourage a student to work hard, or harder, or to reduce the level of force a student is using.

The teacher is the primary role model for students in training classes. When a teacher is willing to address the three objections openly, without stigma, the students will follow suit. A teacher should be willing to be hit, and to hit – never hitting too hard, but willing to take hits that are too hard and then correct the student. The teacher should be willing to openly discuss injuries they and others have had and create an environment where working through injuries is perfectly acceptable, while also taking care not to injure another student. Lastly, the teacher should not be afraid to fall down, have fun, be submitted, or be thrown. This will ease the level of embarrassment within a class as the teacher shows it is ok to be thrown, to submit, and to admit a punch is too hard for them. Removing the ego from the teacher is more important than removing the ego from students ... students will follow the role model. If the teacher is at ease with certain things the student may be fearful of and develop filters around, the student will be as well at ease as well.

Lastly, a facilitator of a process like the CLM must remember the difference between being a teacher and instructor, and seamlessly glide between each state to keep discipline in their classroom while educating students and letting them explore.

Fear statements are the first obstacles in any class and the most often heard. The first statement is the fear of coming into physical contact with another person. Healthy humans naturally do not want to injure other humans. Humans are naturally averse to injuring another human. Most people simply do not want to impact (read: hit) another person. You should be glad to get students like this – the student who is hesitant to contact another person is going to be a long-term thoughtful student who will not cause problems for your school by getting into fights. It is the student who has an unnatural hesitation about contacting another student the first time you should watch. Preventing the over-zealous individual from injuring another student is why Pramek classes start slowly and relatively softly.

Most often, it is not a question for the trainer of a student who does not wish to hit, but about an over-zealous one who has no reservations about hitting another student. This is a good student to have, but a student who must be managed in their study. The first key is for the teacher to use this student as their demonstration partner and let the student act as they would with a student. When the student does this, the teacher must begin a process of correction. For example, in the EPL, speed is addressed. The student must be educated on the speed of their activity within the confines of the training lesson. This student should be constantly corrected on their speed and power and communicated with to work more slowly and less aggressively. Directing the student toward maintaining a form or targeting a specific body part can slow the student down as they are given tasks. Most importantly, whenever a teacher works with a student as a training partner, the student training partner must be taught how to teach the lesson, and then placed with another student to replicate the lessons learned. If the student is brought to 50% speed and asked to target specific places on the body, when the student goes back into the class the student must take the lesson back with them.

Ask the student to demonstrate what they were taught regarding, for example, speed and targeting and form, to their training partner. This will focus the student away from being overzealous in striking, and instead be possibly overzealous in teaching the other students. If the student shows they are overzealous again, the teacher should step into the situation and ground the student ... that is, bring them back to the lesson task. And, when the time comes to move to 75% or to work in fatigue testing within the DPT, that student should be allowed to go first in order to release any pent up frustration within the exercise geared toward higher speed and impact.

The most effective way of overcoming "I don't want to hurt him" is to simply have the students begin at a slow speed with light impact: light pushing and prodding with a relaxed hand to comfortable areas (the chest, ribs, stomach). The ribs are a good area to start because the student will possibly laugh and loosen up. Once the student feels comfortable with light contact with a relaxed hand, move to non-comfortable parts (the neck, face, eyes) with light pokes and touches. Once a student feels comfortable with this, begin lightly slapping both areas. Eventually the student will gain comfort with these physical contacts. Do not worry about telling the student to open their eyes – you should want to remove the flinch outside of the eyes. It is natural to close the eyes and for a new student, closing the eyes when struck to the face will save you downtime in class while they adjust their contacts or stopping to fix 'water in my eyes' after accidentally getting a finger in the eye. Intermediate and advanced students should be trained to work with eyes open, but not new students. They should get over the flinch with their eyes closed and only then work toward their eyes being open.

Once a student is comfortable with being 'hit', then get the student to do this with another student. You are the teacher – the student will trust you and the environment, and the fears of embarrassment will begin to melt because of the realization they are there to learn. Ask the other student to recreate what you just did and convey to them that they had just learned; now they have to teach. Watch this interaction carefully. The next time a new student has the same issue, get the student you originally did this with to perform the task and tell the new student, "_student_ had this same concern and I taught him a method for getting over it. _student_, show him what to do." You have now reinforced to the new student that its ok (removed fear 3), that you have taught how to get over it and that student is still in the class (so number 1 and 2 fears must be unfounded if _student name_ is still in the class). You have also made a teacher out of _student_, who originally did not want to perform these tasks.

When a student has gone through this process, they will know their prior injuries will not be affected if they report them, and they will not be embarrassed because the training is controlled. This is a procedure you should follow all of the time so that students learn a procedure to help other students. A teacher perpetually creates teachers out of students, even in the smallest of interactions and guidance. The ultimate goal is to create a teacher out of a student so that your style will expand. Students will train with someone they like who is of mediocre skill more readily than they will train with someone they don't like of high skill. Personal relationships are the keys to getting past the three objections, seeing them as the obstacles to freedom that they are, and pushing past them.

Chapter 22: The teacher and the student

A student's their worldview will constantly shift between being the student and being the teacher. A student will eventually, if given time and encouragement, teach others and then leave their studies to learn under a new teacher, or a new system. Eventually they will teach this as well, if allowed; or even if not officially, they will inevitably teach what they learn to others. This will inevitably lead to repeating that cycle, as the student studies art after art, under teacher after teacher, becoming a teacher on their own.

Sometimes, the two roles will become one, and indistinguishable.

This state, of oneness, in which a student learns as they teach shows a level of understanding beyond that of the teacher or student state. While a student, the individual must learn from another person or set of methods called a style or martial art. The student looks up to the teacher, viewing them as a source of knowledge. While becoming a teacher, the student must be concerned with the learning of others, instructing them while adhering to the rules that govern teaching. The teacher, in most cases, recognizes the position he or she holds in the training room and in the interaction with their student and must keep this position until the student is ready to move to another position. A student who is consistently shy or unwilling to work with hard impact should be kept with similar students until they show a willingness to work at a harder impact level. There is no shame in working slowly with a student…there is only shame in losing a good student because they were rushed into a situation they were not ready for.

A true teacher is not only a teacher and instructor, but a student. It is only when the ego is removed that the teacher can become a student of what they are teaching. As a teacher, one may be wrong. In Pramek, the years between 2007 and 2010 were spent reforming teaching methodology as Matt Powell did experiments teaching classes in a variety of ways - some correct, some incorrect, to find the mix that would create a better learning environment. Adapting, adjusting, applying principles and theories, the teacher becomes a student of their own adaptation of principle and theory. Within Pramek, this is the highest goal we can attain, because it requires an in-depth understanding of the theory and principles and relies on constant adjustment, as well as physical ability to use movement to apply these theories. The teacher studies themselves, their students, and then uses the theory to adjust themselves and others in real time.

The EPL and DPT: Supplementing the Teacher Student Relationship

The CLM was not created in a vacuum. It was born of the need to structure the relationships between the teacher and the student. This relationship can become difficult within the confines of martial art because of the physical and psychological nature of the instruction. It is unlike other schools of learning, for example, a sport like tennis, where a student is challenged mentally and physically through exercise, but not through physical interaction with another person in a combative manner. Martial art and combative instruction goes to the core of human survival, and therefore demands a different structure than most learning methods.

Learning is an individual's interaction with knowledge. When you learn, you understand the knowledge being transferred, whichever learning profile you belong to. These profiles are determined long before the student arrives in the classroom and begins interacting with the teacher. Students learn either through sight, touch, or by hearing. An understanding of these is vital to the relationship between the teacher and the student, and therefore the relationship between the student and the information being taught. The greatest information is worthless if the student cannot interact with it, and understand it fully.

The CLM was developed to address two questions that exist in teachers and students.

One: How is the knowledge of the student being tested?

Two: How is a student learning?

This may seem backwards, and often in the media we hear the negatives of "teaching to the test" and how it creates students who are not truly educated. This may or may not work within the realm of primary school education, but it certainly does not work in survival training. In the realm of combatives, the test is survival in a situation where the student could die. In movement health, student's training should result in being physically able to function at an advanced age as a quality of life issue. As such, we should teach to the test, and not test to what is taught. Thus, using the strategy of the EPL, we first determine the goal, and then we teach to the goal, which is survival.

We do not bend the goal to the teaching.

We bend the teaching to the goal.

Primary school education is not an absolute – one can live an entire life with little to no education, or classroom testing. One cannot live with little to no survival skills, especially for someone who is thrust into situation which constantly endangers them. Training should be a shortcut provided by other's experience so the student can learn to survive without unneeded injury created by 'learning on the job.' This is why educational models exist.

In the reality that is martial art learning, these two questions are determined by certain parameters in order to guide the transfer of knowledge from one person to another. Within Pramek these are: structure, method, retention, and relationship. Each affects the other, but the relationship between the parties within the transfer can radically alter the other three. The structure of the transfer of knowledge (e.g. progressive versus immersive) is addressed within the EPL and DPT, as Pramek begins with progressive and ends with immersive. The method of knowledge transfer (e.g., procedural versus perceptual) is addressed within the EPL, with a premium placed on perceptual, but a realization that some basic skills must be procedural in nature. The concept of retention, or is the information being retained and more importantly, is it usable, is addressed within the DPT through a testing program. Lastly, there is the overarching question of the relationship between the person facilitating knowledge, and those gaining the knowledge. When a teacher has a structure to their teaching, a methodology, and a method of determining retention, the teacher must then look at how the student is learning.

Chapter 23: Learning profiles within CLM

While generally considering "styles of learning" within combatives education you need to look at the profiles, as the student will tend to fit a profile for how communication must flow in the classroom.

A student will generally fit one of three profiles:

1. Visual Learner – learns primarily through sight and observation

2. Tactile Learner –learns primarily through feeling, performing tasks

3. Auditory Learner – learns primarily through hearing

This is common knowledge in most of the education world and the reader is encouraged to research this on their own. It is best to quickly lay out the general verbal and behavioral cues that will assist a teacher in profiling their student. A student can also learn valuable information about how they learn simply by paying attention to their own verbal and behavioral cues.

Visual Learning Profile

Verbal Cue: "I see what you mean." "Could you show that again?"

Behavioral Cue: Will ask for reading materials and manuals, lead group

conversations, talks on the phone to the teacher and classmates, reads forums and magazines, uses fingers to plug ears when distracted, excels at explaining the lesson; verbs and descriptors used in verbal communication

Auditory Learning Profile

Verbal Cue: "I hear you." "That sounds about right." "Could you say that again?"

Behavioral Cue: Takes copious amounts of written notes, asks for instructions repeatedly, closes eyes while listening to the class lecture, asks for podcasts, will go to other classes and ask questions, excels at writing out descriptions and diagrams of lessons; verbs and descriptors used in verbal communication

Tactile Learning Profile

Verbal Cue: "I feel what you." "Could you do that to me again?" "Let me feel."

Behavioral Cue: Asks to be part of demonstration, consistently wants to work with training partners, is physical in interactions with others, shuns the lecture portions of class, excels at demonstrations but may lack ability to teach technical knowledge through explanation; verbs and descriptors used in verbal communication.

Interactions with these profiles are a matter of observation and interaction by the teacher. When a teacher identifies the cues, the teacher should take time to observe the student, their verbal and behavioral cues, and then utilize interactions that best benefit the student's profile type. For example, demonstrating on a tactile learner, or drawing an in-depth diagram for a visual learner. The teacher may record a lecture for the auditory learner.

Observation and patience are the keys to the learning profiles that the teacher identifies in students. It is a trial and error method, as the relationship between the student and teacher is not dogmatic – it is not a magnet and metal, but it is comprised of emotions, personalities, and experiences. Thus, a teacher must take time to identify the student's profile and work with it, but in order to fully train a student, the teacher must familiarize the student with his or her learning profile, suggest research outside of this manual, and encourage research so they student will be efficient in their learning.

When a teacher knows the profile type, and the student knows the profile type, the communication between the two is light-years beyond an instructor who teaches the lesson plan, and a pupil who struggles being an auditory learner in a classroom of tactile demonstrations. This is the folly of being only an instructor, as it tends to produce short-term students who are frustrated, and a school wrought with student churn and bad finances.

There will be times in which the student's profile must be challenged by the teacher in order to challenge the development of the student. We must create a problem-solver in our work with the CLM. The student must be made to face every obstacle, even when they themselves are the obstacle. Often, a teacher needs to teach the entire class using a particular profile, or ask a class of visual learners to close their eyes and listen, then visualize using their imagination. A student needs to be able to create mental trial and error exercises, to rehearse and test, all without having to touch another person. A student who can visualize never stops training and so students must be encouraged to visualize. By challenging the profiles, the teacher can assist a student to become a better fighter and warrior, via their ability to engage their eyes, ears, and hands – as opposed to only their hands and legs.

These profiles, while generally recognized as the most common learning types, are not the be all and end all of situations in which a student may not have another method in which they learn. Many are familiar with "doodling" and drawing on paper or processing, or activities by which students learn through processing visual and aural information, and then scribble and doodle as a tactile means of working through the information and processing it. The student should never be expected to stay within that profile. Many times a student may jump from one to the other, based on subject matter, presentation, or the presenter. Often the student may tire of one way, or have a moment in which they find they learn better in another manner, and for that time their profile may change. A student should be encouraged to look at their own profile cues – even to be open to the teacher and other students pointing out the cues, and perhaps challenging the student to try another method of learning.

Most teachers will find that students will stay within their basic profiles the majority of the time. This would be fine in a world where combatives did not include physical contact, but it does, and a teacher must be able to take the student through all three profiles in order to ensure they are providing a well-rounded education. So, a teacher must understand how they are communicating with their students in the class, and how each student is experiencing the education.

Cone of Experience

One aid a teacher can use in looking at how to address learning profiles is the Cone of Experience, which was an attempt by Edgar Dale in 1946 to diagram communication methods and the general ability of students to remember conveyed material (see below). This diagram shows that when a learning method is abstract, such as reading, or one that is tactile, such as actually performing the task, the amount of knowledge that is remembered is vastly different. In making the assumption that most people are familiar with the concept of "People remember 10% of what they read, but 90% of what they do", a teacher can utilize a tool such as the Cone of Experience to demonstrate to students what communication actually is the reality of learned skill. When viewed through this prism, communication is not just the teacher teaching and the student listening – it is the means of knowledge transfer.

This manual can be used as a simple knowledge tool, where the reader can read the information developed by Pramek from experience. The reader must use the information. As is taught in the Pramek EPL, Theory + Movement = Application. Theory is dead without movement…the reader must use their own movement and teaching to fully utilize the theory.

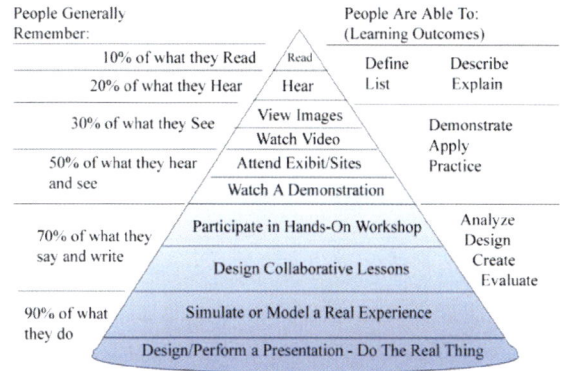

Dale's Cone of Experience

The Cone of Experience, or in Pramek terminology, "CoE", attempts to demonstrate communication and level of understanding from the form of communication. There are many forms of the CoE in the educational world, spanning many different topics and types of teaching. In reality, one should look to the general concept of the CoE as a guide. In the graphic shown, the CoE is explained in general educational terms utilizing Edgar Dale's version. A person learns different tasks in different ways and then remembers information given to them when they make actual use of the information. For example, a person wanting to learn about a car engine will gain a lot of knowledge from a book about the engine, but will gain more knowledge about the engine by actually touching an engine and working on it. But, when you understand the engine, the theory of combustion and how the engine functions, the parts list … and how they interact with an engine, and then the student begins to work on the rest of the car, the student is learning at a higher level because are applying theoretical knowledge. They start with a base of knowledge, and real life information builds upon it.

Pramek puts a premium on manuals, videos, and in-person training because it has been found through internal research that students tend to learn best by being exposed to all three learning profiles, and thus they are then exposed to each level of the CoE. In many arts, there is nothing informational; there is only the physical. For rapid skill attainment, in the case of soldiers or law enforcement, this learning method combined with constant testing like those methods of the EPL and DPT are effective. In other arts, it is only informational, with very little real-world, scenario-driven training and testing. By utilizing all levels of the CoE in communication, the education is well rounded for either style of teaching

When a student can read material, they can reference it and attention-weight it in the EPL.

When they can see it and hear it on video, they imprint it and make it into their own.

When a student comes to live training and actually works with an instructor, the student can learn differentiation, unitization, and be instructed through the tactile approach in person.

They will actually perform it, and then be physically adjusted by an instructor and other students. In doing this process, they will remember and internalize at a higher rate than other students.

And, finally, through the DPT, the student is tested thoroughly, and their perception is pushed to the limit through tension, stress, fatigue, nervous arousal, and scenarios. This hones the student's skills and testes what methods and techniques are autonomic. So that when there is a real-life situation, the student is prepared.

Many martial arts have manuals that are visual tools that please the visual learner – but could they be read aloud to assist the auditory learner? How is the instruction on the video communicated? When an instructor does a public demonstration, how are they working with the audience? How do they adjust their demonstrations and interactions with students? This is the level of education, and organization their presentation, that a teacher must think of. When a teacher thinks of a student's CoE and their communication, they can begin to radically alter the student's perception of education. Within Pramek, we look to a version of the CoE that is more geared toward the conceptual learning method.

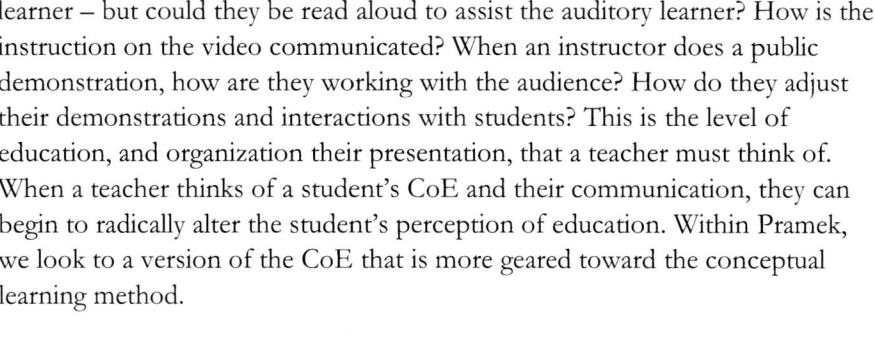

Pramek CLM 'Cone of Experience'

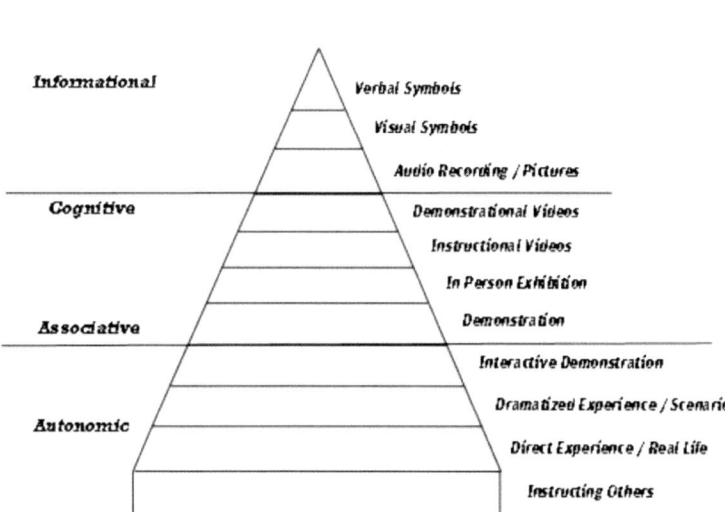

In Pramek, we must look at the general methods of learning a topic such as martial art, health and fitness, etc. The student is taken through all phases of the CoE, leading to a more thorough, in-depth method of instruction that gets results. This is the most optimal manner overall in which the CLM is operational, and why it works. When the EPL and DPT are viewed from the outside, they seem to be difficult methods of learning. But, viewed through the CoE, you begin to see that, scientifically, all of the styles of learning are contained within the EPL and DPT ... that the Cone of Experience is progressed through in an understandable way. This is why it is important for a teacher to not view a student as another dollar sign or a profile that is difficult to deal with, but as a person representing a challenge to be accepted and worked with in the classroom.

Within Pramek's CLM Cone of Experience the type of experience ties to the stages of the EPL, moving from the cognitive to autonomic. But, first we need to make note on the definition of experience. While similar to Dale's original Cone of Experience, Pramek's process is more geared toward martial art instructional methods in modern media format.

Verbal and visual symbols are descriptions, or diagrammatic theory, which may lead to audio recordings like a podcast or book on tape, and eventually a martial art manual that shows general techniques. This would be informational, moving toward a cognitive understanding.

Demonstration videos would be the equivalent of watching techniques online or seeing a foreign language video. An instructional video is a video in one's native tongue and is an in-depth demonstration followed by video instruction.

An exhibition would be seeing someone at an event or seminar performing, versus a demonstration where one is teaching a large group at a trade show or conference, but one does not actively participate. In these types of experiences, one has moved from a cognitive understanding, of just seeing, to a more associative understanding and can begin to see causation in what is being taught.

In the development of the autonomic phase, you move to an interactive demonstration, where you are actually involved and physically performing a task and are asked to repeat the task. This may be learning a technique in PBL as is referred to in the DPT manual, or a method in EPL. At this point, the motor patterns begin to be autonomic, in that the physical iteration creates neuro-pathways, as discuss in the EPL. Finally, once a person performs under testing, such as a method like Pramek's DPT testing methods, which are activity- and scenario-driven, the person has moved to a truly autonomic phase. But, it is only within real life, survival situations that you can truly understand what you have been taught, and whether you have truly internalized it. This is, for the student, the point where the rubber hits the proverbial road, as they reinforce neuro-pathways; refine schema, etc., through actual experience, where success or failure is not dictated by the teacher's critique, but by a teacher called pain and injury.

Tying the learning profiles together using the CLM

The CoE is a guide – it is no different than a belt system for learning karate, in that it guides the teacher on their learning path. The CoE allows the teacher to look at the how, what, where, when, who, and why of what they are teaching, and structure accordingly. If the teacher has a classroom of auditory learners, then the teacher must be adaptable and ensure that the tactile portions are combined with communication that caters to the cues given.

One must always remember – no learning profile is better or worse than the other. Stephen Hawking is unable to use his tactile senses yet he has revolutionized his chosen field of study few have attained and popularized his work. Tom Cruise was barely able to read the scripts due to dyslexia, yet he is among the most successful actors ever. If a teacher begins to discount a student based on a learning profile and only works with certain types, or types they feel comfortable with, they aren't really a teacher … they are a class leader and shortchanging the student and themselves. More than likely, those students will be stunted in development and will not make good teachers themselves, as they are only able to learn, interact, and replicate the knowledge they have learned in one profile.

A teacher should be able to explain what they are teaching, write out or draw a description, and then demonstrate the topic of discussion to touch every kind of student and learning profile, as well as challenge oneself to be a better teacher.

Teachers must try to stop viewing martial art as punches and kicks, and instead views it as an information transfer no different than learning how to cook, writing a novel, or performing math. Doing this, they can challenge themselves to begin incorporating time-tested methods of education, science, and processes to test theories. This challenge is why there is one level in Pramek's CoE beyond "real life", and that stage is teaching. It is not higher, but beyond because when a student teaches, the student engages all levels of experience. The student must recall that which is read, seen, and done ... tying all of the learning profiles into one moment, when the student becomes teacher. The simplest method of tying the profiles together is the use of the Pramek CLM equation:

$$Theory + Movement = Application$$

This equation encompasses both the CoE and the learning profiles and can act as a guide for the teacher to ensure the student gains a full-spectrum education, from verbal to experience. The abstract levels of the CoE are covered in the theory stage of teaching. The teacher can write down and explain the concepts behind what the student is doing.

A block is a wedge in physics, and a strike is an object in space with a trajectory.

A throw is not a throw, but is a removal of equilibrium.

One doesn't blink because they are scared...they blink because the nervous system dictates to do so and must be trained not to.

When a student has knowledge, the student has power over how that knowledge will be used. A medical book is filled with knowledge, but without human hands to hold the scalpel, and experience to make sure the scalpel is used correctly on the right muscle or organ ... the theory is worthless. With this in mind, it is important that a teacher make every effort to be a sponge for knowledge. This knowledge does not have to be in how a student throws the best right hook, but, through physiology, where to target the body to throw the hook for the maximum amount of damage. Theory allows the student to write notes, verify statements in books and in conversation with others, to hear a lecture and gain a deeper understanding of the information being taught. Within the EPL this phase is often heavy in the attention-weighting phase, as the student learns the initial goals, the methods, and techniques. As an example, the Pramek student and a Brazilian Jiu Jitsu student will learn the theory of a lever. The Pramek student will learn the various classifications of levers and force couples, while the BJJ student may learn the basic theory of fulcrums and simple levers.

Regardless of the depth or complexity of the theory, the student is gaining a theoretical knowledge that they can read as well as write down, as opposed to a very general concept of a technique. Descriptions can be honed through discussion of theory, and the theory tested a variety of ways, becoming a method or technique. A lever is a theory that becomes a technique. A technique like a crane kick or a spinning back fist is not a scientific theory found in a theoretical book in a college library. These techniques are an expression of experience and may have some theoretical basis but are not pure theory. Recognition of this assists the teacher in conveying the information, while giving the student more options in learning.

Movement is the stage in which you look at the physical manifestation of the theory in the movement of the teacher and your own personal movement. In terms of the analogy with medical knowledge, these are the hands of the surgeon schooled in the theory of surgery. Students must study how to bring the theory to life within their own movement. In the example of the lever, the student learns to use their arm as a fulcrum point, and how to adjust their own movement with the fulcrum point relative to where the force will be applied, and how it will be applied, such as using the hips to drive the sitting arm bar in BJJ. Utilizing the theory in Pramek, the student may learn to use their thighs, knees, or their heels to change the nature of the lever classification. Exercises may also be used that strengthen a student based upon the theory and its associated movement.

This may be physical strength through exercise and weightlifting, or exercises based on biomechanical efficiency. In the movement phase, the student sees the exhibition and demonstration of the CoE and potentiates the memory of what they will remember. In EPL terms, students work through the imprinting and differentiation phase, as they make this theory their own and differentiate between what works and what does not. For students who fit the tactile learning profile, the movement phase reinforces what they have seen in the theory phase and the same holds true for the visual and auditory learning profiles.

Theory and movement are then combined into an application. This is the surgery itself in terms of the medical analogy. The teacher has given the student the anatomy book, and taught the use of the scalpel, and must now give the student the reason to use both … the goal of the surgery. Within the application phase, the student ties together the theory and the movement to achieve a purpose or goal, e.g. using a mechanically sound strike to attack the vestibular system. This is the interactive demonstration through real life experience in the CoE, as the student has an actual application for their theoretical knowledge. In this case, it is the lever, which the student applies while in interaction with another student in a practice session. The student hones their movement, refines their knowledge of the theory, and coordinates the two into one application.

This is the distinction between the instructor and teacher, as the instructor will generally give the information that is movement and application, as theory is not a readily available subject. The student must seek out much of the theoretical knowledge, either from other sources or must begin the process of their own development. While some may laugh in the martial art community at those who "create" ideas and theories, in reality these are trailblazers as they move toward the full education of their students. Moving from instructor to teacher, you take on the burden of transferring more than just a punch in the nose. A teacher must look at the learning profiles, compare their own teaching method against the CoE, and work toward the education of the student on all levels … not just the physical application of technique.

For the teacher it is best to remember the Pramek equation, because it engages the student in all three profiles. In the graphic above, you see that with Text/Verbal Symbols to Motion Pictures, within one theory, the student can read and hear the explanation and what is occurring. They can see the diagrams, ask questions, and listen to answers. In theory, modeling can occur, as skeletons and various learning aids are used, such as a pistol, rifle or knife. In theoretical modeling, the concept of what is occurring and the underlying principles are explained.

In movement, the student is able to take the theory and begins to make it their own in their movement. In the EPL, this is referred to in the attention-weighting and imprinting phase, as the student works to combine the theory or the goal, and combine it with their own movement to accomplish a task. Finally, within application, the student is able to take both and begin to achieve the goal they have set for themselves.

Chapter 24: The Ego

Often in teaching you will encounter an internal struggle with the ego. In this encounter questions of self-doubt and self-reflection abound.

'Am I teaching properly?'

'Why are students leaving?'

'Should I ever teach that again?'

'Why can't I handle my class sizes?'

The interactions between students and teachers become important in keeping the ego in check as the student will often be able to communicate to the teacher what the teacher doesn't readily see and know. Many times teachers become so caught up in the class that they miss the finer parts of teaching – talking to the students.

This is where the instructor and the teacher are very different.

The instructor exists to teach a class, whereas the teacher exists to teach, but also learn from those being taught, and what is being taught...and how they are teaching it.

The ego can be a big impediment to personal learning as the teacher must largely remove his or her own personality from a class. When the teacher makes the classroom environment personal, and personalizes relationships with students, the teacher can begin to lose their grip on educating themselves. Personalizing a relationship with a student is not just getting beers, being a sounding board for the student, or a shoulder to cry on in hard times. Interactions within the classroom can lead a teacher to personalize the relationship based on reactions to the students' actions. When a student acts up or out, doesn't understand something being taught, or is trying to "show off", this can lead to personalization as the teacher looks at the world through the filter of their experience, and not the objectivity of what the classroom dynamics actually are.

Rarely do students misbehave or are consistently slow in picking up information being transferred. Students rarely "show off" if the teacher is controlling the classroom and the pace of education and information being presented.

It is a good rule to classify student so that the teacher can properly control the class. Students are generally classified as below average, average, above average, and fast.

•   Below average will be the slower student, who has no experience or has physical limitations or limitations that must be adjusted for.

•   Average is the general student, with little martial art skill and no physical limitations.

•   Above average is a student with a medium amount of experience and no physical limitations or limitations adjusted for.

•   Fast learner is the student with a higher level of experience and no physical limitations or limitations adjusted for.

Often a teacher must remember to teach not to the slowest student, nor the fastest, but instead teach at the pace that average student can learn at. This gives the student who catches on fast the time to refine their methods, while allowing the slower students to work up to the pace of the lesson. It is up to the teacher to communicate to the students that this must be the goal, and use proper communication such as methods in this manual in order to do so.

This can be as simple as communicating smaller lessons to the students. The slower student should be placed with an average student and they should focus on the obstacles the slower student has, while above average students should be placed with the faster learning students to focus on smaller areas of refinement.

This is where conceptual learning methods such as the EPL make a difference, when students can be asked to address areas within the EPL. For example, a below-average student may need more attention weighting and their training partner is asked to work within the attention-weighting. The faster student may need differentiation and the training partner asked to work within the confines of differentiation. In procedural-based learning, the students would need to repeat techniques, whereas in perceptually based learning the methods can be focused on for the individual student.

Often the slower student needs the imprinting phase more than any other, as they must make their own what they are seeing the teacher, or the other students, do. Many times student fall into the trap of trying to copy and mimic what others do, whereas imprinting teaches them to make the method or the lessons their own.

A teacher can only do this is they can remove their ego from the situation and see the issue as the student's issue, as the EPL teaches very specific methods for educating a student. Within the EPL, the teacher cannot go "wrong", as there is a control for this within the EPL as the student must be refocused on their attention-weighting, imprinting, and further stages. A teacher is an instructor who has the experience to notice where the problem areas are with the student, and adjust their teaching appropriately.

If the teacher takes the "one size fits all" approach of procedural learning, then they can end up with a student who has not fully realized their own personal potential to imprint the information on their own body.

A teacher must remember that they cannot see through the eyes of the student. They do not know the bad day the student had, difficulties in the past with techniques or methods, or other filters the student has between them and learning. If a teacher becomes objective, and looks at the subject matter, and adjusts the EPL to the student, then the student can begin to focus on themselves and make the methods their own ... as opposed to trying to make one thing work. This will only waste the time of the student, leading to frustration and the student's mind wandering and attention not being paid to the EPL.

This will quickly be noticed as the student moves through the EPL and DPT – if a student has not made the methods their own and progressed, they will not be able to advance beyond the next stage or phase.

The teacher must remember to remove the ego, see the student objectively, and stick to the methods within the CLM to ensure the student imprints the information being transferred. In this the teacher will find success with each individual student, allowing the student to remain an individual employing methods and concepts, instead of being cookie cutter cutouts of what the teacher is teaching.

Where Do We Go From Here?

These are not easy topics to discuss. The thought of classifying students, working with their physical or psychological filters, or using unfamiliar terms can make both instructor and teacher very uncomfortable. When we take on the responsibility of teaching others it can become daunting, almost insurmountable, and sometimes it is much easier just to teach as you've always taught.

But don't listen to that - it's your own filters. It's your experience filters convincing you that it's easier to stay inside the proverbial box than to step outside of it. Shoes that stay in the box never see the road or trail and are never worn in. They never travel, they never break a lace, and they never wear down and have to be resolved.

What are our lessons but a student's favorite shoes to travel with?

Take the information from this manual and do as you will, but remember that you are not dealing with a student. While we refer to students in this manual, whether you are an instructor paying your bills and keeping students, or a teacher who has many students...you are teaching human beings. You are teaching your father, friend, mother, spouse, or child. Think of these people when you teach. Every day you have interactions with others that guide how you will deal with them on the next interaction. People have bad days, they have hard times, they have moments of realization and doubt...and they treat you accordingly.

When students are viewed in the same way, we realize that they treat not only you accordingly, but the material you are teaching, in a similar fashion. A bad day that isn't solved at the school door may lead a student to miss the one lesson they will need most when they walk outside and are attacked; they fall or perform a bad lift.

We, as instructors and teachers, hold a special place in the role of human development in ensuring that people pass the test of survival. We help ensure that they survive the fight, that they go without injury in the work out, that they can move with a full range of motion no matter their age. When they do - they pass on lessons to the next generation without the filter of exhaustion brought on by the past.

We do not teach martial art or fitness -we teach survival.

There are many topics we have not covered. They are important, but the lessons in this manual are greater in numbers and in substance…so supplements to this manual will be forthcoming. The most important concept to look at with this manual is to look at the ideas within it and not focus on what is not covered - but to act as a student and teacher and ask, interact, and learn.

The hardest question within this manual is 'how do I ensure a student will walk out of the school and remember the lessons.' The EPL and DPT answer some of these questions, but the deeper side of both process lead us back to the question of neurology. While neurology is addressed within the EPL, a process that has not been discussed in these manuals exists to ensure that your student makes their study a way of life. After more than a decade, Pramek developed a method of learning that ensures the student makes their fighting style, their sport, their fitness a daily practice. This method is addressed in the next manual in the CLM series.

Never forget - the theory of this manual is reliant upon your ability to combine movement with it. That movement is in the physical sense, but more importantly, movement in the teaching sense. You must have a sense of urgency to help, a sense of urgency to lead a student past their filters, to realize a sense of freedom. When we remember this - we remember our teachers who only wished to help and assist us in our lives…and use a process like the Conceptual Learning Method to refine what we learned and pass it on more effectively.

Without a student a teacher doesn't exist - so when you have no student, remember you are the student and strive to attain a higher level of self-realization in regards to who you are, what type of learner you are, what your filters and experience are, and how you can take these lessons learned in the dark of being alone to shine when you have a group to teach.

With students after a seminar

Teaching a student at the Pramek gym in Atlanta

The first CLM seminar in Cleveland Ohio

Matt teaching somewhere in Europe

199

A magazine article on Pramek

PART 4:

WHY MARTIAL ART?

Part 4: Introduction

When I began this book, I looked back over three years of notes. It was a few years since the last release of a CLM (Conceptual Learning Method) manual. So, I started by rereading the previous three books. After that, I poured through the parts of CLM 1, 2, and 3 I left out of those books as well as the editor's notes. Searching Google drive, my hard drives, my Dragon recording system, and my Evernote, I found I had two books close to being finished. Both books would need editing, adding to a point here and there…or so I thought. The two manuals, one on Strategy and one on movement, were great books I'll eventually release. Unfortunately, they didn't answer the question that had bothered me for years: why does someone learn martial art, and when they learn, could there be a better way of teaching them?

I then came to a problem I couldn't solve…a chicken and egg question in my writings. The previous books, for all their great concepts, consisted of mechanical knowledge. The EPL posed a new method of teaching and the mechanics of learning while the DPT answered the questions of the mechanics of testing. The Teacher and the Student discussed the mechanics of the relationship between the learner and the lesson creator. In each there were elements that were not mechanics, but like all things in Pramek, mechanics is of primary concern. These three books could make any martial art better, or teacher grow. But they lacked something, and that something was answering an important question: 'why?'. During the period I was working on this book I was the student of other teachers and I found the conundrum again: why was the information being taught and learned? It was a question I had never asked in CLM 1, 2, and 3.

Not the how, or what, or the who, but the why. I found this question eating at me after leaving a weekend certification from a great fitness program. The education was in depth, the instructors masterful, but no one ever asked me 'why are you lifting a kettle bell?' Everyone focused on the mechanics of the legs, movement of the body, or the strategy of gaining strength. Yet, in all the instruction, the question of 'why are you doing this' was never asked. After I left, I communicated with the instructors and asked them about this. They invited me to write articles for their website addressing it. This is the mark of great teachers and I was honored to write these articles asking this question, not just of them, but their entire organization…and their clients. I found it again in a mechanical breaching class, and I ask a lot of why questions, and that organization asked me to consult for them in designing class structure.

So, when I sat down to plan how to construct CLM 4, I threw out the two books close to completion. I decided that I would not repeat a mechanical book and instead would do what I should have done at the start: ask why. Within the why we learn more about the answer to the 5w's: the who, what, when, and where that make up a why. We may ask 'who?', but when we ask 'why' that who, we get better answers. When one can answer the why...they can tailor the teaching to address the '5Ws' and create a strong student. People's capabilities, fears, and their past all lead to understanding why they are learning. We not only assist the student and answering these questions, but we also answer the questions for ourselves as teachers. Who are we teaching, what are we teaching, when are we teaching it in their life, where are they in their learning...all key questions in finding the answer to why they are learning?

This questioning led to a breakthrough I had a year previous about and the CLM. In martial art, we ask students to act based on what they see and what they wish to occur; but rarely do we ask the student to act based on the opponent's viewpoint. Yes, we teach counters, but counters are after an action has been taken by someone else. I questioned whether something I had found my mistakes in classes I taught whether I should study a different way of teaching. A methodology based on the viewpoint of the enemy, leaving behind our own viewpoints, experiences, and past. I pondered the question of if I become someone else, what fears from my past could I leave behind because I act based on the opponent's viewpoint, not my own?

As I developed the EPL and DPT, I taught them differently class to class to test my theories out. I found that when I asked a student more of a 'why' of their action, they changed. I didn't ask 'why did you do that technique' but the question of 'does that technique fit into why you are learning a martial art?' I sought a deeper question of 'why'. I wanted to go beyond 'why do I use this technique' which is a question of training.

Take this question, for example. 'Does that technique fit into why you are learning your martial art?' This, for many students, would be a question of what you trained in and the meaning behind your training. These reasons may be that you were bullied or beat up when you were younger, so if you are facing that fear, do you really need ninja smoke bomb training? This may seem facetious, and it to an extent is, but the 'why' goes back to our education and how it takes place. That question, that 'why?' is uncomfortable - it makes you wonder, for a moment, did you need to learn everything you've learned? What fight are you training to win? The one against your past, or the one against an opponent? For many of our students these are difficult questions to face.

We also focus on creating better students because within this focus we evolve into better teachers. But this book is not about creating better students or becoming a better teacher or instructor or coach. That's done, with EPL, DPT, and The Student & The Teacher. Within these three books are the keys to creating better students and being a better teacher exist.

This book is about the environment in which we train and for which we train.

The environment may not be what you think. You may think of the environment as a home, a street, or a competition mat. But the environment where combat takes place, the fight, is more than that - it is where we exist. The fighting environment is in our mind, our psychology, our neurological pathways, and training room. We pull each of those into that home, street, or competition mat where we fight. The fighting environment is our relationships with our training partner. It is our combative interaction with the enemy or opponent. The fighting environment contains the answer to the 'why' of how we train, the 'why' of what and who we choose to engage, the 'why' of our psychology. This is the environment where we exist. Exist. Remember that word because it will come up again. Not the street or home, but our existence, and the 'why' of our action in our existence in the fight.

A bit different from the first CLM books, huh?

As you progress through CLM 4, reflect on CLM's 1, 2, and 3. Compare what you are reading to your understanding of the CLM. This book's study of martial art draws attention to the concepts of not only the fight...but ourselves.

Think for a moment - what is your concept of the 'self'? That 'self' is what you are fighting for.

You may hear, 'you fight for the man next to you' or 'you fight for the woman you love' but when the chips are down, and the damage done, your brain separates from the mind. The mind's needs become separate from the brain's wants as it struggles to survive, the body gasps for air and works to contain blood loss. The concepts of friends or loved one's being the reason you fight disappear and the nature of being an individual organism surviving becomes the primary reason for the fight. This is the environment where the fight takes place – our existence, to live on, breathe oxygen; and the training must reflect this state at some time in your martial art career. At some point, you must learn to fight for you…for your oxygen, for your blood not to be lost, and embrace what the means for your training.

Only then can you move on to studies that do not strictly address these reasons.

You may become lost in this manual if you are unfamiliar with CLM 1, 2, and 3. While it is not a prerequisite, you should take time to get the previous three books as this will help you understand what CLM is. You'll find that the more you understand the previous books the better this manual will be.

If you are a teacher reading this: as you read, put everything you know to the side. Suspend your unconscious brain and how it wants to compare this book to what you've read or seen elsewhere. Instead, for a moment, just embrace the concepts and the methodologies within CLM. Sit with CLM 4, put it down and come back to it. While other martial artists and teachers write their memoirs, I set out with CLM to develop something beyond me. I wanted something not only for my students, my teachers, my system, but for martial artists in general. The CLM method is two decades in development and pulls from a variety of disciplines and sources. I took a lot of bumps, spent a lot of money, trained with some amazing (and not so amazing) teachers across the globe to develop CLM. What you are reading is about Pramek. CLM is about martial art and the science behind it. Everything within the CLM can be used to create better students…and to make yourself a better teacher.

For students: use this manual in forming a basis for your studies. Most systems and styles contain few concepts like CLM. Most arts have a basis in procedural learning methods, which is discussed in previous CLM manuals. CLM is perceptual, we look at the overall context where action takes place, and the underlying concepts behind that context. CLM is agnostic, it can be used as a baseline for teaching and learning any art. Take the CLM and compare your training to it. When you aren't learning a technique, use the EPL to find the root of your challenges. If you can't overcome an opponent, refer to the DPT and see where the gaps in your training may be. If you have a teacher you can't get along with, but a system you enjoy, use CLM 3 as a roadmap to understanding the relationship. Apply the concepts to your training even though your training may not be based on the CLM. You'll be better for it, and if you find it helps you, recommend the books to your teacher.

For those people who have come to the CLM having read my non-martial art works, you might be confused, even taken aback. CLM is where I began and even today where I exist. CLM is a method for teaching something as central to your life as breathing and food. The need to defend yourself is as hard wired into you as hunger. You are composed of millennia of neurological wiring refined to create an efficient hunter, fighter, soldier, or warrior. Modern society has conveniences that clicked some of this innate ability off. Study the CLM processes and methods. Remove the martial art side and apply the principles to your own pursuits, be it getting better at your job, achieving more, or being a better parent. The possibilities are endless if you step back from what you want to accomplish and focus on the method by which accomplish it.

Enjoy

Matt Powell

Chapter 25: Martial Sophistry

In ancient Athens, the sophists taught because, as teachers, they were paid to teach. The sophist taught rhetoric to the well-to-do who could afford the lessons. The primary basis for their teachings was the art of rhetoric, or persuasive speech. At the time rhetoric was popular amongst those looking to advancement in politics and business. The sophist taught the 'how' of persuasively speaking ideas and thoughts. This was done through rhetorical arguments, the teacher arguing points to show how to argue, or the technique of argument. Regardless of the subject of the argument, even if they did not believe in the points they were espousing, they argued. It was a course of teaching that carried a financial, not to mention time, price because the ability to persuade others was considered priceless. The wealthy young, even the masses, followed the sophists to listen to their arguments and the technique of their arguments. The arguments seemed strong as these were teachers who understood wordplay and debate. They could make anything seem logical, their reasoning appearing resolute. Even today this capability is still priceless.

But there were those who found a different path.

Some in Athens, men like Socrates, were not fond of the sophists. Men like Plato saw the sophist as a teacher, but not a philosopher. While the sophist taught what those with money wanted to hear, Socrates taught what people needed to hear. Men like Socrates stood in opposition to the sophists even at the risk of their own reputation. Think about it for a moment…making a living and reputation by telling people what they need to hear, not what they want to hear...something even today is unpopular.

If we bring this historical lesson forward to our current times, it reflects upon the teachers of martial arts as well as subjects like personal growth or politics. While a teacher may want to teach a solid yet unpopular skill, it can be a very difficult path when the bills must be paid. Often, students pay to be taught what they want to learn, and the teacher must look for a balance. This balance, this state of equilibrium is sought somewhere between what the student needs with what the student wants so the student continues to come and train. Schools would shutter their doors across the world if the student were told what they needed to hear. Balance, a word, a concept that great teaches seek regardless of the system, style, or subject matter.

More and more, through internet videos and magazine articles, we find teachers in a state of imbalance. This is a topic I discuss a lot in CLM, and I have often heard that I am beating a dead horse. If you find the balance to be important, keep reading – if not, skip a few paragraphs. The fact is that many teachers are out of balance and today's online, like-driven connected world drives this imbalance. I am often glad I did not come up learning to teach today, but instead in the late-90's and early 2000s. In opposition to today's connected culture, in those days we had dial-up, newsletters, and email where we taught the world what we wanted it to know. Today, with YouTube, streaming, and Snapchat many instructors and teachers capture what others want to see. This imbalance forces many teachers to weigh curriculum toward what the student wants to learn because it attracts more students.

A student may want to learn to show certain aesthetic skill through a movement or technique. Even if the method being taught is bad for the student in terms of actual self-defense or their physical health, the need to keep the lights on often outweighs the need to educate the student on what they need to learn to survive. This cycle is how we come to find so many arts that seem so 'unrealistic' yet attract so many paying students. In many ways, the modern martial art sophists do as the ancient sophists did. They teach what the student wants to hear, like techniques that don't work in real life, even when the teacher doesn't believe in it.

They teach it because it creates the revenue they need to live.

I've often stated that Pramek is not the best emissary to the martial art world at large because we stand in opposition to the current sophists of the industry. Let's not forget, the sophists of the ancient world had a profound impact on the modern world. But, in Pramek, we aren't about rhetoric, the likes, or the views. Pramek's engagement with the student centers on what the student needs to learn without a care about the 'want' of the student. In the Directed Perceptual Test, the student's favorite moves are tested and often shown to not work. Instead of letting the student continue to believe in a failed technique, we take them back to the Efficient Perceptual Learning model to show why it doesn't work. CLM, when properly employed causes the destruction of the student's ego-based techniques. This isn't popular, and many schools shy away from CLM because of this. As a student once told me, 'what you teach is controversial, and isn't exactly liked by liked teachers.'

As I replied to that student, 'that's why I have a day job'. I don't want to teach what people want to be taught. My aim, Pramek's aim, was to teach what people need to learn – mechanics, biomechanics, kinematics, psychology, neurology, etc. This means a training environment which can be uncomfortable as it does not cater to the wants of the student. The answers the student needs must often be extracted from the student through a process of engagement that in many systems would too deeply hurt the pride of the student to risk it.

In many systems EPL would take too long, DPT would be too tough. The CLM curriculum engages the student's intellect and asks the questions about the 'why' of their martial art. CLM ignores the sophist draw of teaching to teach, showing technique to show technique. CLM shows what they need to learn and if they wish to find other subjects, they find it somewhere else. For the CLM, the science is the answer, the hypothesis the technique. As we often say in Pramek classes, 'try it!' We want the student to explore the concepts, find what fits their usage. Then, we utilize the DPT, a scientific process of testing the hypothesis you might say, finding the answer to the question of survival.

My first realization of our teetering popularity this was when I sent out a poll to newsletter subscribers asking what they wanted more of in Pramek. Now, keep in mind, Pramek is my creation. I could just license it, restrict its access, sell it out or just sell it…but instead I spent half my life working on it and showing it, many times at a loss. When I asked people, in the poll, if they wanted more CLM (which most did, with more mechanics), one guy left feedback 'I come to Pramek to learn to fight, not all this philosophy. Stop trying to be Tim Ferris and stick to what you know how to do. I want to learn to fight a larger opponent - why don't you do topics like that?'

Here was someone who didn't want to learn what I had to teach, nor did they want to draw from Pramek something they could use…they wanted it their way. I was to do as they said. A few friends of mine said, 'well if they want combatives, maybe that's what you should stick to.' I took notice and after that poll we released only a few more reality-based fight videos. I then decided we would focus on what people needed to learn. Pramek became about the CLM and incorporated more sportive martial art, to strike a balance. Over time we have continued to transition to almost purely educational and with little reality-based products for the public. I don't know who that anonymous guy was, but I appreciate him every day for teaching me a lesson.

CLM doesn't care what someone wants unless it is wanting to learn to be better. For a teacher, engagement through the CLM means learning what fight the student fears most and teaching how to win that fight. When a teacher loses this concept and focuses on the want of the student instead of the need, they begin trading money for training instead of money for education. They cross the line backward, from a teacher who looks out for the student to the instructor teaching the curriculum for the check.

In our view, in Pramek, because the realism of a student's survival, what 'works' is the highest power to which a teacher can answer. A one-year instructor who asks 'why' and focuses on it is more of a guru than the thirty-year 'master' who focuses on the 'what'. Survival on the battlefield or survival in the sport ring, it does not matter, the why must still be examined. The techniques that 'why' created must be honed. If it can't be taught through the EPL, and tested successfully with the DPT, it must be reevaluated.

Such a process attracts only certain kinds of students who wish to understand at a deeper level their capabilities as well as find greater abilities. Therefore, Pramek has no belts, no sports…everyone is a winner and a champion if they are finding out more about themselves. No, I am not saying 'everyone gets a trophy'. Your belt, your trophy, is surviving a violent encounter. What I am saying is that in Pramek we engage those who wish to be engaged in learning. In this engagement, we find the strength to act as a sort of martial art Socrates, questioning the modern martial art sophists. We measure success beyond money or a student's feeling of success.

Within the world of Socrates and ancient Athens we find that Socrates only fully engaged those who wished to engage fully. If one did not wish to engage and find the questions behind the answer, Socrates moved on to one who did…even if he didn't teach many people or make much money. He wanted students who wished to learn. Today, in our quest to teach, it is our job as teachers to find what the student wants to face in their unconscious mind and turn that knowledge into training that is enjoyable so that they wish to continue. I have seen many new students who want to become a YouTube star with their technique and ask, 'Can I put that video up on the internet?' Upon deeper training and reflection, they realize this is about more than looking cool. Martial art is a gigantic life lesson, and that lessons starts somewhere in their distant past catching up with their present self in the form of a fear. When the fight they fear is found and they learn to face that fight…they no longer want the 'flash', they seek further answers to their own personal questions. I have spent a lot of time with advanced UFC fighters and they are the same after fighting that one fight they must face – many seek, read, study, look to develop themselves beyond fighting.

Those MMA and UFC fighters have been a source of radical change in the martial art world in the past two decades. The martial art world has changed, from board breaking competition to UFC mega pay-per-views, but the strike...the strike never changes. Sure, the strike is the application of force, but the teacher must find where that application is best suited for the student. The application of the strike, what the strike is accomplishing...not the strike itself. The questions must be asked why that strike, who is it hitting, where on the body is it hitting, and what happens after it lands? These are application questions.

Many times, over the years when teaching strikes, many students ask, 'How does this strike work against a bigger opponent?' They aren't worried with the technique - they are worried about the bigger opponent. That is the fear. Anyone can teach a strike, but not just anyone can teach a student to get over their fears...and that kind of education sticks with a student. Within this the teacher becomes not just a person, but an experience, that the student never forgets. What is meant by an experience, not a teacher or person?

I recently watched an old interview of Don Rickles on a late-night TV show. The host read off the list of names Don had worked with and quickly said the name 'Frank Sinatra'. Don stopped the host immediately after he said that name. Rickles replied: 'Don't just run over his name fast. Frank Sinatra, he was the greatest in the world.' How strong of an influence was Sinatra to create this response from Rickles? What were the memories, the lessons learned, that he would stop on national television to correct a host in front of millions of viewers?

The experience Sinatra provided to Rickles should serve as a role-model for us all, in every facet of our lives. Sure, Ol' Blue Eyes could have taught Rickles to sing or dance, but Sinatra taught him something different. Sinatra taught something that touched Rickles soul in a way that decades later he still made sure that Sinatra's name wasn't passed over.

Rickles had an experience. Rickles was touched to his core.

Does martial art affect your life this deeply? Does it affect every facet of your life so much so that you are changed at your core...or is it just a 'hobby'? Do you see martial art in everything you do? If we cannot find the martial art purpose in the most mundane of things, then we must ask if martial art truly provides a life changing experience. If it doesn't provide a life-changing experience for us, as the teacher...then how can we expect it to provide one for a student?

How has martial art changed your life? What is the experience you pass on?

That change in your life should be the core of why you teach and why you learn.

Somewhere along my life's timeline martial art infiltrated every facet of my existence. I was consumed with it, but that 'it' wasn't martial art. 'It' was the elements I was finding within martial art that changed how I looked out at the world from where I was in my life. This viewpoint in Pramek is expressed by theory, movement, and applications, solutions. My 'Sinatra moment', if I can borrow from Rickles actions, is when someone minimizes martial art to me, calling Pramek 'karate', or 'it's just learning to hurt people' comment.

It's so much more…or it should be.

It should apply to any facet of life, from moving better during the day to looking at a problem at work through theory. We should find where it touches our lives, such as the explanation of theory, and study those areas it touches. Your movement is not the movement of another, no matter how much you wish to emulate them. This realization is empowering, you are yours, your movement is something you control when nothing else in your life is under control. This is something life changing, something others who do not study movement lack. How you apply a lever is your application of physics theory and that application is created by your mind and movement. This is control over not only yourself, but of another body a control you create. This is a control you create and something others do not have as they copy their teachers.

Control, be it over yourself or another, is a concept that most do not grasp. You have, through your study, the ability to exercise control when all seems without control and is chaotic. Control over your movement, your mind, your application of theory, and your survival. Martial art speaks to our primal self where our deepest darkest fears live. In those depths of the unconscious mind, where our fears lie in wait, we find keys to our survival. We can control these memories and how they affect us, exercise this control in other areas of our lives. If we can survive the physical threats to our lives, get past our past fears, then those lessons find a home guiding the most mundane of daily tasks. Life is a study of martial art…a study of control. Martial art should permeate everything from getting out of a chair to how you interact with others.

I use meditation to calm the mind before a long day or teaching a class, or before writing a book such as this. I was once told that meditating while eating was possible as well. At a cursory level many think of meditation as sitting on a pillow in a room, but like martial art, it has applications beyond the rigors of working or writing and can be utilized to enhance a meal. Some sophists may teach meditation because it is the 'it thing' while ignoring the enhancements it can make to something as important as a meal. Similarly, one could teach martial art because MMA is the 'it thing' while skipping the strength it creates through the exercise of control. Without its knowledge, without the control it creates, we perish in the face of a disciplined enemy, be it a person or life's trials.

Many times, life's trials are deadlier than that of a robber. I have sat with friends, as well as their loved ones, as they pass. A book I recently wrote was inspired by a dying friend. The challenge these situations create pose a much larger threat to our well-being than any adversary we face in martial art training. Grief, loss, pain - these enemies require control to overcome, to create peace with, or defeat much like the 'larger opponent' students want to learn to fight. Few studies are worthy of so much time as the study of control taught by the challenge of martial art. Teaching this control…learning this control…this is our Sinatra moment, when an impression is made that never leaves.

This control is why we study martial art and how the question of 'why' changes our reason for studying. Our job as teachers is to equate balance in what the student wants to learn. Blending their need of education with their wanting to learn. Their feeling of accomplishment in an unrealistic technique is not as important as their survival. Yes, we should tie survival to the subjects they enjoy, but do so because it keeps them learning what they need to know. If we do not ask the question 'why' of a student, we may lead them down a path they enjoy but will hurt them on 'the street'.

Many would say, 'yes, I understand, but I will lose students'.

Now you may need to ask yourself your own why. I am sure the same was said to Socrates and Masaaki Hatsumi. The sophists always had more students than Socrates. Hatsumi's schools never gained the global power of the UFC. But we cannot trouble ourselves with today if we focus on our legacy. Today's work will build the legacy of tomorrow and our work live on in the years after we are gone. If the student sees your legacy as something, they want to learn...they discover what they need to survive and why in the process.

That is a gift worth trying to give.

Chapter 26: The Why

Students come from various walks and stages of life, hoping that martial art will help them solve challenges in the life they experience. As we discussed in The Teacher and the Student, we teach to create a relationship that is symbiotic. But there comes a time in any relationship where the past of the parties involved must be questioned and analyzed. Say, for a moment, that something goes missing from your house during a party. You later learn that one of the guests in the party, someone you had a great time with, previously went to jail for theft. Would you not wonder, or perhaps see this person through different eyes were you to meet again? The same must be said for a student - we must know their history before their history makes itself known in a way we would want to avoid. A student has things they need to learn, challenges to overcome, or they would not come to a martial art school. When we focus on the reasons of those involved, we deepen the understanding of the relationship. We begin to ask questions to define the difference between the mechanics of the technique and the technique's application and find elements of the 'why'. Often these two terms, mechanics and applications, get confused but they are vital to understanding the student. The application of martial art skill is at the basis of the study. Martial art is not the technique…martial art is the environment (physical, mental, spiritual) surrounding the training and use of the technique. The application of martial art answers the question about how the mechanics the martial art will be used.

Does the student see martial art as a means of feeling secure, or winning a match? Each has its own style. A student wishing to learn a sport like kickboxing versus a reality-based style will learn very similar mechanics. The kick, the strike, the clinch...the mechanics are interchangeable between the two styles of martial art. The application is the dividing line. The environment determines the application, the application determines whether to use a knife hand chop or a jab…a groin kick or a roundhouse kick.

When a student comes to Pramek the first question one should ask is not 'what do you want to learn', but instead, 'why do you want to learn?' and then 'how do you learn best?' I've heard many teachers through the years ask, 'what do you want to learn', only to be answered with the phrase, 'how to punch.' Think about some of the 5W's: who, what, when, where, why. Who they want to punch, why they want to punch them, where that punch would take place…all seem to be unimportant in the world of 'what do you want to do learn.'? 'What do you want to learn' ignores the why and reinforces that what. For a woman wanting to defend herself, the 'what' isn't as important as always remembering the 'why' of her study. The 'why' would provide a what, when, where, and who that gives her the knowledge she needs.

These questions are incredibly important. The '5W' questions provide us the most in-depth answers we can have about our students and sometimes these questions show us a student who shouldn't be trained. For example, who bullied a student, or were they a bully? When was a student abused or were they an abuser? Where were they abused? What did they use to attack, or defend? If we don't answer these kinds of questions, we can end up teaching the wrong thing to the wrong person.

Students will have a variety of answers to the 5W's. The most important thing to remember when this conversation takes place is that, long before the mechanics are discussed, the application of martial art is what must be discussed first. Many times, students eat the menu not the meal, they mistake the mechanics for the context in which they take place.

A technique is not an application…it's a technique. An application is an answer to the question of why. How many times have you, the reader, said you study martial arts then someone says, 'oh, you do karate?' People see martial art as 'karate' because, well, what could be the difference, right? They think of technique – kicks, blocks, chops. We think we know the differences…but do we? The application is what is important and why answers what. For example, a student may need to learn self-defense, but they confuse sport styles for combatives training. The training works in the training room and on the mat, so the reasoning goes that it must work in a real-life situation…until it doesn't.

This is a hard lesson to learn, that mechanics are not the application of martial skill. Often this lesson is learned too late and at great cost. To avoid this lesson, and many others, the 'why' must be established. The state of action, or the why, and its presence in training must be central to training. How actions will be taken and why they are taken become the defining questions that must be answered. But the state of action within martial art can become confusing as students are kept or lost, schools open or close, and reputations become more important than the reason they are established.

Think about the sophists from earlier and think about the state of martial art today. While I endeavor with these books to write on topics that transcend current technologies, the demonstrational sophist is not a new phenomenon – only monetization for making videos is. The internet is filled with sophists. They teach what the student wants to learn, or worse, what will make the sophist appear intelligent to the public at large. Worst of all, they teach what will make the student look good with no application in mind. If a video of a student performing a good move on the internet gains likes and hits, the training environment or video editing that created that move are less important than that moment in time.

We see the moment in time when the camera was rolling, and technique was on…after 15 retakes and breaks. This moment doesn't show every student and their capability in the school. It shows just one moment, and for the martial art sophist, that one moment is enough and should be repeated. Within this structure we find the problem with many system's belt structures, as proficiency instead of competence is chased. The student has learned something that works until it doesn't when they need it to most.

I personally saw this early in my martial art career with a competitor who became a friend in another system. He was well respected for this martial art skill outside of the style he was learning, and he embraced fully the new lessons of an art that was based in his homeland. The knife work of this art was questionable in its effectiveness…but it looked great on film. He knew it, but he became trapped by social media's approval of his aesthetics.

Overtime he became a bit of a knife defense master in this art and he and I would often argue about how effective it was. At the time I focused little on knife work as my teachers had told me to focus instead on mechanics. He, on the other hand, loved demonstrating knife defense and appearing in multiple instructional videos. So, it was a shock to many in his system that on a cool fall night he was stabbed to death behind a convenience store. No one really knows why he went back there, but everyone knows what happened – the knife master was stabbed to death by a robber. I read the police reports – he wasn't ambushed and hit in the head or anything like that. He simply tangled with two guys and one of them stabbed him to death. All the videos, glamour, accolades regarding his videos and in the end, it didn't save him. His technique might have been visually impressive, but his application wasn't realistic. What does it say for a system when its knife master is stabbed to death? It says that the system is teaching something fundamentally flawed.

The reason, the 'why' of our action, is more important than how we act. The 'how' is a means to achieve a Goal. If we do not understand the reason why we act, then we can quickly become lost in the combative interaction and training. We can lose ourselves, years of practice, and possibly our lives when we lose our Goal. If you do not understand why a student is acting as they do, what they do in their action means little.

So…

Understanding why = survival.

Survival = life.

Life = control.

Control = martial art.

So, what is martial art?

First, we need to answer what is survival.

Chapter 27: Levels of Survival

Let's take a moment and do a 30 second personal inventory.

What is your biggest accomplishment until this point in your life? What do you consider being most valuable in your life? Are you happy or unhappy with your studies, your job, your relationships? The answers to these kinds of questions say multitudes about where you are in your life now…the person you are now, your essence, the reality of your life…your being. To be is to exist, to occur, to have a state. It's how we exist, live, how we occur.

These kinds of topics often make people uncomfortable because they cut to the core of a person. But, for our purposes within the CLM we must address the question. 'Being' is about a place in time, in our lives, our training, our understanding of the self. The elements of life that make up the state of 'being'

Think about the following terms that describe time for a moment: 'now' versus 'then' versus 'will be'. 'You' in the future is your action in this moment. What you do now creates the future and conversely the past affects what you do now. When we analyze combative survival, being able to exist within the fight means walking into the fight not only with a plan, but without fear. The you that you walk into the fight with is you that is stuck fighting. If it's an uneducated you – you're in trouble. Fear is a tricky thing and in fighting, fear for one's life isn't always the biggest concern. Fear for one's life seems so far in the future as we think of death being natural, but fear of reputational damage is immediate. While this may seem trivial, for many, reputational damage, perhaps getting arrested, is enough to create a pause in their willingness to fight. We must put fear in perspective in terms of the concerns in our lives. The 'you' that you walk into the fight with might not be the 'you' that walks out. We must look back all these concerns, get back to basics.

To teach a student to act in the moment, first the student must be taught about their survival.

First, we should admit something that for some may become uncomfortable to admit. Your brain and your mind are not the same thing. For the sake of moving forward, we will use the Descartes concept of the brain and mind. In this concept, the mind is where your consciousness exists. It is the place where your ability to reason and live beyond basic instinct are held. Your mind is the center of your consciousness and self-awareness. Your brain is where neurons live and the governing force over the operation of your body. An easy way to think of this is you and your dog both have brains, but your mind allows you to draw a distinction between your mind and brain. Your dog, on the other hand, has limited to no capability to do this. Even when your dog performs a behavior that seems to show intelligence, this is the brain of the dog bringing forth memories and instinct about the behavior they must utilize.

Do they learn, yes, but this learning is based on fear, food, pleasure, and reproduction. I have two dogs, and have had two dogs before them, and two dogs before them. In the end, they are still Pavlovian in nature, and the Pavlovian response isn't a bell, but survival instinct. Pain, pleasure, hunger, procreation, security…these same driving forces exist within you, but you have the 'divine spark'. You, a person, have that 'thing' that allows you to understand you can live beyond these basic drivers. This manual doesn't seek to give a philosophical explanation of the soul, mind, and what differentiates us from animals. This doesn't mean they are any less important in God's creation - they have a brain, some animals have large brains, but only a primitive mind.

One way to think of this concept is that your brain is the hardware, your mind is the software. Anyone who has ever seen a dying person who has massive trauma to the brain, or large amounts of oxygen or blood loss, understands this concept. The brain operates separate from the mind. The brain, when the body has taken massive amounts of damage, will do anything to distribute blood, oxygen, and protect itself. Agonal breathing and its symptoms are an example of this. The eyes are wide open, and they may be seeing everything, but the brain's need for survival, which is the intake of oxygen, takes precedence over what the eyes see. When the mind cannot reason or have a conversation with an attacker who has damaged the body...the brain will still operate, gasping for air to operate. The brain will still run the body when the temporal lobe is damaged beyond repair. If this were not the case, then it would seem comas would not exist.

This may seem extreme, but we must go to extremes to understand survival. You can be brain damaged, unable to communicate, unable to exhibit emotion, or unable to reason...but you will still breath, your heart will still beat. Your brain will still allow you to exist, in a physical state, while levels of outward intelligence have disappeared. I recently was talking to a nurse who works in critical care and she was telling me about a patient who could not communicate, follow any auditory cues, but their brain was still running the body. The patient had a stroke that had destroyed parts of the brain, and subsequently the mind, but the doctors were continuing to operate on the brain when it swelled. They still drilled into the skull to relieve pressure because they had not been told not to by family. They were keeping the body alive, the heart beating, the clinical definition of death driving them trying to prevent a 'death'. The machines were feeding oxygen to the brain, but the mind was gone. The patient was an organism, just blood and electrical impulses to the heart at that point.

That is not a being we want to be.

This may seem graphic, but survival is a relative term, and this is something we must understand in defending ourselves. You can survive a near-fatal assault only be left with a physical existence and a mind having disappeared behind the curtain of injury from oxygen loss or trauma to the brain. Therefore, in Pramek, we teach that you must do anything to never be put in a position where you can be 'choked out' or 'knocked out'. In Pramek, except for in controlled environments, we do not cut off oxygen to the brain in training. In these two states, you are left completely defenseless as the brain is unable to engage neurological defensive methods and the mind cannot process the situation. This is when the body is the most vulnerable and why these situations must be avoided at the cost of even death.

Death may be preferable to a life lived on machines allowing you to exist physically but nothing more. The assumption of this book is that you are learning to defend yourself to live a fulfilling life where you can create, find joy in your friends and family, perhaps write your own book. It is with this baseline, the fine line between the brain and mind, survival, and existence, that we talk about life in terms of Levels of Survival.

I came up with the concepts of Level of Survival (LoS) after struggling to define quality of life for other projects I was working on. As I am ever more clinical than poetic, LoS seemed to fit, and then I divided it into three sections (short, medium, long term) in describing the concept of what I was trying to work on. I started at our immediate needs, like wilderness survival with the 'rule of 3's'. The more we can remove worries from our daily lives and look at what the bare necessities of life are, the more we can make good decisions about the important decisions we face and worry about. If we are meeting our bare necessities and we are content, then we can focus on achieving Goals beyond our bare necessities. Think of it this way: many people confuse the sandwich for their dietary fuel. If food is a fuel and our bodies are cars, many people eat for a Ferrari when they own a Chevy. To subsist, one only needs a certain number of calories a day. But subsistence is defined by the needs of the person eating. If someone is training for a marathon, they will have different dietary fuel needs than someone who never goes to the gym and only walks 30 minutes a day. In other words, it all comes down to necessities, or what it takes to live what one might term a basic life. No frills, nothing extravagant beyond their needs...simply basic.

I'm guessing that I'm not telling you anything you don't know, but let's look at this in terms of the decisions we make in combat. Why strike if you only need to grapple to win? Why use a complex choke if a strike will do? Why eat like a marathon runner when you will never run a marathon? Why turn the decision of your clothing for the day into a morning long decision when you only need to wear a shirt and tie? In life, when we understand our basic needs and live in a way that allows us not to be worried about beyond the basics needs of life, something interesting happens we are free to focus on the things that we really need in creating the life that we really want.

I live quite well, I won't lie. But I don't need much to live the life that I want. There is an element of humility within this thought process. It's not easy to say, 'I only need ___ to survive' because we are conditioned to think we need more. The LoS system of viewing your life is not meant as, 'this is it, you're done, never move forward', but to instead act as a baseline. In the LoS system, there exists a base level that says, 'I own/have this, it's all I need, now what do I what beyond this?' I once had a student with one pair of shoes, one pair of pants, two t-shirts. His life fit into a suitcase and he was, in a sense, semi-nomadic. He had no home other than people's couches, where he worked to earn his keep. He lived a life of travel and no attachment. Later, when he began to focus on a career, he found a career that was nomadic as a truck driver. He learned to love golf and skiing because of the company he drove for - so he had the finest golf gear and the finest ski gear.

A guy living in a tractor trailer had the finest set of golf clubs and skis, a pair of pants, a few shirts shirt, and some shoes. We would often laugh that he had photos around the US and Canada of him golfing on the finest golf courses but always wearing the same clothes. For him it was traveling and experience, not material goods, that made for luxurious life. His life was basic, his needs simple, and he had a few non-basic items he needed to live his basic life.

While we should never be happy with 'just enough', we should endeavor to recognize that, in survival, too much can be a detriment. Everyone has seen the person with multiple knives on their person - one knife for each pocket, the belt, a boot knife, and a knife on a chain around their throat. To be effective, one would need to train to fight with each one - training the draw on each, it's mechanics, how to utilize that weapon. The Pramek view would be one knife, maybe two knives (one in the waist, one in the boot) and driving the fight to the accessibility of the knife and training on only one or two knives and the mechanics. A collection of knives looks great, but is it needed? As my friend Kelly McCann often says, 'beware the man who only owns one pistol, he's probably really good with it.' All we need is to know how to use what we have well, and drive the fight, or life, toward what we do well.

In the end, LoS is about life, life is about survival, and martial art is survival. Most people never get the life that they really want because they never get past the life that they have. Be it a job or martial art studies, we become entranced with the now and don't look to the future beyond what today tells us to worry about tomorrow. To think about the arts, we want to study in the future, and then to plan when we will - this takes a level of dedication few martial artists have. Most instead focus so much on the feeling of victory in the art they love and then neglect the chance to increase range of motion or increase cardiovascular health found in a different art. For many of us, we become complacent in our current study and then, time passes, and our physical ability to study other arts is impaired by age and injury.

Age matters. Rarely do we sit and think about the 'why' of today and tomorrow. We don't analyze the 'why' of our study today and what our 'why' may be in the future. I have known few people who begin to prepare for those future needs arts even if just in research. Life is remarkably similar as we don't know what we truly need to survive daily because we are so focused on today's needs. Sometimes one must step back and ask what is 'enough' and what is 'more than enough?' What is 'too little' and what is 'too much'? Each person will create a different answer.

I have had students with more money than they knew what to do with and rarely came to class but spoke to me about how class was so good for them. Conversely, I had a student who owned two pairs of shoes, two pairs of pants, a few shirts, and a coat - he spent his money on his martial art studies and travel. What is profoundly important? Self-worth or self-knowledge? Total knowledge of one art or cursory knowledge of as many arts as possible? When little is very important, anything over 'very little' is considered a luxury. This is an individual decision.

An important lesson in life is to know what one needs to survive and to comprehend that things beyond are luxury and probably unneeded to just subsist. Those luxuries become a choice one can choose to make. Why do you study martial art - to protect what is yours or to learn about your capabilities? These are two different reasons to study martial art and they lead to different paths of study.

In our paths, we should look to our reasons for study from a different direction. We should look at them in terms of our survival as an organism. This gives us an idea of the training that we need to undertake in our martial journey. This is the process that led me to developing the system of Levels of Survival to understand our needs. They are as follows:

- *LoS 1 is immediate term survival, to have food, shelter, and ability to procreate.*
- *LoS 2 is medium term survival, such as health and fitness, to create longevity in life.*
- *LoS 3 is long term survival, generally psychologically based for mastering a task, need for community, or creating a legacy that one can pass on to another generation.*

With this in mind, let's look deeper at LoS.

Level of Survival 1

Conceptually, LoS 1 is about more than the basic survival of the organism. If someone is starving, then it is highly doubtful that they will put a premium on exploring their own thoughts in mind and strengthening their fitness so that they have a longer life…because they are worried about food. So, we must determine what our LoS 1 immediate needs are so that we are better able to transition to a new plane of thought. LoS 1 needs or wants are where most people spend most of their time. Worrying about money, food, sex, ego, these are all basic aspects of our existence, thus these are LoS 1.

Candidly I've never met a student that could long-term balance their martial art studies with a bad financial situation or terrible relationship at home. They become too busy discovering things about their finances or significant others to discover things about themselves. In class, if they are overweight, they worry about their weight more than they worry about their technique because they are self-conscious that everyone else is conscious of their weight. If their significant other, even their boss, is mistreating them they will bring that rage into the training environment and find training less and less joyful. Later in this book we will talk about student disclosure. I am sure many instructors and teachers, regardless of system or style, can related to the above circumstances. Training is filled with big traps and distractions, and everyday life is the primary reason most people do not continue their martial art study or achieve other success in life. They are too busy trying to survive, not only as an organism, but survive the circumstances they find themselves in. When we look at survival from the basics, within this definition we see that we can't confuse the menu for the meal, the steak for the calories, the heated home for the mansion.

There is a base level and then everything else.

Ask yourself, for LoS 1 what do you need to live comfortably? How much money? What kind of shelter? What spiritual relationship? What relationships in your life, both close and in general? What caloric intake? List it out, check it off, see what you truly need to have a happy, fulfilled life with less worry today. Try it for a week or two. LoS 1 survival means that we do not look at fashion, we look at clothing. We do not look at restaurants in LoS 1, instead we look at the quality of the diet. LoS 1 means differentiating between living and luxury. When we do this, we create a baseline for our lives and on top of this baseline we can make decisions that are educated and thoughtful because we are no longer concerned about immediate level survival needs.

If you worry about the bills being paid - what martial art seminar you will attend next should be the least of your worries. Let's focus for a moment on a word in the definition: immediate. You will find in LoS 1 that when all else is lost, this is what you will be defending. Your immediate needs: your home, your family, your food, your water, your friends, your religion, your nation, your ideals...these are immediate safety. Within LoS 1 you find a base level martial art - combatives. There are no cool axe kicks and fancy triangle chokes - LoS 1 is eye gouging, knife hand chops, quick ways to ground and pound, and groin kicks. LoS 1 is the style of fighting that you will have when you are clinging to what you have, like your own life and breath, not a fancy car or a fancy belt given by a master.

I recently had a police officer student of Pramek tell me about a fight he had with an armed subject. I asked him about what his thought were during the struggle. He said it was odd because he had two thoughts. The first was controlling the subject's weapon, and the second was 'who will take my dog if I die?'. When you ask yourself the question of what it is that you are willing to die for, within the answer you will find LoS 1. Do your techniques match this? Do you know how to disable eyes, create a knock-out, complete easy chokes to disable the airway and breathing? Do you know the defenses against 90/90 unarmed attacks? Do you know where to cut to maximize bleeding? Do you know how to use basic weapons culturally available to you and defend against them? Would you risk your loved one's safety on an 8-step movement chain technique for knife defense? Then combatives might be for you.

These are serious questions for a serious style of learning to defend yourself.

In terms of LoS 1 survival, we ask ourselves what our most basic needs are. Once we realize our most basic needs, we can organize our lives to make sure that the basic needs are met. For martial art, our LoS 1 is about basic needs. In LoS 1 we find the definition of combatives. In LoS 1 martial art we find the definition of doing 'anything' to never be put in the vulnerable positions where the brain is cut off from its oxygen supply. In sport, one may be knocked out or choked out because a referee is present. In combatives, in real life outside of sport, this is not an option, as the organism that is the body would be vulnerable to attacks it cannot defend against. We should train to protect themselves while putting an enemy into a position they can be terminated without resistance.

Terminate may seem a strong word, but words are important in teaching martial art. For example, 'opponent' has a sporting definition, 'enemy' does not. While many words are used for reality-based martial arts, from aggressor to an attacker, in the end they are an enemy. They are a person, group, or organization who seeks your end and is hostile to your existence. In combatives we must remember, regardless of words, we are facing an enemy. The enemy either knowingly seeks your end, or, in the way they fight, they show a wanton disregard for you as a human being with a family, religion, culture. Psychologically one must be willing to make the distinction between an enemy and opponent. If a referee is there to stop the fight, you have an opponent. If no referee exists to stop the fight, and an action such as being knocked out, choked out, or facing massive blood loss can kill you…you are facing an enemy. No, third parties or those around do not qualify as a referee. A referee has a moral and ethical duty to stop a fight when you are unable to continue - a third party or crowd does not. Reality-based arts must make proper use of words and definition, understanding the scenario.

These definitions do not include 'techniques' because accidents happen in sports where people die or are permanently disabled. These definitions are about the environment where the techniques take place. In Pramek there are entire directions of study for techniques to be used within this scenario, to kill or maim the enemy, or rob them of the physical, mental, and spiritual ability or will to fight. But these techniques are taught within the context of LoS 1, pure survival against an enemy. Many of these techniques can be used, albeit differently, in sport, but in LoS 1 they are applied for the destruction of an enemy.

Once we determine LoS 1 and have fulfilled the study of martial techniques that protect our immediate safety, we can begin to study LoS 2. LoS 2 is a bridge…it is the current self in a lot of ways. We learn from LoS 1 to get to LoS 2. Without LoS 2 we cannot get to LoS 3. While LoS 2 and LoS 3 are not time specific, LoS 1 is. Los 1 is right now, it's your ability to breathe, to walk around, to eat, to procreate. LoS 2 and LoS 3 are not time specific as they are further out in our view of time, in a sense, not being time specific, they are life specific. Once you've gotten past your fears of the challenges in life that endanger LoS 1, you're able to focus beyond it into studies of LoS 2 and LoS 3.

We move through our martial art study in phases and in coordination with our life circumstances. Combative arts are generally harder on the body, focused on the violence of our actions. These arts can be taxing on the emotional and physical state of the student. As students' progress through programs like the CLM DPT they come up against psychological barriers not found in other studies. They move into fatigue, high levels of stress, and scenarios which test their mental wherewithal. All of this is done in the pursuit of being able to take the physical and mental battering of realistic combat that an enemy may bring to threaten the Level of Survival 1. In my own personal experience, having multiple concussions and numerous other injuries, and seeing the injuries other artists absorb through years of the combative styles, LoS 1 is a taxing study. For many LoS 1 should be studied to competency and then moved on from.

Level of Survival 2

Let's take the advice from above, and every student of martial art would be able to defend themselves in an LoS 1 manner. They become confident in their ability. Now what?

Some artists move into pushing their body harder and soon find arts that are less about combatives and instead focus on challenging the physical conditioning of the artist. This can be seen in LoS 2 concepts like cardio kickboxing, and sportive arts often seen which are heavily influenced by rules of engagement like boxing and Brazilian Jiu Jitsu. Within these arts high levels of associativè and autonomic understanding, as well as athletic ability, are needed to compete in the art or style. Other times artists often find themselves unable to practice LoS 1 methods in full-speed sparring and begin to focus on LoS 2 arts. These arts have elements of sparring where there is full contact with other artists while avoiding the high levels of possible injury found in combative arts. In LoS 2 arts, students find the ability to have full contact sparring under rules, or they find athletic and physical attribute development.

The physical attributes of LoS 2 arts are incredibly important in the bridge along the path that is our martial art journey. In LoS 1 and LoS 3 we find the beginning and the end, but the in-between, the physical and psychological attributes that come from LoS 2 provide a strong foundation for the bridge. These arts form a strong personal foundation for a student, tested by physical and psychological setbacks in competition. Losing in competition, losing in timed drills for exercise, moving beyond the physical plateau of a personal best - these are challenges for the mind and body. They often work in concert with the other areas of our life as we are tested by life's challenges at work, home, and in personal relationships. Just as within Pramek we teach 'if you can touch the ear, you can move the head' we also look at LoS 2 challenges. The thought 'if I can win this competition, then challenges at work are no problem' is a positive outlook that correlates our martial art study to our personal life, linking success in one and success in another. I know many Jiu Jitsu students who are successful businessmen, tying their overcoming the challenges of one, sport, with the confidence to overcome the challenges of life.

Level of Survival 3

Remember, LoS is all about the needs of life above the baseline and our needs change as we age. In LoS 3 styles of martial art the 'why' of training is different from both LoS 1 and LoS 2. LoS 3 styles are usually for the level of mastery of self and the art. With life experience comes an appreciation of martial art beyond that of the younger self looking to fight an armed opponent or an edge in competition. As one ages, not in physical age, but in martial experience, they tie their life experience in their art. They may seek to find a spiritual point to their study and seek arts that enhance this a cultural study. Many students may find that the lessons of another culture resonate with their own feelings or experience and see it as another level of learning and draw closely to it, to the point of their identity changing. I have even seen long term history students study a culture art to understand a culture's history better.

The LoS 3 student may enjoy an art's community of peers and the comradery it brings. They may work extremely slow, having fun, experimenting with techniques unsuitable in LoS 1 and LoS 2 arts. The study is different as the student looks at their long-term study of their LoS 3 needs for understanding their inner self. In these arts, realistically, a greater emphasis should be put on the experience more than the application. Few would use Tai Chi in a real fight, but the study of slow movement and meditation in movement has an appeal brought on for those limited by age, injury, or the need for refinement of technique. For example, in Pramek, a LoS 3 student may only look at the mechanics of every method, or use strategies designed around understanding the biomechanical structure of an opponent and seek to do as little as possible to win the combative interaction. They may forego the devastation of a strike to the brachial plexus or a violent choke to cut off an artery. They may just explore, to see what they can do with only biomechanics, kinematics, or principles of physics like a lever or pulley. Within LoS 3 we see a high number of exploratory arts or arts heavy in cultural basis but lite in the physical stress of LoS 1 or the competitive functions of LoS 2 styles.

Creating a differentiation

Within these LoS definitions one may ask, 'What about MMA and UFC? Aren't they sportive, but people get really hurt?' With this question, we come back to the answer of 'why'. Why are you in the fight? Why are you training certain methods? For safety reasons in training, in Pramek, a teacher or instructor may say, 'that's not allowed' because the safety of the training partner – but never the rules. I hold myself to a general rule in this consideration, because though organizational fights like those found in UFC and MMA competitions are highly violent, if you can't do certain things to your opponent, they are not truly LoS 1 styles. Some arts as they are taught may contain LoS 1 elements, but if the 'why' is not pure survival - they are not LoS 1 as they do not instruct the student to use any Tactics or method to survive. One can say 'that's not allowed' due to safety and still teach LoS 1. LoS 1 styles see no rules as being the rule where nothing is out of bounds in training except for safety. Conversely, the LoS 2 style is different - the 'why' is to win in competition, or to be in better athletic shape. Certain rules to protect participants, with bans on certain techniques or methods are highly damaging and, in a matter of speaking, shortcuts to end a sportive fight. This is vastly different from concerns for safety.

If an art is not regularly teaching concepts like eye gouges, knife use, or beating someone's head against the ground in a manner to cause damage - they are not training the neurology of the student to perform such attacks under duress. While some LoS 2 arts may incorporate potentially LoS 1 methods, such as chokes, they must be trained regularly in their context. If they are not trained regularly to full effect because they are considered 'too dangerous to use', then the style is still in the LoS 2 category.

Most people never genuinely think in terms of Levels of Survival because their day-to-day lives, or their training in martial art, doesn't require them to. They only concern themselves with these concepts when their life is in danger, when their health is failing, or they feel no sense of purpose. It is important to explain to students their 'why' of training and to set them up for success at the very beginning by understanding LoS and that they can rarely address LoS 1 concerns with a LoS 3 art, or vice versa.

It would be difficult for me to count over the years how many people have told me how fearful they are of crime and wish to understand how to protect themselves. Then these same people immediately go and find a LoS 2 or LoS 3 martial art. In doing so they ignore that fundamental boxing and wrestling, basic combatives, would allow them to succeed in the immediate term and address how fearful they are. While we should strive to confront fear with confidence, confidence must be focused on skills that are applicable and not demonstrational-only in nature.

When a student with LoS 1 fears studies a LoS 2 or 3 art they put the proverbial cart before the horse. These students are never challenged with the 'why' of their study, or what they want a martial art to become in their lives, because they are too worried about addressing the LoS 1 concern that they have.

But, if one never addresses the original reason for training, they will float martial art to martial art, looking to solve the question of LoS 1 personal confidence in LoS 2 and LoS 3 systems finding spiritual or fitness benefits, but little combative capability. Each has its place, but a place must be made for them in the life-time of a student's study.

Remember, martial art is as much about timing in the strike as the timing of life.

Defining the LOS blend

To review, we can define the arts as follows:

LoS 1 Martial Art - combative styles for near-term survival

LoS 2 Martial Art - fitness or competition-based sport style

LoS 3 Martial Art - in-depth study of martial art information

There are many arts that are blends of LoS. LoS 1 and LoS 2 blend if the purpose is recognized and one uses elements of combative methods in their sport-based techniques. Remember, neurology is the key. As stated previously, if an art isn't teaching the combative end of a throw and is instead teaching the sportive result, it doesn't matter how great the throw is – the combative element is lost to the neurology of the practitioner. Think of it this way – if I train to gouge the eye then throw 1000 times, and someone else trains to grab the collar then throw 1000 times, what do you think we will do in a real-life altercation? Sure, we will both use a throw, but how we get to the throw is completely different in terms of damage to the body. This is a popular topic, street vs. survival, and in the end, no matter the blend of LoS arts, neurology rules supreme. Repetitions to develop neuropathways is hard to argue with.

Furthering the discussion of LoS blends, the study of psychology or limited range of motion movements in an LoS 3 art may have benefits in an LoS 2. These are general classifications and while individual arts are not listed, the methods held within different styles have the capability to be utilized across classification. You can learn important techniques, strategies, and other concepts from any art and therefore learning from any art is important. Our purpose in defining a classification like LoS is to define the 'why' of study.

For a true martial artist - martial art is life. It doesn't matter the study; martial art becomes a lifestyle. For the combatives student who problem solves everything, the MMA student who changes their diet to reflect their training, or the cultural student of LoS 3 who is enriching their lives - there is no difference. It is all about the 'why' and the application. A 21-year-old student in the military thinks differently about martial art than the MMA fighter, and both think differently than a 52-year-old student looking to understand their own mental capability in meditation. Some arts transcend all three levels, and this can usually be seen in the age range of the practitioners. In Pramek, a student can study combatives, utilize the science and athletic aspects in sporting competition, and in advanced age use the art to further their understanding of psychology. In BJJ, a 19-year-old student in US Army basic training is learning a different BJJ from a 26-year-old MMA competitor. Each of these are learning a different BJJ from a 60-year-old student who enjoys the community and the study of movement.

The Understanding of LoS arts

The purpose of classification is to define the concepts of the study. The classification is made for a reason...so we can better understand the needs of the student and their 'why'. If a student has LoS 1 needs, they should not go into an LoS 3 art until the Level 1 need is met. If a student is concerned about LoS 2 issues, such as their cardiovascular health, placing them into an LoS 3 art for 'fighting' is not going to create a positive outcome in 'scratching the itch' they have in their 'why'. When a student understands the difference of 'why' between the arts and can identify their personal 'why' of the martial study, they can identify the direction of study they should undertake. When a teacher understands the 'why' of what they are teaching, they can gain and keep certain kinds of students and then the focus of their system will grow as the students wish to continue to study and develop their art.

In CLM 3 we discuss the reasons students leave teachers. One of the reasons is the teacher no longer has anything to teach the student. This comes back to 'why'. A teacher may know 30 years of advanced joint locks to teach, but if the student is looking to become a better athlete and use combative study to do it, the student most likely will leave. The student will leave eventually for an art that is more athletic in nature and the teacher will have wasted their knowledge on the student. In addition, they will waste the time of other interested students as the teacher attempts to alter classroom curriculum to keep the one student. Is it a waste? Some may find this term a little insensitive, but if you keep one young athletic student and lose two older interested students who didn't want MMA incorporated into their LoS 3 study - is this not a waste?

This could be the definition of the phrase 'stay in your lane'. If the purpose of an art is to create better athletes, then the instructor should not pretend to teach street fighting methods or spiritual insights. Don't be a sophist, teaching anything to anyone who will pay money - instead, teach to the people who want to learn what you teach. Outside of location and demographics, I have seen many failing schools with incredible teachers bring on other arts to bring in more students, instead of truly focusing on increasing their visibility to bring in a greater number of students. There will always be someone who knows more about what a student wants to learn if you have the wrong student.

As we discuss in CLM 3, brick and mortar martial art schools are on the decline and what we covered is one of the biggest reasons. If you can't keep your school open teaching what you love, ask yourself, 'Which is more important - what I want to teach or making money?' Beyond keeping a school open and putting food on the table, the understanding of LoS classification is vital to understanding how to have the student 'be' in the moment. What are they afraid of, what fight do they need to fight - and are they in the right class to do so? The importance of this classification is so you can best understand the needs of the student and the student can best understand what they need. All students should start in LoS 1 and every 'martial art' school should offer an LoS 1 class and ask students to attend it, even if only for a few classes. If a student is in great physical condition from your kickboxing class but is injured on the street outside of your martial art school - what has been accomplished? If a student has a higher-level understanding of self from their classes, but loses a part of that self in a stabbing they never prepared for at the grocery store - what has been accomplished?

When we can answer the 'why' of survival, be it immediate danger, the bridge to old age found in athletics or competition, or the understanding of self and camaraderie of a training community around concepts and ideas - we've answered some big questions of what to teach. Different students have different needs. I know a very well-known UFC veteran who rarely does martial art anymore and focuses on competitive shooting. He only teaches martial art to students he genuinely wants to teach but has found a new challenge in the mechanics of shooting and love the community. This individual has found new teachers, a new group of friends, and a new level of training. He knows his 'why' and he uses the challenge of LoS 2 as a means of training to perform advanced shooting under stress and movement. He knows his 'why'.

Answer the 'why'.

'Why are we here' is a big life question… 'why am I in this martial art class' is not.

Chapter 28: A concept of martial art.

Over the years, as I studied various styles, learning from different instructors. My personal martial art study is rather like a pendulum. Swaying away from the mechanics and teaching methods of the Western styles to the Eastern arts and the ideas of the East like 'Zen'. In both methodologies one point I continued to come back to is the concept of 'noise' and how much noise exists in martial art and combative training. We often hear people say, 'cut through the noise' and this is what I continued to come back to in my search for finding a bridge between the great martial art of the East and West. In the world of martial art, how do we find the elusive state of 'flow', of 'being', not reacting, just acting on what is observed. But, by the same token, how do we remain vigilant and ready to act in a violent manner without looking too deeply into what combat is.

This is a balance of the self – the authentic person we are today.

Professor Maung Yi is famous for saying, 'in a fight, if you start thinking about your mother, you have already lost'. If we dive too deep into the waters of looking internally, we find the onion to be composed of endless layers. But if we do not do this internal search of self we can become uncentered. This is common in many Western arts and commonly displayed in the MMA world of big muscles and aggression. Anyone who has been in true combat know that throwing one's self at the fight in typical MMA fashion can quickly result in great injury. This method of fighting says a lot about the person who is throwing themselves into the fight, their experiences, training, and confidence in their skill. Conversely if one does not throw themselves into the fight offensively, and becomes overly defensive, one can quickly be overwhelmed and lose confidence.

Whether the person is confident, or unconfident gives rise to the question of where the self, the fight, the opponent's self exists: time. But, before we can even think about the student and the time in which they exist in the fight, we first need to understand the concept of a fight. What is a fight? This is not about the unorganized brawl, but about the Tactical decision to engage in combat and win.

First, as we have discussed in previous CLM books, let's not use 'fight'. A 'fight' cannot be broken down into segments and studied. Instead, we look at a combative interaction, and I encourage you to read previous CLM books to understand this concept fully. A combative interaction is not about victory or defeat and should rarely be categorized that way. When one thinks in these terms, they lose touch with the reason they are there in the first place.

Ask yourself a question: what is victory or defeat if you are defending your child? If you are defending the life of a child and you lose your life in the process...did you win, or did you lose? If one thinks of a fight in terms of winning first, and Goals and strategies second, they will end up using their techniques for no true purpose. Techniques and methods exist in a pyramid of action defined by what we know about the fight.

The Pyramid of Action

The Egyptians did not build the pyramid from the top down. The top was the last piece of the construction as it is for all pyramids. The base of the pyramid is the foundation for the entire structure. It is must be strong, wide, and capable of supporting the structure above it. From the base, the rest of the pyramid can be reached and built upon. One can climb to the top or back to the bottom with ease as the sides are built at an angle that is defined by design. It is within this design that we find the Pyramid of Action, or PoA.

How do we use this to teach or learn? One of the most popular questions teachers of martial art are asked is, 'How do I fight a bigger opponent', and since it is a prevalent question, we will use this as our basis for explaining the

PoA. Certain questions need to be asked to answer this problem, and the answer lies in a more effective answer than 'let me show you how to fight a larger opponent'.

Let's assume, for a moment, that the student is of average height, perhaps 5'9 and 170 pounds. We already see the conundrum of this question in the defining a larger opponent. What is the definition of 'bigger'? So, we will further assume they mean someone who is over 6'4 and 250 pounds.

If one were to rely primarily on techniques to answer the question of fighting a larger opponent, then one would train in primarily fighting larger opponents. This poses a problem because what if most of their training partners are their own size or not what they define as 'larger'? The student would end up with no experience in consistently fighting a larger opponent. While many techniques, like a strike, can be applied to a larger opponent, a rear naked choke cannot without the enemy being mechanically disadvantaged, exposing the student to prolonged attachment to the enemy. If the student has been taught a large quantity of choke methods, the quantity doesn't answer the question of getting the opponent to the ground, by attacking the legs for example, which is a Tactic. This begs the question, has the student learned effective leg attacks? How will one attack the legs and where will they target the legs? Will it be from the side, from the front, or will the student attempt to get behind the opponent and attack the back of the legs? As you can see there are a lot of questions that are reliant upon techniques within this model of training. Within this paradigm the student's ability to gain victory is tied to knowledge of techniques.

If we shift the paradigm, using the PoA, we see that first we must build an effective basis for action. The PoA exists to reduce the number of available options the student must focus on, so they can focus on what is needed to accomplish their Goal. If the student acts based on a Goal when faced with a larger opponent, the student will do what must be done to achieve a Goal. The student with a Goal will take certain actions and look for certain openings that achieve the Goal. Conversely, the student without a Goal will often be overwhelmed by the availability of options and will delay while searching for the answer, giving the opponent time to act unpredictably. This action leaves the student constantly reacting, versus the student with a Goal, who acts for a single purpose, making the opponent react.

In the PoA, the student should be first asked what Goal is. In the Goal we answer the questions of the environment. The why must be answered first because it gives the student the ability to understand their Goal before they engage in combat. Why do they have to fight the larger opponent? Is the opponent robbing them or attacking them while drunk? Are they in a parking lot, kitchen, or bar? What will be accomplished in combat and why act? If one is defending a child, then their action taken will be different from preventing a robbery. Each will give a different Goal, where defending a child against kidnapping may mean a fight to the death while preventing a robbery may require the student to fight a delaying action to get to a public place and call for help. With an understanding of the environment a student can limit their options outside of their technique capabilities and focus what is necessary in the situation.

Strategy is the well-informed child of a Goal. The Strategy chosen will determine the options available. If a student decides under no circumstance will they go to the ground, because doing so could mean severe injury against the larger opponent, the student will do everything to remain standing. If the student happens to end up on the ground, the student will use only the options available to get back up. This ensures the student remains focused on their Goal and sees part of their Strategy as never going to the ground.

The PoA also limits the number of techniques the student must neurologically call up during the fight. When under a high amount of duress, and physiological reactions such as high respiratory rate (all of which are measurable in the DPT), the brain's ability to use fine motor skills and engage complex techniques becomes impaired. If the student decides not to fight on the ground, the student has reduced the number of techniques they must neurologically call up under duress, instead they focus on the techniques they need to win the fight.

Options begin to shift rooted in the foundation of Strategy. In the case of the larger opponent, defending one's self, versus defending a child, creates vastly different Tactics. If the Goal is to survive, and the Strategy is to get to a public place away from the attacker, then getting an obstacle between them and the attacker becomes their Tactic. If their Goal is to protect their child, and their Strategy is to kill or render the attacker unable to continue the attack, then Tactics change drastically. Choosing an obstacle to get between them and the attacker versus finding and employing a weapon become the selected Tactics, instead of just fighting wildly while their child is in danger.

There is a clarity of Tactics when the Strategy and Goals are defined. Within this clarity, and a limited number of options, we come to techniques. The first question we must ask when it comes to techniques is not 'what technique to use against the larger opponent' but 'what technique would work best, and have we trained it?' Techniques reflect training, and training is the reflection of the teacher's understanding of the material. Rarely would someone expect a world class sambo competitor to teach a reality-based self-defense seminar about surviving a carjacking or kidnapping. Their training environment was not based upon the carjacking. In the training environment, the Goal is to win on submission or points. Their Strategy is to use throws or take-downs to do so. Their Tactics develop around this Goal, what wins 3 points versus 1 point, and using this knowledge to create a foundation for techniques.

Some fighters are better at throwing while some are better are submissions and pinning, and their techniques develop around this. They train these techniques over and over, against a variety of training partners, and the good sambo competitor will work a Strategy to achieve their Goal, using Tactics to get to their best techniques. In sport, we find the state of action as the result, a win or lose, is known - the only unknown is the response of the opponent. This unknown response can be mitigated if the student constantly plays their game, forcing constant reaction by the opponent.

In reality-based martial art and self-defense we cannot create techniques for situations we have never faced. This poses a problem for many students – they can train for sambo throws every day, but how does one train for a sudden attack in a subway or driveway? If we follow the logic of the sambo player and the PoA, we find the techniques employed exist for one reason: to win a match. For real world altercations, the why behind choosing techniques is no different…they must be trained. They should be chosen for their purpose as they are the product of the Tactic. Strikes to create distance, such as a jab in sport, are different from strikes to win a fight, such as eye gouges and ocular hooking.

Back to our original subject, a bigger opponent, we can solve this problem very quickly through a series of PoA questions. To answer, 'kick them in the groin' would be a disservice to the student because it never discovered the true reason the student needed a question answered. A groin kick, which is always a great technique, requires medium distance, many times the length of an opponent's arm. If you are 5'6 and the 6'3 opponent can reach you, they can grab you...and what if your Strategy were to flee to a public space or protect a child?

To determine what action to take, we should first determine why it needs to be taken.

The PoA when utilized is an effective method of doing this. To utilize the PoA in training, ask:

> 1. *What is your Goal?*
> 2. *How will you achieve that Goal?*
> 3. *What can you use in your environment or knowledge to make that a reality?*
> 4. *What technique do you know that can assist you?*

Answer just one of these are you are already ahead strategically of your opponent. To learn more, I encourage you to discover CLM 1, 2, and 3, as well as our video series where we show this in action.

Concept of time in Fighting

The pyramid is a method of organizing a fight. Think of your own life for a moment when you need to get to a business meeting or a family dinner, but you didn't plan properly. If your life is unorganized, you may end up running late, having a bad mood, or the most dreaded organizational obstacle of all may strike: the inability to find your keys. But, if you are organized, paperwork is pre-printed, clothes are laid out, the children are ready, and the keys are beside the door. The PoA is the layer of organization because each layer of the pyramid creates a vital ally for us in a fight.

That ally is time.

I once told a student that time was his primary ally in a fight. Why? Time is an ally because to gain time for one's self was to take time away from someone else. We exist in the same universe, so we are in the same time frame in terms of the clock, but in terms of the effectiveness of our actions time is utilized differently. When one understands time is an ally or enemy, it forces one to use time effectively or ineffectively. Time adds options, points of escape, weapons, friends, luck, and for some, the supernatural. My student scoffed at the idea, stating, 'If I'm overwhelming someone, and outweigh them by 100 pounds, what difference does time make?'

The answer, I told him, is found in a delaying action in the fight.

With enough time, they can get away from you.

With enough time, they can go and find a gun.

With enough time, they can find someone to help them, or reinforcements to arrive.

With enough time, your energy will sap, and the 100 pounds will become a liability.

Time is power in a fight.

The Ghost Division of World War 2 is a perfect example of this. The blitzkrieg, or lightening war, was defined by the 7th Panzer Division, called the Ghost Division. The Ghost Division led by Rommel moved with speed and shock through the battlefront, sometimes outstretching communication and supply lines, to overcome the enemy. Even when the British counterattacked and stalled the 7th, Rommel reacted by bringing up artillery and his anti-aircraft guns into the fight against the British. This was reaction defined by action, making use of organization and speed in the time the battle took place. Patton worked in a similar fashion in breaking through to Bastogne.

For martial artists, though smaller in scale, time is about ending the fight quickly because that is our primary Goal. What if either commander had hesitated and waited? The longer one is in the fight in an unorganized manner, the more opportunities there are for the fight to go wrong. In combatives, the longer the fight goes - the greater likelihood the opponent is to go and find a gun, a friend, or for you wear down and become vulnerable. In sport, the longer the fight goes, the more likely you are to make mistakes that cost you points before the clock ends. Taken to a larger scale such as our martial art learning journey, the more time we live the more time we may have to study all the arts that amaze us.

Time determines, and in many ways is, the mechanics of the fight.

In mechanics, motion is the change of a body's position over time. Everything covered in Pramek's UOS, from the levers to strikes, is measured in time - displacements from a strike, acceleration from loading and unloading, distance to targets. In human equilibrium the body position changes over time, the center mass shifts, it can be shifted by applying force over time. With enough time, we can gain mechanical advantage and with enough time, we can increase the advantage by applying multiple force vectors.

If we are to gain time, then we first must not lose it. The first way that we lose time is to become overwhelmed by the situation at hand. If we gather too much information, we may have a difficult time deciding what is the 'right' information and what is the 'wrong' information. In terms of combat, this often happens when we abandon the GSTM construct and give ourselves over to disorganization. This occurs when we do not know a why or can't answer what is the Goal or what Strategy will we use. Without a 'why' we might let the fight go as it will, delaying as we choose options - missing opportunities that could lead us to a short victory and reduce the amount of time that things can go wrong.

In Pramek we speak often about the GSTM because the GSTM gives us access to time. The first way we gain time is to have the fight happen in such a way that it is understandable and correlates to our 'why'. We gather information before the fight and simultaneously process information we are seeing about our opponent. We make decisions based on this information that result in actions that we judge will put the opponent in a reactive state. Then, when we act, we are in a constant state of adjustment and revaluation. All of this takes place in time.

But a fight can't go on forever - at some point it must end. While we all love an underdog or an upset knockout, most of the time, be it points in the twelfth round or blood loss, the person who has had more time using their preferred methods will win. This begs the question of how is this time found, and more directly, how do we create time in a fight?

First, we must understand how we our brains respond to the fight and what processes take place mentally during the fight.

Chapter 29 The Concept of OODA

The nature of action is the creation of reaction. We know from Newton's laws of physics that an object at rest will stay at rest or in an uninterrupted straight-line motion unless acted upon by another force. Your creation of reaction is an action you take that causes a reaction.

So, what happens when someone acts?

First, let's get to the psychological basis of action, how the brain views information. The brain must go through a mental process to understand a dynamic situation such as combat. This process is commonly referred to as the OODA loop. OODA was originally developed by United States Air Force Colonel John Boyd as a means of describing the decision-making process used by fighter pilots. For the sake of brevity, as there are many sources on the OODA loop, I am not going to go into a deep definition and explanation of OODA. We will use a basic understanding of what the process is and then look at how it relates to the state of action. Over time I've written several articles about OODA, as have other Pramek instructors like Aaron Cowan and Dr. John Landry, and I encourage you the reader of CLM to go out and research OODA. The following is the basic understanding of OODA that is often used in Pramek classes and seminar.

Observe - seeing and processing the information and stimuli in the outside environment

Orient - acquiring a problem and comparing the problem against one's own experiences

Decide - comparing the information against possible solutions and possible actions to take

Act - acting based on the decision, then reengaging OODA to test the result of the action

Here is a diagram (reprinted with permission) from our good friends at Sage Dynamics which visibly explains OODA in more detail:

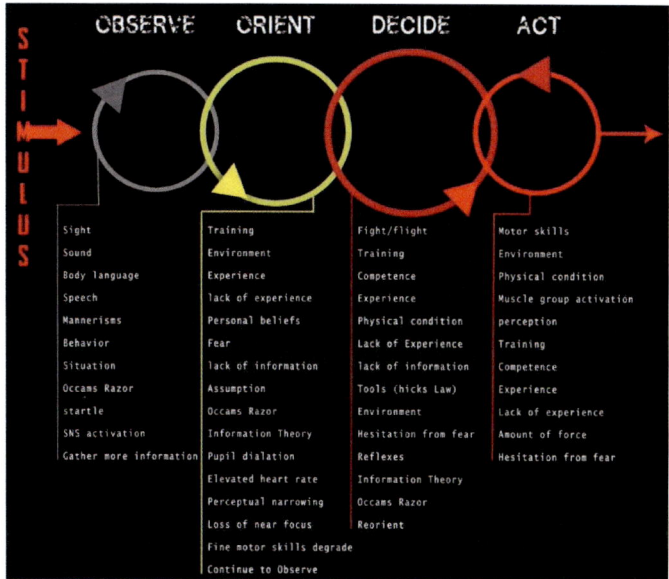

It's a lot of information and instead of diving into the subsections, let's instead ask: how does OODA work in real life?

A real-world example would be observing someone hanging around the door to your apartment complex or business. You orient on this person and compare this person against your experiences in the past. This engages the decision-making phase of the loop, as you decide if this person is a threat, and if so, compare the situation against possible actions you can take. You then transition into action where you take an action and re-enter OODA in terms of comparing your action against the result of your action. You don't consciously know that you do this - it is how your brain works, contrasting the information the conscious brain takes in against the information the unconscious brain holds. Your brain is a giant 'assumption machine', making assumptions about everything based on the past. Even down to the way you sleep, as your brain processes the day through the hippocampus, your brain is designed for OODA. We live observing the present, evaluate based on the past, decide based on the past, and act based on the past...and then do it all over again. It's who we are.

Is OODA applicable?

Why are we pointing out OODA as a standard to understand and not making one up or looking to other methodologies for understanding combative action?

To choose a methodology that is specific to one martial art and describes that art, versus taking a universally recognized methodology, would limit the ability of the student to understand the fullness of a topic. Are there concepts like OODA in the martial arts? Of course, but OODA gives a scale of study unmatched by anything in the martial arts. There are thousands of works on OODA one can sift through and look for applicability, or comparison to other processes. This process is now used for all kinds of subjects, including industrial and business processes. OODA became popular in firearms instructional usage in the mid-2000's as shooting instructors began to study the concept. It was invaluable in understanding the complex decision-making process that was involved in the deployment of the firearm, acquiring the target, making the decision on whether to fire the weapon, and then the action during, and after the trigger pull. This led to OODA being brought over into the martial art world by combative organizations that were engaged in the shooting world, like Pramek, as the applicability seen in shooting meant it could be used in martial art.

OODA is real, it does happen, and it can enhance your capabilities both pre- and post-interaction in your ability to process the results of your techniques. For many of you, this may be a process that you've seen described in business or read about in an article on a blog. At its core, this process is describing the human experience of a highly stressful situation and how the mind-body makes decisions. Pramek, in 2010, began incorporating OODA into our teaching methodology and experimenting with OODA in Pramek seminars, but also by teaching for other organizations, such as Sage Dynamics. This gave a deeper understanding of the applicability of OODA in terms of actions being taken by students. In Pramek we have seen OODA repeatedly in a variety of situations. One thing we have learned is that the best students and fighters are able to functionalize OODA into a means of gaining valuable time or advantage.

The primary challenge with OODA is that it is an unconscious function based on previous experience. While it is a function of the brain, OODA does not seem to be actionable. No instructor has ever told anyone, 'Looks like you are stuck in Orient' when talking about OODA because OODA has not been developed as a method of conscious action. It has been developed as a means of explaining an unconscious process. So, while we might not say someone is stuck in Orient, we can look at a training scenario afterwards, and study our judgments or performance based on OODA. For example, if someone is slow to the strike an aggressor in a scenario, this may be because they have little experience in the Orient and Observe phases, making their Decision to strike slow. This shows us that while OODA is not an action plan, we can use OODA as a training tool to apply to the process of fighting.

We can't utilize OODA in a way like the Methods section of GSTM, where one can practice certain methods to achieve a Tactic. The Observe section of OODA can be trained, and it can become an attribute to help you see potential dangers - but you cannot win a fight by being better at observing. One still must move from OODA to GSTM or use OODA to create GSTM. In the end, your OOD's effectiveness is gauged based on the success of your A, or Action.

OODA describes your decision-making process - it is not your action. In educating a student about their behavior within a combative situation, OODA is an important tool. It's professionally researched, and it can be broken down into teachable segments. It helps the student to understand the nature of their action as they are educated on how they make decisions upon which they will act. The better the understanding of OODA, the more instructors and teachers can use it to help students become faster in their action.

Feedback Loops

Within OODA a person can become stuck in the decision-making process due to the many possible actions one can take. Therefore, the student must have methods of reducing what they attempt to access. If you have learned too many techniques you can enter a feedback loop of technique where you compare techniques to the situation, try a technique, compare to the situation, technique, compare to the situation. This is where fighters can become stuck in their decision-making process. When one utilizes concepts and principles, like those within the CLM EPL, and uses a limited number of highly violent or effective methods, they are more likely to achieve an advantageous position. Therefore, in action, it is often preferable to fight based on one's GSTM instead of engaging the fight as it goes. Bringing the fight back to one's strengths not only is effective in controlling the fight, but it also avoids the pitfalls of the OODA loop and how our brain and bodies process information. We can over process information, as discussed in our Organizing the Fight series with increased heart rate, respiratory rate, etc. The brain can take in so much information that it can no longer effectively process all of it.

We cannot consciously utilize all the information that comprises OODA to create a plan. Instead, our nervous system and mind combine, with the brain relying on previous experience and our nervous system allotting energy supply to the body to perform tasks. OODA is a concept we can use to understand how we make decisions, but it is not a means of making decisions because it is unconscious. To make decisions, we must develop mental models based on our previous experience, be it real or imagined.

Earlier we looked at the past and how the brain operates based on the conscious-unconscious brain communication. When we have experienced a situation enough times, we create a mental model. A mental model is an assumption we create based on our experience in the world.

Look at this photo and you will immediately understand mental models. Looking at that photo you assumed an outcome. You might've seen this happen or experienced it, so you developed a mental model that allows your brain to make a quick overarching assumption about the situation and then move on to act accordingly or analyze it more fully. Our brains are chaotic places – simply sitting in silence can be difficult. If we allowed our brains the time to focus on everything we see, we would consistently overanalyze. Hick's Law is commonly referred to in this situation, as the more available choices we have, the longer we will take to make the 'correct' choice. This is fine within certain aspects of our lives, like buying a cereal, but not in a violent engagement. We have many frames of reference in terms of cereal selection, but few have experience to call upon in terms of a violent altercation. This can lead to what is called a 'feedback' loop, or 'analysis paralysis' where a person consistently tries a high number of solutions on a problem with no success yet continue to try the same solutions again.

In combatives training we often see the same solutions being tried repeatedly. These loops are created by unconscious processes we've trained repeatedly in response to a situation. The action taken is ineffective, but the person takes the same action again, repeatedly, or variations of the same action that still do not work. This continues until a corrective action solves the problem the feedback loop was attempting to solve. There are a variety of ways the corrective action may be found, such as being consciously decided upon. The student and the situation will dictate how this corrective action is found.

FEEDBACK LOOP

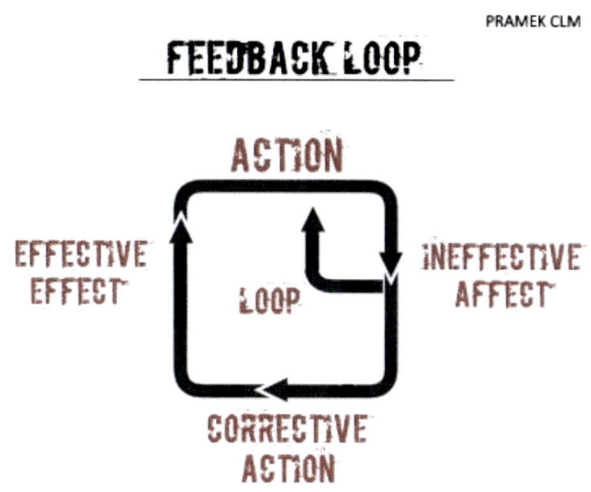

In firearms training, we see feedback loops during malfunction clearing (repeated 'tap-rack' instead of ejecting the magazine), or in a hand to hand altercation where someone repeatedly tries a throw or hold, even if it doesn't work. We often get stuck in a feedback loop because we visually see that our action is not working, so we start over. We may make a conscious decision to change what we are doing, or we stumble into something that begins to work, so we switch and begin processing again.

We see this often in Pramek full contact classes using Spartan Training Gear or similar gear. Most students are accustomed to training against another opponent, but outside of full contact fighting, students generally don't go full force for fear of injuring the training partner. But when students use safety gear that allows for high impact levels, they become overwhelmed by powerful impacts they don't receive during regular training. Once overwhelmed, they quickly develop feedback loops. Holding and delay-based wrestling moves become common as students frantically search for a solution.

Generally, the situation causing the feedback loop will change because the attacker will move to a position of advantage or defense which the student is familiar with. When this occurs, the student will usually bypass the feedback loop and become active in the fight again.

But what happens if we can't work through the feedback loop?

On occasion people stuck in a loop will just quit. We see this in training when someone can't solve the problem in front of them. The most common is attempted take-downs being blocked or stopped and it becomes a loop. The student can't work through the feedback loop and many times they simply stop and begin looking around, bewildered. This is the onset of one of the most feared phases of action in martial art, if not in most parts of life. This phase is a phase of action beyond a feedback loop which is the most terrifying: panic. What is panic? We must first start with anxiety to determine what panic is. Anxiety is a natural burglar alarm – the brain's 'bump in the night'. It lets us know something is wrong and gives signals to the nervous system to employ defenses which have previously worked even if not against the exact present threat. This is called signal anxiety, or the signaling of the body to react to anxiety.

Two reactions are possible when we have panic-inducing anxiety. First, the mind can be overwhelmed with stimuli (for example, at the sight of a massive injury). People often say, 'he froze when he saw blood.' The mind becomes fixated on these stimuli instead of continuing to act on the surrounding threats. Most often this is because the mind has no experience to draw upon for, as was stated earlier, an assumption about what happens next. Panic is an action; unfortunately, it is an action that does not address threats. In this panic, a student stops acting and begins thinking about the stimuli rather than the threat, leading to physically 'freezing' because he can't process past the stimuli he has never experienced before.

The second reaction occurs when signal-anxiety-based defenses are overwhelmed. In this situation defenses are ineffective, leading the anxiety to switch from reacting to the threat to reacting to a realization of possible annihilation by the threat. People in highly stressful environments often act without thought to their own safety because their defenses have been trained, and thus they have experiences to relate to and act on. But when their defenses are overwhelmed, they realize they could die; this realization becomes so overwhelming they stop acting in hopes of surviving. This may lead to a 'hunker down' or surrender mentality, or irrational behavior such as fleeing a safe area to try to save themselves.

Few have a frame of reference for a violent altercation because it is an uncommon occurrence. Without this being a common occurrence, and without realistic training, one may become caught in a feedback loop. Once caught, they lose valuable time in combat or go into a panic from a lack of frame of reference to act on. Below is an example of what it looks like going from Signal Anxiety to Panic.

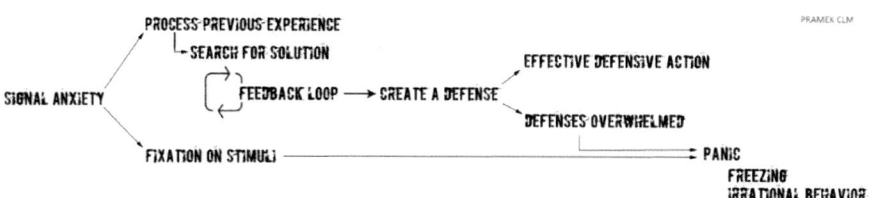

We all fear we will freeze when it counts most. Now we know why this happens.

Signal anxiety is a well-known concept in psychodynamic theory. It triggers a psychophysiological response to danger and is as old as biological life. The better the signal anxiety the more likely an organism's is to survive to pass on its genes. Humans are one of the evolutionary pinnacles of this process. Signal anxiety seems daunting but can keep us alive. There are however times when there is a true surprise and an overwhelming attack. This attack overwhelms our known and trained defenses. Such an event is most properly termed traumatic and can be psychological and physical.

The key to overcoming these states is the development of mental models we can apply to a variety of situations, reducing the number of available options that may not work…and replacing them with what is known to work consistently. Many are not able to attend simunitions courses or reality-based self-defense courses with full protection equipment. This means that one must use alternative means to prepare for the worst with the tools they have at hand.

One of the ways we can prepare and become faster in action is to create mental models for our actions and reactions. If we look at most scenarios we may face as a civilian or law enforcement, we can create a general plan of how we will react. This will give us valuable time to see outside of the effects of our sympathetic nervous system, analyze information, and act accordingly in a way that will best guarantee survival. Here are a few methods of developing mental models you may try to start getting your reaction time faster.

Making visualization part of your practice is one you or your students can use. If fighting is about time, we can't go and get into every single fight we could ever face, experience it, develop a mental model based on the experience, and then wait for the next fight. Based on how likely someone is in a developed country to experience a violent crime, one would have to live a thousand years to have a high enough number of situations occur to develop a mental model for fights based on experience. Either this or become a criminal who each night goes out looking for a problem with the populace. Instead, we must make use of our imaginations to create mental models.

Human minds have the power of conceptualization and perhaps all people develop an inner mental life. They form mental models. Think of the concept of the "theater of the mind" or creating a location or scenario in your mind. It begins in early childhood and develops from then on. Psychoanalytic Object Relations theory is the scientific and artistic conceptual outgrowth of this process. Within the individual, emotional value is attached to internal mental models that have helped defend and give experience information to the developing person. The solutions of the mind help broker inner and external conflict, and in so doing reduce anxiety and return a person to emotional and cognitive homeostasis. We are all model makers...and we must use this to our advantage.

Vince Lombardi once said, 'practice doesn't make perfect – perfect practice makes perfect.' Many times, people practice looking good but forget why they are practicing. Do not practice just to practice – practice for a reason. Visualization is an important key to developing models about how to act in a fight. We can't live in a fight, so we must train when we can. Take a few minutes and visualize a scenario you may encounter on your known route to places you will go today. The sounds, sights, smells. Are you in a familiar place, like a family business? Where is a weapon? What would your breathing be like? Who would be the enemy?

In combatives we can develop new mental models to help better protect us from danger. Inner visualization is a well-documented process that improves the performance of a learned physical task- for example shooting a basketball. We must apply it to our given course of study. This is also where principles become more important than techniques. You will find that applying every technique you know in your visualization practice is rather difficult - because it requires you to visualize the technique the aggressor might use. Instead, think in broad strokes, to the lever, wedge, screw, equilibrium, general combative strikes as you use your visualization practice. Within this you will find you are able to use gross motor skills, large movement patterns, 'big weapons for big targets' as we say - and you will focus less on trying to do complex chains of movements to defend yourself. Visualization is about exposing your mind to the situation and understanding it, not using every technique you know perfectly against twenty ninja warriors in your dreams.

Part of developing a mental model is experience, real or imaginary. Your body can familiarize itself with situations and stress through visualization. Just as the image of the child at the stove is a point of reference, visualization exercises allow you to create a point of reference for combat. If today is strikes and elbows day, then close your eyes, visualize a scenario, and perform your practice under the imagined stress of the visualization. You will find there are certain things you can always do, such as changing the angle of an elbow, that you can create a mental model to always get faster in response. These models can help us in avoiding panic when otherwise we may freeze and search for a solution we may not have.

When it comes to the fight, you know your strengths better than your aggressor, so play to them. Play to your strengths in training by developing a base model, creating your 1 tool for 10 jobs. Some people are extremely fast strikers, or left handed, or for some their experiences at work with loud noises puts them at a great advantage at not being startled. Yes, this is real - people who work in loud environments, such as construction, have a quite different startle response than those who do not. This is a strength if one is attacked by surprise - it's one more thing not to worry about, as you can weaponize the movement through training at work by bringing your hands up to a defensive posture, versus someone who is frightened by a vehicle backfire. A self-evaluation is important…be honest with yourself. This student may need to take this into account in their visualization exercise. Realize your strengths and make your models fit them. Encourage your students to do the same once you have done it and can show them how. Your solitary 'shadow boxing' training time and your visualization exercise should revolve around playing to your strengths. It's what you are good at, so it should be your first resort. If you are an incredibly fast striker and a weak grappler - where will you gain more time in the fight versus where will you lose it? Regardless, your mental model for any situation is to take time into account and make what gives you the most advantage your baseline to work from.

If you are engaging your visualization exercises, you should also put a premium on moving to a position of superiority. In your exercise - look around. If you visualize a garage, your home, next to a vehicle you just pulled over - where are you in the position of superiority? Look around in your 'theatre of the mind' and see what the best direction for movement is and where to drive the fight. These days the internet provides hundreds of hours of videos of real fight and altercations on in real life. If you utilize outside sources, such as videos on the internet to supplement your visualization training, you might look at what is most commonly effective and incorporate this into your training. Ask yourself - why throw out all that information for a someone's word? The people in the video, are, in effect, your teacher in terms of your visualization exercise. If you notice a successful trend, remember it. People may be different, but they are more alike than you think and as you watch videos, you will find this to be true.

A small percentage of the population has any advanced martial art training. If it works in Bangladesh, China, and Britain - chances are it'll work for you. Combative interactions and people rarely change just because of the continent. Combative interactions are still confusing, still exist in a place and time. Develop a mental model by visualizing the most common responses. Looking for the most common occurrences within a situation allows us to pre-plan responses, such as working toward our strength or moving to a position of superiority. This allows us a general template we can plan to address the maximum number of situations, allowing us to be faster in combat by reducing available decisions that could overwhelm us. When combined with actual training, this gives us confidence in what we train, and acting effectively consistently.

Within this we find some keys to OODA by taking it from a concept to a teachable process where we can affect the different phases. If you know by experience that if you see someone doing _x_ that you will always do _y_ actions, you reduce the amount of time it will take for you orient and decide. This is not the same as __x__ and __y__ technique in terms of Action, as we have addressed in the EPL. If someone pulls a firearm, and you always decide on a certain Tactic, such as moving to cover, this is different from the disarm. Remember, based on the way that your brain functions, you will still move from Observe through Orient and Decide to Act. Visualization and creating a mental model don't stop Observe. But, if you have certain situations in which you will always act a certain way, it is possible to move from Observe to Act immediately as the decision is based on a previously utilized one.

Lastly, OODA is not just a term that should be used in a class - it should be recognized as the time saving concept that it is. The faster you can process information and move through OOD and get to an effective A the better. As a student of Pramek once said, 'I can tell you this - pulling out a baseball bat and swinging it at someone will change 9 out of 10 fights'. The simplest tool that applies the most often is usually the one that will give you the most time to transition between OODA stages and reduce the possibility of panic. Remember, panic is like a vampire when it comes to time. It drains it from us as we not only lose time to act - eventually we are unable to recover the time we lose as we become stuck in the feedback loop.

Stopping panic

If we are going to stop panic, we must first remember Hick's Law and apply it to our experiences. We must reduce the number of available options that may not work and replace them with what we know consistently works. This is usually done through realistic training. Unfortunately, many people can't attend reality-based self-defense courses. This lack of realistic training can lead to freezing or fleeing in a real-world encounter. Those who can't attend good training must use whatever tools are at hand to prepare for the worst. Thus, the most important key to remember is Hick's Law - limit your options to the best, most general options - and use those.

The idea of a limited number of options and decisions begins in the EPL and DPT. In the EPL we study the concept of how much a student can neurologically learn. We use Differentiation to differentiate between what can work and what won't, and what will hurt us and what won't. This process removes unneeded methods or techniques. In the DPT we analyze how much a student can perform in combat. This process removes possible techniques based on their effectiveness. Our Goal in using the EPL and DPT should be to constantly treat techniques like we discuss schema in the EPL - we want to refine them and find what works.

Most teacher and students want to learn new techniques and new ideas, but this can be a distraction in terms of the OODA loop. One must remember a student will learn new ways of observing, orienting, deciding, and acting due to new ways of looking at the world from different arts. In learning new arts, we learn new ways of making decisions, and then we gain new layers of neurological pathways of techniques. In life, if we are not looking at Hick's Law, soon we have OODA for driving, OODA for a fight, OODA for a sport fight, OODA for playing baseball, etc. The fewer layers we must dig through, the better our action will be when the time comes.

As you learn different systems, ask yourself - what is the purpose of adding new information? If one is unsure of their capabilities or has not learned to fight the fight, they need to win to overcome their fears - adding options can have a degenerative effect on their martial learning. As discussed in the EPL manual, 10 tools for 1 job are not the same as 1 tool for 10 jobs. We cannot get so tied down in new ideas of techniques, thinking we are adding to our ability to act effectively; and become more reactive due to an overabundance of choices. An overabundance of possible Decisions in the OODA loop works against the Action of the student.

OODA and time.

OODA creates time.

No, it does not add seconds onto a clock, but gives access to the usage of time you might otherwise not have had. Many have felt what seems an excess of time when we are organized as opposed to feeling rushed when we are unorganized. Bringing this into the combative realm, when we are overwhelmed, we are not processing the events happening around us. Have you ever been hit a few times before you realized what happened? Ever had an opponent attempt a throw and you are suddenly in an arm bar and not sure what occurred? Have you ever been holstering your weapon as a police officer and trying to recall exactly what just happened? Our perception of time matters and our perception changes when we are unorganized or ill prepared. Lets, for a moment, pretend that you will never be unorganized after reading this book…you will always be ready and not feel rushed. The question becomes what do we do with the time we have, and more importantly, how do we get more it?

These are questions answered in both complex and simple ways. The complex way would be ideas like those of Zen and mindfulness. To exist within the moment, to study without judging, to sense the nature of the combative interaction and gain more understanding from it. Conversely, the simple explanation would be to fight more effectively, to cause more damage, and slow the opponent. Both explanations have strengths and weaknesses.

Unfortunately, for the western student, mindfulness and Zen are concepts many will come into only cognitive contact with. They breach associative on occasion, through meditation, but for the most part these are concepts written in a book, perhaps spoken of by a teacher, but rarely associated with the Western arts. A quick query of internet search engines for Zen within the western martial arts found few results…search results were based on the ideas of the East, and Western arts that did use the concept did so from an Eastern perspective. Due to a cultural understanding based on philosophy and religious belief, the Eastern arts are filled with concepts of Zen in training and in combat. There we find a concept of Zen and mindfulness in martial art that go beyond associative to autonomic, even from childhood. In my two decades of teaching and learning Western arts, these powerful concepts are rarely found or taught. To 'exist' within combat…this is often a strange concept due to the chaotic nature of the actions that confront someone within combat.

I use the statement 'within combat' because, in a fight, we are within the combative situation. We are not observers or coaches on the side screaming instructions at ourselves. We are in the experience, existing within it, acting, and guiding or being guided. It takes two to tango, as the old saying goes, and fights don't 'just happen'. There is Newton, cause and effect, a catalyst. The person who is mugged on the streets is as much of a party to the fight as the mugger when the victim doesn't prevent the crime by taking proactive measures. The victim exists within the fight and sadly time is usually spent on the defensive. The victim's history, psychology, neurology, fears, memories, and doubts exist within the situation, swaying the fight in one direction or the other. The person with little martial art training and little fear will have the advantage over the person with training and lingering fear from a previous time they were mugged. The person who grows up to be the bully will relive a life of successful bullying within the interaction while the bullied will become bullied if they are not taught to defy this psychology. But the bully may just as well overstep their confidence in the face of someone who has defied their past of being bullied and fights back. Everything we are, who we are, and who we will be exists within the fight. It is one of the few places where our primal nature can exist, and that nature has no right or wrong, only action...and time in which to exist.

When one moves beyond the fear of combat, one can begin to exist within the fight in a controlled manner. The primary difference between controlled and uncontrolled is the difference between active and passive interaction with the fight. When a person decides to engage the fight mentally and physically, they actively control their fate as they can make decisions on how to manipulate time. In this active state the person is making decisions and engaging what the fight is. Those doubts, fears, memories, even their internal chemical releases, are all faced and at least partially control by the active student. This self-control is not enemy-control through GSTM and is no substitute for the experience of a fight and the associative understanding of techniques, but it is a start in being able to exist within combat.

Without a willingness to actively engage the combative interaction, one becomes passive...the engagement happens to them. This is like the difference between amateur and professional athletes. The difference between players in high school, college, and the NFL is a matter of what they do with time. An NFL offensive line coach once told me, 'the game is so much faster for someone who is in high school versus the NFL. The game happens around them so fast they run out of time to act'. The longer they play, the more games they play in, they gain experience and the slower and more manageable the game becomes. Think about the first time you drove a vehicle. Remember how fast driving seemed the first time you were on the highway, your parent or sibling barking orders, the surrounding cars changing lanes? You can visualize how an athlete such as a high school player would feel in a college, or at a higher level of speed and complexity, an NFL game. When one has trained repeatedly at either a very constructive level or high stress level, the fight is much slower for them than someone who with no exposure to fighting. The one bringing the baggage to the fight has their hands full and will first need to drop the baggage before they can use their hands to fight.

Without fear one can act, but without doubt one can act boldly.

When one has experience and has fought previously, they lose some sense of fear in the fight. They know what a fight is like and as we discuss in the EPL, they move from a cognitive to an associative level of understanding the fight. They begin to understand, 'time after time, if I do __x__, then __y__ will happen.' It is only when one has experienced enough associative acts that they begin to remove personal doubt in their own abilities. They can say, 'I have done this technique before, and this is what happened.' It is the removal of doubt that allows the fighter to stand taller, or to take the risk that the other fighter might not take. Jon 'Bones' Jones, for all of his faults in the UFC, is famous for his unorthodox style and while many would emulate it, it is difficult to duplicate. They can do something that looks similar, but they will draw back to what they know - the basics, the punch, the kick, the throw. Jones, it would seem, has trained utilizing his unique physical gifts in a state of unorthodoxy so that he has become comfortable with it and is willing to take risks. It seems he lost the doubt that his methods will work, thus, he tries new methods, and he acts boldly. An opponent's fear of his capability becomes a confidence in what those capabilities can create. Jones exists within the fight, he adjusts within the fight, he takes chances within the fight. He is 'in' the fight, a state of being, where adaptation is not a defensive tactic but an offensive methodology.

There are many fighters like Jones, and more than that, there are many athletes like Jones. These are athletes who exist within the moment in their competitive sport. Their experience, physiology, self-control, OODA, an understanding of skill...they own it within the combative space. To achieve this level of existence proper training must be employed. If we are to reach a state of 'being' within the combative situation and explain it in a way that matches the mechanical styles of the west, we must not only develop a new way of looking at this state...but also a way of teaching it.

On Finding time

 Defining the concept of action in martial art is not only a matter of the defining the person and the environment but also that of time. Time and timing in martial art are very different. Timing, be it when a strike is thrown or when someone leaves the fight, is different from the time in one's life in which the fight takes place. Time is not about the age of a student, but about defining where a student is in their studies.

To truly study the martial arts, one must study themselves. I have found these many times in my own study and as the author I take the liberty here to digress. In my early years, I was heavy into sport training but over time became obsessed with the mechanics of technique and the science of biomechanics. As time moved on, I was exposed to the spiritual, 'energetic' topics of study and briefly began to follow this path. Unfortunately, I found my lifestyle, which at the time involved an unhealthy amount of partying not conducive to fully developing these topics of study. My teachers told me 'don't force it, when it's your time it's your time' and I paid attention. After mechanics, I dove into the concepts of adult learning and pedagogy and developed the CLM, turning my seminars and classes into labs instead of training rooms. During this period, the topics of study were not the students Four Confidences but instead focused on developing the CLM. After this I went into the reality-based side of training, working toward applying what I had developed into the more stressful situations, teaching firearms, and other weapons, and how to fully develop methods to destroy the enemy's mind, body, and soul. Then, I moved toward the psychological aspects of training, during which this book was written. One day I plan a return to the spiritual arts but am not sure when that time will be.

Life spans periods where our mind, studies, and environment bring us to different explorations of training. Within these cycles we find timing. Timing makes the most of time. At the right moment in time, with the right teacher, if our psychological state rings with the vibration of a teacher's classes and lectures, we find harmony. For many, someone to tell them where they are in life does not fit where they are in their studies is never found. Many people study the wrong art at the right time, or the right art at the wrong time. This shows that answering 'why?' is important for not only what you study, but when.

Training speaks to our place in time, finding timing in time. Martial art is not about learning new tricks or techniques, but about fully absorbing the 'right' ones that we are taught. It's about finding what makes sense for your place in time, your physical stature, your confidence. For a good teacher, matching timing of instruction with the time in a student's life is so important. A good teacher seeks to match the 'why' to the training. If one is to absorb and make training a part of their daily lives, one must first be in a position in life that allows them to absorb the maximum amount of information. If our 'here' is to be secure, and our 'there' to be understood, our place in time must be important to us.

Time = distance

For a moment, think about your last sparring session. When were you on defense? When were you on offense? How many moves ahead were you able to think in each case? Did you have the knowledge, the experience, the ability, and the capability within the match? Did you walk in knowing that you had these? Did you move the fight into the direction of your confidences? Do you know why you were sparring - what was your end Goal, what methods, Tactics, Strategy did you use to achieve this?

These are questions that give us time in the fight.

The fight only moves too fast if you are behind the fight. If you are ahead in time, the dynamics of the fight change quite dramatically, and your ability to exist within the fight changes, as does the nature of action. Stopping the fight from moving too fast is determined by preparation. Think in terms of your daily life and how you prepare for going to work, or taking your child to a recital, or doing a home project. If you prepare everything ahead of time, your plan tends to come to fruition. If you are taken in by the noise of the day, you might put your plans off until tomorrow...or still accomplish your plans in a haphazard manner. Fight preparation is similar with the fight prep being realistic, reducing the number of concerns one has about surviving, so one can focus on the preparation for surviving.

The less time we spend deciding on options, the more time we have being effective against an opponent as we drive toward our Goal, leaving others overwhelmed by decisions.

Chapter 30: The here and there of combat

We live in a world of distraction, from technology in our hands to technology on the monitor screen we read. It would seem for those who begin training in martial art that distraction is a more powerful enemy than the opponent or aggressor. The mental distraction of figuring out what the other will do, how will they act, what will a student do to counter...and these are distractions that occur before the fight even begins. Once strikes and kicks, combined with increased heart rate, respiratory rate, and panic set in... distraction becomes a prime enemy to conquer. In the reality that is martial art training where we see ourselves does not matter as much as where our opponent sees us. That 'where' can be a multitude of concepts...where we are in our training, where we are in physical relation to them, where we are in relation to where they see us in their world, etc. We can think we are the greatest fighter in the world, we might even be...but if our opponent is seeing differently than what we think about ourselves, then in reality our viewpoint does not matter. In the end we are facing an opponent, so why not see ourselves from the viewpoint of the opponent?

If we exist 'here', and the enemy is our 'there', then we must work to be able to see ourselves outside of ourselves. The student must be able to see themselves as they are but also what their opponent sees them as, which is another form of here - from a student's there.

In Pramek's concept of being we must first inspect ourselves outside of our own mind. The student must be asked to identify what the enemy sees in the student's 'here'. We must first view ourselves and consider where we are...and then inspect ourselves and our capabilities. Our own mind is working through the filters created by past experiences. These filters are making us act based upon previous experiences, the assumption machine as earlier discussed. Unless we are facing the same situations repeatedly, like the movie Groundhog Day, we must remember we exist in the present. When we make a 'wrong' move we are not only on the defensive against the opponent...we are on the defensive against our own mind.

To get beyond this concept of constant filtering and interacting with our past takes a long period and training. This would seem an obstacle in getting a student to move quickly through the EPL and DPT. Many times, I have asked a student about something they did wrong in sparring, only to have them answer,

'I knew the moment I did it that it was wrong.' How would they know that it would be wrong unless they were recalling previous training experience where it was 'right'? When a student is constantly fighting their own experience, judging their actions, they exist in a state that is backward looking. They begin to fight themselves and the enemy. They become stuck in a loop of experience, then a memory of the experience. They have an experience then a memory of that experience. Each time they train and spar they are stuck in this loop. After the training, they reflect on what they did, making plans about what they will do next time based on the previous time.

If they have a positive outcome, they will be more likely to repeat the same techniques or methods in the next situation...though it might not work. If they have a negative outcome, they will reflect on this, create self-doubt, and then try to perfect the methods they did incorrectly because, as a student once told me, 'it must work, or I wouldn't have learned it'. In this mindset, they do not progress because they are trying to perfect something that which was previously done incorrectly. Instead, the student should be taught to move beyond the past, not 'try again', but instead perform a completely different method in the situation or future situations. For the student who constantly tries to fix their mistakes the fight is never new, but is a repeat of the last fight, with them chasing success or failure based on the memory of the past.

Reflective states are ineffective in training, they encourage the student to 'try again' using methods that didn't work. They are perfecting something that if it had been done differently it would work, but only done differently in that past moment in time. This forces the student into the past instead of looking at each new engagement as a place they are using their full capability and knowledge through adaptation and GSTM-based thinking. Directing the student to use the knowledge they have gained to where it is most applicable is an important part of stopping reflective training. We should endeavor to have the student look at the common themes between fights, finding where a technique works 90/90, not on one occasion. But they should not only look at the common themes between fights – they should also look at the common themes about themselves. The student should begin to not reflect on what they did right or wrong, but instead, what their training partner saw in what they were doing and analyze from that standpoint: a student's 'here'.

Where is there?

Now we begin to get into the crux of CLM 4, our 'here' and 'there'. We've focused a lot on the here thus far – LoS, OODA, etc. We must begin to look outward to find inward now. As you begin to delve into the following concepts, remember, this is a place to look out from, a place to view your training from. It is not set in stone, or the only way to train people – it is instead a lens to look through on our learning and teaching. Taking even a fraction of the concepts in this book will create a better student or teacher, but the beyond LoS, OODA, sophists, etc., the 'being' concept creates incredibly well-rounded students and teachers.

So, you are 'here' and 'there'…

You exist in your 'here', but you also exist as your opponent or enemy's 'there'.

Let me repeat that: you exist as your opponent or enemy's 'there'. Yet, we focus so much on the 'here', where we are in our time and timing, that we forget we are seen from someone else's eyes, experience, time, and timing. We forget to look at ourselves as 'there' for another person. [I'm going to take a moment here and prepare you. You are about to see a lot of 'and ". At first this may be a little tough with your reading, but when you see the difference between 'here' and here, it will make more sense. – Matt]

In Pramek, being is to move beyond ourselves, draw ourselves from outside of our previous successful or unsuccessful experience, and instead exist within the situation. Fighting based on the past and our own viewpoint is one dimensional. By seeing ourselves from the opponent's eyes, we can fight in a fuller spectrum. We can see the fight in a way that we have not seen before because we have a new set of eyes to inspect ourselves: the eyes of the enemy or opponent. In viewing ourselves as we are, replete of ego, understanding our experience, we open ourselves up to inspection. While we may want to become better through understanding our faults, in combat, there is another person viewing, seeing, and inspecting us. To get to our Goal, we need to become the enemy's 'there' instead of being our 'here'.

The concept of being 'here' or 'there' is a difficult one to grasp at first.

A diagram may make this concept easier to understand and realizing this new training model.

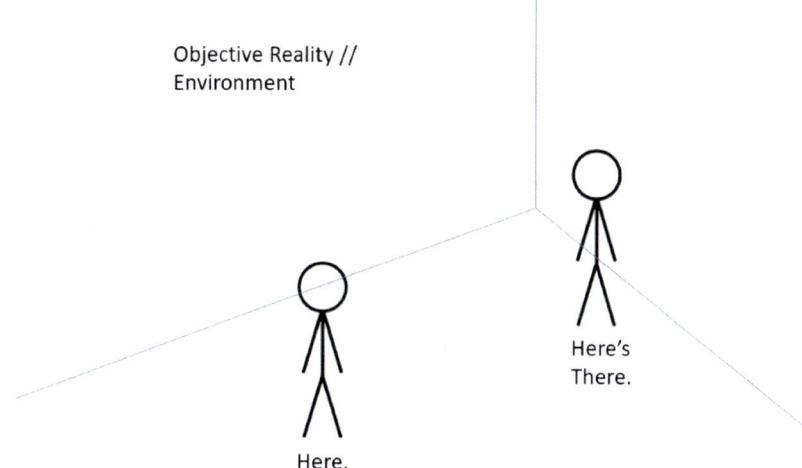

How good you think you are matters little if your opponent sees weakness in your 'here'.

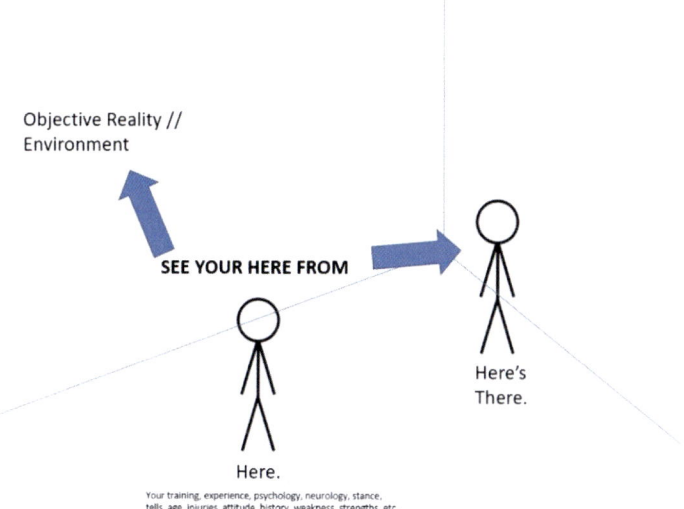

It can be extremely effective to see ourselves from our 'there', or the eyes of the opponent at all points of training. In this model a student must be trained to be constantly adjusting their Tactics and methods based on what the opponent is seeing. The student must question their actions based on where the opponent sees weaknesses, instead of where they identify their own weaknesses as being. Where one feels they are strong makes no difference if the enemy sees it as weak. It only matters how the opponent feels about the fight, and how the opponent sees us and our actions within the fight.

We often view fights in terms of us being in our space and the enemy in their space. In this model we are constantly acting upon what we know, what we see, and within the space that we exist. Unfortunately, as discussed previously, in most situations we bring a lot of emotional and neurological baggage to the fight and must take time to cut through those filters. In the 'here' space we are limited because we ignore the fact that the enemy can see us and act upon us as well. We think in terms of what we will do in our 'here'. Instead, we must look at the terms of how the engagement exists in space and then use that understanding to bridge the conceptual gap that exists between our self and our enemy.

There is no reaction in martial art - there is only the action taken and the action that counters that action. This may seem strange, but in basic Newtonian physics an object does not react to the force applied to it but instead acts in concert with the force exerted upon it. An object's action is governed by its properties, such as mass and position in space. If an object is against a wall, then the object will act in concert with the force applied and then act upon the object (the wall) it is placed against. In the combative space, our properties are variable. We are, as a human body, mass. We have a position in space, such as our position against a wall, but our center mass in terms of equilibrium has a position in space as well, it's just within our overall mass. We have other properties one may not think of, such as experience when certain forces are applied as well as how we will act after that force is applied. Other properties such as our neurologically programmed techniques, or our memories of past experiences will dictate our actions.

Remember, there is only action and action that counters action. 'Reaction' is taught, learned, or it is agreed upon in terminology with a student. This terminology is damaging to a student as it allows for the acceptance of filters they must go through to act. When a student is taught to react, they think reactively but in reaction, they lose time. Reaction, by its very nature, is just action happening between two points in time, and in a combative interaction, that time is the beginning and the end of the interactions. Between those two points of time our properties determine the direction we will go. If a student has many techniques, but a limited amount of experience under duress, the student will take more time in OODA to decide an action.

If a student is taught reaction and reaction time, they also lose the ability of foresight. An example of this is found in 'reaction time' testing, where a sound, such as a buzzer or bell, is signaled and the student must react after the sound. This seems like great training and looks great in demonstration, but it is not instruction and teaches little in terms of combative reality. The bell does not have experience that guides its behavior. The bell does not have a physical body that shows what kind of attack it is preparing to deliver, nor does the bell communicate with the student. The bell exists as a Pavlovian device...when the student hears the bell, the student must react to the bell. Does it speed up a student's reaction to the device - yes. But this skill is difficult to translate, other than physical speed, to a body wanting to attack. A body has signals, it translates into physical action the mind's thoughts.

With a bell, the student is never reacting, they are by their very nature acting as they are anticipating the bell. They are only acting in concert with their anticipation. But a bell is not threatening. It's just a bell, and it causes the student to become absorbed in their 'here', instead of the 'there' that threatens them. Perhaps, during martial art study, it is better to throw out the bell entirely and replace the bell with a person. This creates a student who can act quicker based on the signals they view rather than translate the Pavlovian response of striking at a sound over to a person preparing to strike and reading their signals.

If you are 'here', then you only control what is 'here'. That 'here' encompasses your location, the environment, and self. You act based upon here. If the here is the focus, which in martial art training it primarily is, everything you know about the fight exists within your here and anything that contradicts that knowledge of here can only be understood by your own personal viewpoint. The 'there' is seen as something to react to, but never seen as something that could be understood from the deepest levels and then predicted or acted in concert with.

When we look at an opposing force, we must understand that there exists a gap that is not only time and space but also experience, an understanding of the environment, and a host of other gaps that exist that separate us from the opposing force. When we focus in the 'here', we see the world differently than our opponent. We must instead see the world as our opponent sees it and adjust accordingly so that our 'here' is ready to act. If our Goal is to close with and defeat the opposing force, then the most effective way is to form the closest bond that we possibly can: to view ourselves from the enemy's mind. Instead of being here, and the enemy being there, we must become our 'there'.

Often, we try to beat the enemy or force the enemy's mistakes without asking why the enemy is acting as they are. They may see things that we do not see in our defensive or offensive action that we are executing that we do not know. They may hear things we do not hear as we are verbalizing commands or physically communicating in a way that make sense to us...and we wonder why they are not reacting in the way we wish them to. Within this viewpoint we are not seeing the disadvantages the enemy is seeing in our here and how they will attack it. We may be defending or using a defensive method that may be indefensible and should be abandoned. Only through the eyes of the enemy can we discover this.

There and being

Understanding 'being' is a matter of training more fully. We can only get a student so far if we focus the student on 'here'. I have interviewed many top fighters and experienced soldiers over the years, and most have had the realization that they must see their weakness from the eyes of the enemy. As one of our US Special Forces students told me at a training, 'I always try to ask what is that another guy seeing, and why is he seeing it? It's not about how he's advancing, but how am I being advanced on. I might be doing something I need to change.'

This thought process usually happens after a confrontation. In sport, this process sometimes occurs in real-time during the fight as the coaches begin to shout what the student should do. The fighter can find themselves in an altered state where they see their weakness through the coaches' instructions, even if they do not internalize this is what is occurring. In my own life, I have found this in numerous situations, which was part of the impetus for CLM 4.

CLM 4 was born as much in in the training room as much as the streets of Atlanta while running with my dogs. I found that over a period if I approached a vehicle at a stop light, see the street from the eyes of a driver, I would be more likely to think ahead of the situation and not react to it. In the state of reaction, I would find myself in trouble because of what I saw, not what the driver sees. If this is a state in which an advanced fighter finds themselves, then it is a state we must recognize can be trained in a student from the beginning. We don't have to wait to shout instructions to them. To effect action, we must train through the opponent sights, the enemy's eyes, our 'there' looking at our 'here' in the person that we face.

And many times, the person that we face is ourselves.

If we are unable to deal with how we view ourselves, then the enemy will be even more difficult. We will constantly be fighting the enemy that is our own experience and robbing ourselves of time. I commonly teach this in rape-prevention classes. In these classes, a student is exposed to high levels of verbal discomfort to create immunity to that kind of stress. Notice I didn't use 'stress inoculation', which is a buzz-word within the martial art training community. While this seems a fitting term, it is not accurate in what we are attempting to do. In vaccination, a weakened organism is introduced, and the body develops a resistance to it. The person eventually becomes immune to the organism. For a student to overcome their own fears they must be, in a sense, vaccinated.

In most of Western culture vaccinations are common so the body can develop a resistance to a variety of different potentially hazardous organisms. Vaccination is the introduction of a weakened pathogen, while in inoculation the pathogen is live and at full strength. We don't want to introduce full on hitting and striking and yelling at a student. We want to build them up and build up their confidence. We do this through progressively introducing higher levels of stress, fatigue, etc., through the DPT. When a student is vaccinated, we can break down the various kind of stimuli and the student can develop a resistance one by one. We start with verbal, then move to controlled contact, such as a grab or a push. We then move to impacts where the student develops an immunity to the impacts. This immunity is not only the physical, but the psychological aspects of being impacted and the fears associated with impact.

We then move to scenarios where the three are combined, slowly at first, then at higher and higher levels. The student is vaccinated against these kinds of attacks. This combative vaccination leads to immunization where the student is immune to attacks

Words mean things.

Some students possess a natural immunity to certain kinds of attacks. Why would we focus vaccinating a 6'6 300-pound student to the stress of being attacked by a person much smaller? Most of their life is spent being physically capable of handling an unarmed person who tries to strike them, and they possess certain physical traits, such as range and mass, that create a natural immunity to this. Would it not be more effective to ask the student 'How did you deal with these attacks in your life', understand the response, and then incorporate a knife into the smaller person's attack? Ask the student to use their natural immunity to defend against this situation? We use the EPL and DPT to accomplish this task progressively. In this method, we create a vaccination against that stimuli, while allowing for the natural immunity to stand. In effect, we give a booster and save time in training, allowing them to use what they neurologically are programmed to do through their live experience, only altering it slightly for the knife. I often do this with former football players, especially linemen. They have spent years in a form of combat with another person and have developed programming to do so. Instead of changing them, I adjust them, so their neurological programming is adjusted slightly to a real fight - allowing for strikes, etc., while also using their stand-up push type of method they have confidence in. It is easier to branch from an existing neurological pathway than to create a new one.

Though I had the MMR (measles-mumps-rubella) vaccination at a young age, when I was a child, I still had both measles and mumps. Just because we expose someone to a training method it does not mean they develop immunity. If a student is not trained through Differentiation and Imprinting, as we discuss in the EPL, they are not vaccinated to all attacks - they are vaccinated to that attack, that one attack and that attack only. If the student is trained with another student who is 5'5 and 150 lbs., then the student will learn to defend against that body type and the capabilities it offers in combat. Should someone be 5'8 and 200 lbs. working against the smaller student, without Imprinting and

Differentiation, and in turn Unitization, the student will be relearning to defend themselves. The infection of 'not knowing what to do' returns. They will constantly see each person as an individual to defend against and go into their bag of techniques. Instead, they should see a body-type to work with and adjust their GSTM based on the actions the body-type takes.

Commonly we see in martial art training the student is yelled at, pushed, shoved, and then hit. The student is inoculated against those three in combination, but they have no immunity. There is no immunity because the yelling, or verbal contact, isn't fully explored individually. In their younger life was the student picked on or made fun of, a trigger word not explored, do the verbal commands go to their true psychological weaknesses? You can yell all kinds of things but if you aren't yelling the right things than what does it matter? To go further, if there was a previous experience the student has had, such as sexual abuse, did they disclose this and trust the process of training to safely explore their weakness to the verbal communication around the sexual abuse? What if the person is robbed by the bully from when they were a child and they recognize them? Seems silly, but the point is we must dig deeper into the 'why' of the student.

Take into consideration your most important ally: time. In the most extreme definition, time can come down to milliseconds, and milliseconds can mean the difference between identifying the knife before it's deployed and identifying the knife once it's deployed. The difference between those two is potentially life threatening. Teachers should take care to dive into what makes a student uncomfortable to create an overall immunity. If a student is fully versed in how to deal with verbal attacks, using a variety of verbal commands, the student may never move to physical contact 'in the street'. But if the student is only vaccinated against the phrase 'give me your money' then the student will lose time searching for answers when told 'get in the car or I'll kill you.'

These two phrases elicit an entirely different physical and mental action to be taken. Without the experience, without vaccination, the student will spend OODA in OOD and, candidly time, may not be something the student has to find an Action. I once had a female student who, before training with us, was taken from her front porch and put in a trunk by an attacker. She survived the ordeal but, in my notebooks, I wrote down our conversation in detail as I sought to understand what happened:

Me: 'Why do you think you ended up going with him?'

Her: 'Well, he had a gun, and I didn't know what to do.'

Me: 'But you were near your door, so couldn't you have run into the house?'

Her: 'Yes, but I've never had someone walk up and pull a gun and threaten me.'

Me: 'Why do you think you ended up getting into that trunk? There is a lot of time between him coming up, threatening, you deciding to go with him, and deciding to get in the trunk.'

Her: 'I've never had someone tell me get into a trunk. My head was spinning...I couldn't believe someone was telling me to get into the trunk. Who does that? I've been to self-defense classes, where a guy yells at you, but asked you to get in a trunk? Seriously, who the hell says to get in a trunk when you're on your front porch and his car is on the street? He had a gun, and I didn't want him to get in the house where my roommate was, so I went with him thinking I would just run. I was thinking about the movies, where people are thrown into a trunk, not asked. I was trying to figure out what to do that by the time we got to the trunk, I didn't know what to do. By then, gun, trunk, I was out of time. So, I got in.'

Me: 'Do you think you would get into the trunk now?'

Her: 'No, I know what to do, which is to run a scream no matter what is said, gun or not.'

Me: 'How did you know how to escape from the trunk?'

Her: 'When we were kids, I got locked in a trunk once while playing with my brothers. When they didn't come back to get me, I figured my way out of the trunk with the safety latch. Only problem was this guy had torn off the latch. I clawed all the plastic out of the way since he had ripped off the latch part. I knew I had to just find the release mechanism. So, I traced the latch rod to the lock and manually did it.'

Me: 'If you didn't have that happen as a kid, could you have figured it out?'

Her: 'Probably, my adrenaline was kind of taxed by the time I was in there, so I came down. If I could have shut me up brain long enough, I would have figured out how to trace the rod when I found the latch disabled, I guess. I mean, I've seen it in the movies, so I probably would have tried it.'

Me: 'Where do you think you went wrong?'

Her: 'I've never had someone abduct me from my porch. I saw him milling around, but I live in the city, I didn't take notice of a shady guy walking around my front driveway. That's common, homeless guys milling around, they usually ask for a cigarette and I tell them to go away. So, I was watching him while I was yelling to my roommate in the house to bring me another beer.'

Me: 'You would have thought differently in a dark alley is what you are saying.'

Her: 'I wouldn't be in a dark alley.'

Me: 'But it didn't happen in a dark alley. The signs were all there.'

Her: 'That's why I'm here in this class.'

Once placed into the situation she knew what to do because she had been exposed to it. She had associative experience in how to get out of the trunk but no associative experience in getting told to get into the trunk. Unfortunately, everything before being in the trunk she had only cognitive experience with, so her unconscious brain spent vital time looking for a solution while time ran out. The here in the student's life was consumed by a lack of exposure to what happens. Another important part of this is to note the nature of compartmentalization in training. She knew what to do in a dark alley, but on her porch, she had a different mindset. While this isn't a training manual on preventing kidnapping, it does speak to the gaps of time the student experiences after the moment. She noticed the person but did nothing because it's 'common'. When the situation unfolded, she did nothing because she was stuck in her feedback loop. It is not because she didn't want to do anything, she did, but time ran out as she weighed her options because she had never experienced something like this before.

When we train a student, we must focus on them understanding 'here' at all levels. Our own doubts are reflected in the way that we deal with other people. Ask yourself, if the opposing force can see your doubts, weaknesses, and apprehension...are you truly strong in your 'here'? I had known the student for years prior to her coming to class and she is very street smart and extremely tough. She's been through a lot in her life, so in her 'here', she was tough. In her case she didn't look at herself as a victim, but she failed to see herself as a criminal would see her: as a victim. Her 'here' was safe, it was her porch, but his 'there' was not safe as he saw her alone on a porch.

What can be easily missed is that he acted, and she acted in concert. There was no reaction. It is here that we see the difference between action and reaction. She didn't act in uncontrolled natural defense, what one might consider 'reaction'. She could have created a struggle, fought the aggressor, and perhaps ended up dead. Instead, she acted unsafely in accordance with his wishes. When she saw the aggressor, her action should have been to identify what was happening and to move inside the house and call the police. Instead, she acted in concert with her experiences of this being 'common' and then eventually, she acted in concert with his action.

Sometimes, be it in the mind of a student or the mind of a criminal, all it takes is to act on our 'there' and let the other person act in concert in their 'here'. When we act with boldness, calculating the risk and rewards of our actions, another's behaviors fall in concert with our own and can come under our control. If we treat their action not as a reaction, but an action in concert with ours, we can manipulate their use of time by taking control of the situation. This is about changing our view from 'here' and turning our attention to 'there'…the enemies 'here'. Remember, this concept is not only defensive, but offensive in nature. What options does our 'there' have?

I often do this when walking in a city. If someone has pulled into the crosswalk, I will stop and demand they back their car out of the crosswalk. I once decided to keep a count of the number of people who would back up instead of telling me to walk around. If they had space behind them and I refused to walk forward, I found that 90% of the time they would back up. If they had no space, they would look back behind them, act confused, apologize, and motion me across. While some would view their action as a reaction, I instead view it as an action in concert with my wishes. They are doing as I asked, but I can only ask for action if they have the capability to act in concert with my wishes.

Fighting is no different.

If we act and see their reaction as an action that furthers our ability to gain our Goals, our strategies and Tactics remain in place. We continue to act toward our Goal by choosing the path, not having it chosen for us. If we act and view their action as a reaction, then we become reactive to the reaction, taking away our initiative as we shift to counter their reaction and refocus GSTM. For example, if I wish to disturb someone's equilibrium and move to rotate them, and instead they wrap me up, I don't react to the wrapping. I instead view the wrap up as another chance to disturb equilibrium.

I have chosen my GSTM, I act within the PoA, and continue to work to achieve my Goal. I differentiate between what they do that can hurt me and can't, perhaps delay with a strike, and in those milliseconds, control the fight by forcing them to act in a way that opens their equilibrium up. If we move beyond technique and instead look at strategies and Tactics, every action the opponent take gets us closer to our Goal. If we focus on technique, we will only begin a match of counters, as we move through an A+B=C-E / U = D scenario we have addressed in the EPL.

It is important to remember the laws of thermodynamics here and the concept of inertia. A body at rest will stay at rest, and a body, by its properties, will resist attempts to change its state. Notice I did not say react, but resist. If a force is 1 joule but the object's mass requires 10 joules to move it, the mass resists the force, it does not react to the force. One must use 11 joules to move it, or affect its friction with where it is placed. Objects in motion tend to continue their path unless forced into another direction due to an outside force. In the combative space a body will remain at rest until an external force acts upon it, but unlike an inanimate object in a physical lesson, the body may use internal force to begin a movement in another direction. While this is physical, in the terms of psychological inertia, one does not generally change until given a reason. We must give an enemy a reason to change.

In terms of training, a loss or near defeat will often give someone a reason to shift their training into another direction.... but what if one does not compete? In my experience, many times someone is training in combatives for fun with generally compliant friends and will not attempt to hurt them.

Unless you are given a reason to change - you won't change.

In Pramek we call this personal inertia. This person is in a state of training inertia where they will continue their path until a force changes their direction. Unfortunately, in the combative space, that force may be a force that ends their ability to fight again due to physical damage. A student must learn to be their own internal force, to see their own weakness before the opponent sees them or see what the opponent sees and change their direction to mitigate a weakness. We will come back to personal inertia later, but think for a moment, when does a person, a student…even yourself…have a catalyst for change?

Outside of competition or real-world altercations, the only answer to stopping personal inertia in training and combative methods is to utilize the here-there concept in training. Within this training model one looks to their opponent to guide their training completely, their 'here' becoming the opponent's 'there' and providing new insights to change their training in small increments.

But how is this done?

It's done first by finding our confidence.

Chapter 31: A Foundation for Why

We've established the why.

We've established what being is.

We've established our base needs, and why students train.

We understand 'here' and 'there' and the concepts meaning.

How is all this best taught?

First, we must go back to the concept of 'here' and 'there' in a combative action and the question of where the student exists in the interaction. Where is the student - here, or there? When a student is trapped in the concept of 'here' they will lean toward defensive action because they do not know what their opponent is seeing. Their doubts about their own abilities and expectations of an opponent's strengths will set in then lead to a defensive mindset in combat. For a student to be truly effective they cannot be defensive or offensive in combat, but instead exist within the combative interaction and make decisions based upon where they exist. They should be able to see themselves from the eyes of the opponent, adjust based on what their opponent sees to remove their self-doubt, and then move to a state of knowing the opposing force. While it may be a cliché to quote Sun Tzu in a martial art manual, a quote by Sun Tzu is very applicable here:

> *"If you know the enemy and know yourself, you need not fear the result of a hundred battles. If you know yourself but not the enemy, for every victory gained you will also suffer a defeat. If you know neither the enemy nor yourself, you will succumb in every battle."*

This is the essence of what we are working to attain in teaching our students. To know themselves, know the opponent, and understand what they do not know - these principles will push the fight in such a way as to discover the unknown. Confident fighters push the fight to where they see it as advantageous for themselves. They push the fight to take advantage of time, making the opponent lose time in defending, and then making the opponent work to gain time in the interaction by fighting back from the defense. We know that time is our most valuable ally in a fight, so everything we do should gain as much time as possible. Only by knowing the opponent can one control time in the fight. Only by existing in that time, can on find free from self-doubt. They can own their confidence and begin to control the fight.

This can only be done by teaching the student to understand 'there'. Everything we learned up to this point in CLM 1, 2, and 3 leads us to the method of becoming, absorbing, our 'there'. We must teach the student from the very beginning to first have confidence in their skill all the way to how it was learned neurologically. Secondly be willing to ignore their own skill - and instead, see the fight first through the biomechanics, mechanics, physiology, neurology, and psychology of their opponent. This is total confidence.

The 4 Confidences

Teaching confidence is not an easy task. Confidence is individual by nature and defined by certainty in one's own qualities or skill. One can have confidence in a martial art style but the confidence to deploy such a system is entirely different. To trust one's skill means to trust beyond just the application of a technique, but instead to trust one's self to deploy it effectively. This requires confidence and competence. Within martial art there are four kinds of confidence. Each stand on its own individually, but combined, a student develops a full certainty about their skill. The 4 confidences are defined as:

> *1. Confidence of knowledge*
> *2. Confidence of experience*
> *3. Confidence of ability*
> *4. Confidence of capability*

These 4 Confidences allow a fighter to exist in the fight, as they have a full knowledge of themselves, their experience, abilities, and capabilities.

Confidence of knowledge

Within Pramek theory 'science' is the structured study of the world around us through observation, and, when able, through experience. We combine lessons from a book based on observation and experience with our own observation and experience. In Pramek theory there are sciences we should endeavor to understand:

1. *Biomechanics and Physiology, the knowledge of one's own physical qualities.*
2. *Physics and Mechanics, the knowledge of one's physical qualities when in interaction with another body.*
3. *Neurology, the knowledge of how the nervous system operates and is programmed.*
4. *Psychology, the knowledge of how the mind functions and human behavior.*
5. *Environment, the knowledge of an area in which one exists and fights*
6. *Strategy, the knowledge of how the first five sciences interact within a fight.*

Confidence in one's knowledge creates a fighter that can understand the world around them and the actors, and their actions, within it. They can comprehend the entire situation before them based on the reality that is natural law. Within the physical sciences we find much about an opponent's why. Biomechanics governs their movement and physics governs their physical interactions with another body, while neurology dictates upon which biomechanical movements and mechanical techniques they will utilize. Hence, threat identification for a student is extremely important. Understanding a boxer versus a kicker, or a knife user versus a bat user, leads to understanding extremely specific biomechanical and mechanical actions. Their stances and movement are dictated by their neurology, as they have trained in a fighting form repeatedly to refine schema over time, as is discussed in CLM 1, EPL.

Within the psychological realm we find three keys to understanding how the physical realm will be utilized. Psychology gives us valuable insight into the communication and experience-based reasoning of the opposing force in their interaction with us. Strategy dictates what they will do and why, as a boxer will take a specific stance for a reason, versus a grappler. The farther we dig into psychology the more we find information about the nature of attacks, such as someone robbing an empty house versus someone committing a home invasion while a family is home. The kind of attack provide clues to the thought process of the opposing force and the Strategy they will use to achieve their aims.

Lastly, the environment determines where and how actions will be used, as well as weapons, external dangers (such as improvised weapons within reach), and third parties. Being able to understand the environment provides key information about how the fight will progress, for example between cars in a parking lot versus an officer next to a police cruiser. While each involves vehicles, the environment shifts, as the availability of weapons changes due to what an individual may be wearing.

It is within the Confidence of Knowledge that one gains massive quantities of information and through the EPL and DPT a student learns to process the information in an intelligent manner. The more information one must process in training the more they will be confident in understanding what is before them in combat.

Confidence of experience

Experience is applied knowledge. Within the EPL the student learns how techniques function both properly and improperly and build upon this knowledge. A student begins to understand the Strategy of applying their knowledge and creating a workable GSTM plan. With the DPT, the student can test that knowledge in a variety of scenarios and situations, against a variety of opposing forces. With this applied knowledge, the student gains the confidence that regardless of the situation they face, they can succeed and achieve their Goals.

In understanding their experience, the student can move beyond their fears of combat and move toward existing within the combative space. In combat, the interactions move rapidly and the world in which the student exists becomes extremely fast. Within this state of action large quantities of cognitive knowledge can become a detriment. If a student were to walk into a fight with no training, or in our previous example you were to walk onto an NFL recruiting field, the options would become overwhelming, the speed too fast.

What does one do when this happens?

Drive the fight, or the plays, to their familiar space where they have an advantage.

If we look at the concept of Occam's Razor, a 14th century decision-making process, we find some clue in how to apply knowledge. A simple definition of Occam's Razor is that if there are two explanations for a situation, the simpler one is probably the best. In combat, if you must perform many techniques to achieve a Goal that is achievable by simpler means, you are probably doing things incorrectly. Most students are taught simple techniques at first and then over time they are taught techniques that are more complex. In sportive interactions, where highly violent and damaging 'shortcuts' are not allowed, complex action-counter action actions make sense. Combative interactions, as opposed to sportive interactions, are rarely complex as they rely on high amounts of damage through primarily gross motor movements to create a desirable outcome. For example, in Pramek knife fighting, the primary method of using the knife is not to have complex technique chains for the knife to be effective. Instead, we do everything possible to place the knife, by a slash or stab, into the face of the opponent. Both are ways of achieving the outcome desired, but one is less complex and leaves less space and time for counters, as well as engages neurological mechanisms to protect the face.

Applied knowledge, and the confidence in it, only occurs through the choosing of options through intelligent training. This is the basis of the Pramek 90/90 rule - 90% of the time on 90% of opponents. This high-probability concept is based on experience with applied knowledge.

Confidence of ability

Confidence built from experience leads to a confidence of ability. Ability is larger than being able to fight - it is the confidence in applying methods to achieve a desired result. When a student has trained long enough with certain methods, they begin to develop a confidence in their ability to accomplish a task.

Ability is mental. One can accomplish a task but if their known routes to success are taken from them, their ability is removed. If a student has accomplished a certain task repeatedly in a certain way, they gain the confidence of ability. They know, under the right circumstances, there exists an ability within their means to accomplish the task using these methods. In this state, a student should work to set up a fight or altercation toward their strengths. If they know they need something, for example technique 'A' to accomplish the task because they trained the task in 'A', an intelligent student will find 'A' within the fight. The more experienced a student is the faster they will find 'A' so they can accomplish their task quicker. One can search online and find many videos of ravens performing a variety of tasks with complex puzzles because they gained the experience doing this task repeatedly. There is a confidence in the outcome of their decision if they have the circumstances set up the way they are experienced with. But, if the circumstances change, adaptation is a necessity.

It behooves the instructor to notify a student of these concepts early in their training. Many times, an instructor will let a student 'find' A themselves, and if they fail to, they will allow the student to fail repeatedly and wait for the student to find this. A CLM based teacher will see the student's ability to perform 'A' and quickly show the student 'A' so the student can understand their ability faster. What we train for won't wait. Combatives or sports, a student should know how to think, not fight, quickly. The confidence in ability is the confidence one gains through proper instruction, as they find their personal 'A' and then the teacher shows them how to find it, where to find it, and when to find it.

Confidence of capability

Capability is the physical manifestation of ability.

Capability is the power to do something, versus ability, which is the means to do something or perform a task. Just because a student has the means does not mean they have the power to perform technique 'A'. When knowledge, experience, and ability combine, it creates a capability to act. Capability is when the student understands then physically performs their ability when the situation suites their capability. Physical manifestation of the three confidences is the nature of capability.

The capability to act is a trait that is vital within the combative space. Action is not only physical, but mental and spiritual. A student must be taught that their action does not exist just based on their ability to do something. Students, as discussed in the EPL, have a cognitive ability to perform a myriad number of methods but, without associative learning, the ability means little. Their capability, which is their power to perform it, is based on a foundation of associative understanding of what 'A' will do in an interaction. When a student develops the confidence of capability, they have developed the confidence they can utilize their ability even when their usual trained means may not exist. By drawing on a variety of experience and learned lessons the student can find 'A' within 'B' or 'C' and turn either into 'A'.

Action, or the process of doing a task or achieving an end, is the culmination of the Four Confidences. Action is a state where the student decides to act based on their confidence level. A student should try to only act when the Four Confidences are fulfilled because to do anything less would result in succumbing to the chaos that is combat, or to be swallowed by the 'noise' of a combative interaction.

The enemy of the 4 confidences

A student once asked me, *'Should I study another art while I'm studying Pramek?'*

I asked the student questions to determine his 'why'. The why was simple - he wanted more things to do during the week and Pramek class was only once a week. Since he loved martial art so much why not take another class in another art? He was focusing on combatives within Pramek and wanted to check out a few sporting arts. He was a great student, attentive in class, but always searching for a new topic of study. He had many studies, from astronomy to business, even tracking bigfoot some weekends. He was the consummate student, the kind of student we all want.

As we talked further, we turned the questions to his 4 Confidences and found that in each he was lacking. He still didn't believe that the fight he truly feared (one against an experienced knife fighter) was a fight he could win. We tailored his training classes to further his Four Confidences, put a timeline together, and agreed that after this he should look at other arts. Meanwhile I encouraged his other pursuits, even bigfoot hunting. In discussion we realized his love of martial art, based around learning new techniques, but he realized that learning new techniques wouldn't address the fight he feared most. Instead, he needed more time focusing on a GSTM complex that would address that fight, rather than use that energy in other pursuits. He never found a bigfoot, but he did learn to survive in DPT Scenario training against knife attackers.

For many arts this is not possible. The question would be one of the teacher's ego when the teacher asks why the student wants to study something else. While we've all been there, wondering why a student wants to train elsewhere, I have found there must be a level of confidence in answering: 'no, not right now.' If a student understands their why, and their 4 Confidences, then the answer should be clear...go forth and learn, then come back and let's work on refining what you've learned within your 'why'. But if they are working to answer a specific 'why' and they haven't, and they feel the instruction is adequate - anything else will be 'noise'.

Think for a moment about a static-filled radio transmission on an AM or FM station. You want to hear what the music is, but the static makes it difficult. You hear a word, maybe a verse, but it's primarily static. For those of us who remember turning dials on a VCR or adjusting the antenna of an analog TV, the idea of noise is a very real thing. Static, with images popping through, some voices, then static, then we would adjust the knob or move the antenna. These different techniques and ideas create filters the student must work through. Think of the knobs on the VCR or the antenna being filters. How many filters must one get through to get the clear signal in their mind, brain, and nervous system? When one is focused on their 'why' and find an art that answers it, they have a clear neurological signal. But, when they begin to study other arts, and then bring those arts back to the original study, the static becomes apparent.

I once noticed this in a student who was training in Pramek but attending a sportive style, training camps. In Pramek combatives class when he had thrown an opponent, he would then apply an arm bar. We would correct this and have him kick to the body or head. When he went to the sport style's camp, where an arm bar was encouraged after a throw, he would kick to the head...and rightfully so, be corrected by the instructor. Eventually I spoke to the other style's instructor about this and he noticed the same thing. But we both noticed a lot of hesitation, and this hesitation was magnified during higher paced (this was before DPT) training sessions for both Pramek and sparring in other systems. We both agreed that the student needed to choose, as he was potentially endangering the sport style training partners and becoming miserable at Pramek class being corrected on arm bars and hesitation.

He eventually left both systems and took up another art that was more LoS 3. The lesson here is the neurological noise created by training between two systems, each teaching a throw, but one teaching LoS 1 methods and the other LoS 2 methods. As noted earlier, many arts teach similar concepts - for different reasons. These different reasons were creating neurological noise the student had to filter through. The goal in teaching is to minimize these filters, to minimize the noise.

Elements of Confidence

When we study the Four Confidences, we find knowledge, experience, ability, and capability. Each of these have elements important in studying an art. Learning a principle such as the wedge, experiencing it in combat, developing an ability to use it and a capability to do so - these are psychological and neurological progressions. For a student learning the principle of the wedge, using it in various attacks and defenses means embracing the mechanical aspects, developing a psychological tie to its usage, and neurological pathways associated with schema, imprinting, differentiation. If an individual defensive technique is introduced for a strike, kick, knife defense, etc., this creates neurological confusion.

The technique is based on a specific response to a technique, while the wedge is a general response method that leads to a Tactic within a Strategy that leads to a Goal. The student begins to unconsciously thought-wrestle with, 'Do I use technique A, or do I used a wedge?' The more repetitions with each individually, the greater the time between stimuli and Decision and Action become. Their reaction gap, the time between stimuli and response in OODA, grows as their neurology catches up with the conscious mind processing and unconscious mind finding a solution. Therefore, I recommended to the student that they complete some studies in Pramek, then take the lessons learned to the next art. It's not only better for Pramek in keeping a student, but it's better for the next instructor because he has a student not trying to do two different things at once when said instructor is trying to teach a technique.

An effective 'here' cannot be in a state of confusion about what technique or method to use. Martial art is neurology. Martial art, as it's basis, is taking what is a natural action, fighting as an animal with teeth/claws/speed/strength, and changing this wiring. Martial art at its core is rewiring evolutionary neuropathways and programming them for a different purpose. A person who has never trained, or a student in panic, will fight like a person with no martial art skill - they revert to what is engrained through genetics. A person's true 'here' is that of a caveman until they are taught math, lest we would have been born with math skills. We have the ability and capability to perform mathematical equations, but it is only with theory and knowledge that we do algebra.

Fighting is not like math - you are born with an instinctual genetic ability and capability to fight as a caveman would fight. Within this state of existence there is no theory of fighting with a sword or knowledge of a parry...you swing it wildly and use teeth/claws/speed/strength to overcome the opponent. It is the confident student that understands theory and knowledge, finds ability, and teaches capability that overcomes the 'here' of the caveman. This all takes place in neuropathways. Neurology takes over your processes the moment you wake in the morning. How you get out of bed, reach for your comb, when you reach for the coffee cup that is always there in your cupboard. When you get into the car and put on your seatbelt, neurology is there. When you reach into your pocket to grab your cell phone, neurology is there. When your comb is misplaced, and you try to use another comb and it doesn't do its job, neurology is there. When your seatbelt in your rental car or other family car is different than your daily driver and you can't pull it across quickly, neurology is there. When you forget your knife and you must open mail, so you reach for a knife that isn't in the pocket, neurology is there. When your favorite coffee cup isn't there that is always at the front of the cupboard, but now it's in the wash, and you still reach for it, neurology is there. When you reach to your pocket for your phone that is ringing...but you see it on the desk in front of you, neurology is there.

Martial art is no different. One read of the EPL and you will find how much your neural pathways govern your martial art learning. When you train you are programming yourself? Remember, knowledge is an applied theory in CLM. When you use a technique and it works, and you draw an associative bond to the technique, then do it repeatedly, neurology is there. When you find there is an ability to pull off this technique repeatedly, and then you do it in competition and show its capability, neurology is there. When it doesn't work, you enter a feedback loop, signal anxiety is overwhelmed, and you go into a panic, neurology is there. When you enter OODA, your Decision is based on experience, an associative or cognitive understanding of the situation, and neurology is there creating a path to your Act.

If we look at the nature of panic, as we discuss in this book, we can see a very clear danger to our well-being by too many options. Having little frame of reference on a situation, combined with a high number of options, can create panic. Hick's Law is the definition of using the technique one has used repeatedly and drawn a conceptualized understanding of - the mind, the body, and the brain, in terms of neurology, work in unison to tie everything together for the technique or method to execute properly. By adding too many options panic can take place as the conscious brain is overwhelmed by the information it is taking in regarding the situation, but the unconscious brain searches for an answer among too many options. This is where the noise of knowing too much at one time in terms of martial art can be dangerous.

The key to noise reduction is a simple question: 'why?' Why does one study an art outside of their current study or known studies? Why does one art answer a question the other art doesn't answer? Why does this new art bolster the Four Confidences and not confuse them? Why does this art complement the known options available? Are these options viable, and if so, why?

Ask 'why'. When the crowd cheers, ask yourself why you are there, not why they cheer. When the enemy threatens, ask yourself why you are fighting and your goal, not how you are going to react. When you confront self-doubt, ask yourself your personal 'why?', not how will you pull back your actions, so you don't doubt yourself so much.

When you reduce noise, you make room for action.

'Why?' is your greatest weapon against noise.

Chapter 32: On Action

Imagine the inefficiency of a rudder in the front of a boat. When a student places their own knowledge ahead of their opponent's knowledge, they place the rudder in front of the boat and try to steer. Imagine for a moment if you knew every weakness that an enemy saw in your Four Confidences. Further, imagine for a moment if you knew how the enemy sees you and you acted not according to what you thought was best, but instead based on what the enemy saw as most advantageous for you. What if you were to fully place yourself in your 'there' and see your 'here' from that position? How much information would you gain about your weaknesses and strengths? This is putting the rudder behind the boat with knowledge of the waves ahead.

Being in the fight means not seeing the fight from your view, or the opponent's view, but instead the view of a third party. You know your techniques, you might know your opponent's techniques, but have you asked the question of your opponent, 'What do you think of what I am doing - will it work? Can you defend against it?' This may seem to be a proverbial nirvana of combative fighting, to stop the fight and ask. We know we cannot do this, but we can train in such a way that we come remarkably close.

In Pramek, over many years experimenting with a variety of training methods, the 'here' vs 'there' concept is one that has shown itself time and time again to be the most effective form of training. To see yourself from the enemy's eyes goes direct to the heart of CLM and the GSTM paradigm. To In seeing yourself from 'there' you can adapt your strategies around what the opponent is seeing so that you can blind them with what they cannot hope to see because you have concealed it. To not want to see yourself from their view is an arrogance that you know your weaknesses better than the opponent.

To move forward, to exist within the fight, to be observing, orienting, deciding, and acting in a way that is advantageous, one must accept a simple premise: the enemy knows more about you than you do and therefore, you should pay more attention to what the enemy sees than what you want to do.

Today most of us have seen ourselves on video or through pictures of our training. How many times did you view footage of yourself and think, 'Oh, I should do this' or 'Oh I should have done that?' We cannot bring a mirror with us into every training session, a sparring match, or fight. We can only reflect on what we did by listening to the comments of others and try to correct ourselves the next time around. The challenge is that this process is an inefficient way of training to be more effective. It requires the circumstances to be the same, the moment to exist again, the training partner or opponent to be in that moment again. Then, with the feedback we receive, we try to adjust what we did previously, only to find our opponent doing something they would have not done previously.

This kind of learning is at the core of why we study the 'here' vs 'there' concept. It's why I have worked for years on an up to date, universal training model because many of the contemporary methods of teaching martial art are flawed. Current teaching models allow for the teacher to teach by way of nuance. Students copy the teacher, or they have a reflective training methodology constantly refighting the previous fight. Both methods create a student who is a duplicate of their teacher and self-centered. The student never addresses the training partner until after the action and there is communication about what could be done differently.

To truly exist within the fight, to have the freedom to act, one must gain feedback about their weaknesses not from the instructor, or one's own thoughts about their performance. Instead, the student must, from the beginning, make 'there' the primary focus of training and understand what 'there' sees in a student's 'here'. We must truly remove ourselves from our 'here' and throw ourselves completely into the eyes of 'there'. We must do so to the point that our entire fighting style is designed around what the enemy sees in our here. We must base the most important training phase of our martial art, the beginning, upon not ourselves, or the instructor…but feedback from on our 'there'.

Action Percentages

Over the years, in observation of Pramek classes and other seminars, as well as various other combative arts like shooting, I found something interesting. Education of the student is generally 45% the student judging their own performance, 45% the instructor's correction of that performance, and 5% feedback from their training partner…who they trained against. There is always a waiting for the instructor to come by, give their feedback, when they didn't see the entire interaction take place. In this scenario, 95% of a student's ability to become better is based on themselves and the instructor. A student can wish to become better, shadow box and train in their home, use methods to train their neurology. The need to become better, peer pressure, as well as failure and success, will drive a student to success. But the need to master one's self must also embrace the path of humility that one always has something to learn.

In this mindset, the student turns to the instructor or teacher to show them this humility. But let's look at what a coach or instructor is: an Educator. The student finds an Educator to show them something they do not know, to educate them. Yes, there are different levels of education, and skills in an education, but regardless of their title, be it instructor or guru, they educate. The Educator holds the cards in this relationship as they are the primary point of knowledge. In the instructional phase, the teacher imparts knowledge on the student, and the student is held under the direction and instruction of the teacher.

This creates the next phase of instruction, the correctional phase. Within the correctional phase the teacher imparts knowledge on the errors of the students. After a period, instruction versus correction blend, as the instruction is given, correction advised, instruction from the correction is internalized, and the cycle repeats. Through each phase the primary holder of knowledge is the Educator as the student looks to this 'objective' third party and their experience to instruct and correct.

While the teacher holds the cards in this relationship by having a monopoly on knowledge, knowledge is not experience. The two are different in both definition and in concept. The student can draw on the knowledge of the Educator but until that knowledge is applied, an associative understanding is created. Information taken in by the student in this model revolves around 'the teacher said X, I did Y, and now the teacher is saying that based on the result, do Z.'

But was the teacher there every moment? Sparring with the student, identifying all the problems? No - the teacher was a third party, viewing the interaction, and then filtering their feedback through their own experience as to how they think the student should behave. While this is effective at later points in training, when a student has experience and is able to associate their actions with results, in the early phases of training it is inefficient. The feedback given is based on the student's inexperienced thoughts on what happened and the teacher's experience-filtered feedback on what happened. This begs the question: how can this create anything other than a mimic? In this model, a student becomes a mimic of their teacher first, an independent thinking student second…if at all. The student relies on the teacher as the primary source of knowledge and eventually resembled the teacher.

What about the other student? Were they not in the interaction? Were they not seeing and feeling what the student was doing? Were they not the most important point of feedback? With this much insight and knowledge, one that an Educator cannot have, the other student, the 'there', must be the primary point of education.

Chapter 33: The Communication Based Training Method

As many can attest in a Pramek seminar, we work to ensure the primary point of feedback is not from the instructor, but from the other students. This is done by making the most efficient use of the instructor's time, so they can focus on facilitating a learning environment, not nitpicking the students. Most Pramek seminars are divided into two four-hour blocks. The first four block is EPL based, being heavy in theoretical and movement training. These blocks are separated into two 30-minute sub blocks. The first 30 minutes on the theory blended with movement, EPL based correction and refinement. The second 30-minute sub-block is working with the theory through movement in a mechanical application with further EPL refinement. To visualize this, think of teaching a grab release. The first 30 minutes is the movement involved and the theory behind levers. The EPL is utilized to refine the understanding of the theory through the movement and ensure students can conceptualize what they are doing with their body to create an associative result. In the next hour block the grab release may transition to a takedown, or strikes, based on GSTM. The EPL led process is repeated until the student has a conceptual grasp of how a grab release becomes a takedown, or strikes, or choke - whatever the Goal is, and the Strategy and Tactics dictate. In the end, the understanding is Unitized...that a grab release isn't a technique, but a means of achieving a Goal within a combative interaction.

In the second half of the seminar, the time blocks become shorter to reinforce learning through the DPT. Students are encouraged to experience the theory and movement in mechanical interactions repeatedly, with as many different partners as possible, and EPL based corrections are made on the fly. For a 1-hour class, the blocks are different, but structured similarly. 15 minutes warm up, 15 minutes of the class subject in terms of mechanics and movement refined by the EPL. The next 30 minutes are comprised purely of engagements between students in DPT, primarily timed for a maximum 45 seconds to 1 minute, and then feedback sessions between the students.

Many martial art seminars, while perhaps not organized at this level on time, are by nature based on feedback between students more than the instructor or teacher. Anyone who has seen a martial art training class knows that feedback is given by the other student repeatedly, but the feedback is filtered by the class Educator. The Educator floats between groups, making corrections. Student feedback is told to the Educator, the Educator then responds to the feedback based on the Educator's knowledge. While the Educator may be constantly inserting themselves into the feedback – there is often no real observational, much less associative knowledge, of what the students did.

This is as old as teaching martial art itself through this process. Great students have been created this way since the first time some caveman taught cave children to swing a club. So, why fix what isn't broken? Because learning can happen much quicker when the filters of the Educator are removed, and the interaction as seen and discussed as it was, by the students themselves. This realization led to Pramek developing a new training model almost solely based on student communication.

The Communication Based Training Method, or CBTM, is based not on the knowledge or experience of the teacher, but instead upon the interaction between students. The teacher exists as an independent third party that runs the class based on a methodology and is only present to keep the training room safe, pose subject matter-based scenarios, and to ask one question: 'why?'. Through focusing on phases of OODA, questions, or direction about GSTM, use of EPL and DPT - the Educator acts as a facilitator. They facilitate an environment for students to experience combat according not to their 'here' but based on the feedback of the other student about the 'here' of their partner.

CBTM learning is based on partner communication and correction, the interaction takes places, communication takes place, and then partners are switched. Elements of the EPL or DPT are incorporated, scenarios can be posed, reminders or requests made to focus on an element of GSTM. In the end, for the training class or seminar, the partner communication model is utilized only.

Now, take a moment, and examine what was just written.

When I first did this in a seminar, someone said, 'this is anarchy. How do I know my partner knows what he's talking about?' I replied, 'why do you think you know more than him? He is looking at you, you are not.'

This is not anarchy.

It's structurally putting the student in the 'here' and asking them to remove their ego in the face of something other than their teacher.

Humility becomes an instructor, the partner the coach, the methodology the teacher.

The Educator becomes a third party guiding the class and looking out for safety, posing new challenges and different interactions, and keeping within the concept of GSTM. CBTM works to teach the student to fight based on what 'there' thinks of the student's 'here', and not the other way around. Within this model students are focused on learning about their Four Confidences, dissecting them based not on what they think - but upon what the training partner sees and tells them. But, for this to work, first we must begin with the student to understanding the state of 'here'.

Conceptualization…remember that word?

We found so much success within Pramek with this model, we decided to standardize it. This natural interaction between two students creates incredible insight. It's a natural thing to do, the only challenge comes when one student knows less and feels they have little to contribute. I see this often, a 'newbie' saying little because what do they know, right? Once I encouraged them to show their value, coming from the outside, things got interesting…students were getting better and it wasn't because of my constantly butting in on them. I knew I had to standardize what is a natural interaction, create a method out of it, take what is successful without thought and put some thought into making it successful.

CBTM starts with the student first but not in the traditional way. The student must be brought to an understanding of 'here' beyond their skill level. The student removes their ego, the 'here', from the interaction and focuses only on the 'there' and what 'there' is seeing, feeling, and doing. The Goal of CBTM is to create a student who can utilize the Observe, Orient, and Decide portion of their mental process to create a GSTM platform to Act from. A student is taught to use Observe and Orient to create a Goal and STM complex. Goals and Strategies are created from Observe and Orient. Based on these processes, the student can Decide their action based on an objective viewpoint, where they are using the conscious brain to determine the pragmatic approach to the situation as it is, not what they experienced in the past. Their Tactics and Methods will dictate their Action, and once committed, the OODA loop is acting to not only adjust their actions but also to keep their actions within their Goals and Strategies.

This isn't a long-term process - as we stated, OODA is split second based on the conscious and unconscious brain communicating. With it being so fast, we should work to slow down in the Observe phase and try to Orient and Decide. Training should give a student access to OODA, not make them an unknowing slave to it. Goals and Strategies help with this as we place what is Observed and what we Orient on within the context of the Goals and its creation of a Strategy. The information we take in should work toward a purpose, our 'why'. If our Observation shows we are vulnerable due to location, the 'why' must be a fight based on getting to an advantageous position. The student must be walked through this training by the Educator. To come to an effective CBTM, a student must first observe their own 'here' and the OODA process that defines it. Once understanding how their 'here' effects their GSTM, the student is ready to look at themselves from 'there'.

So – how do we get there?

How does CBTM work in the real training room?

First, disclosure.

Getting to 'here'

A student's past is their primary weakness.

Before ever stepping into the training room a student must be encouraged to take a full personal inventory to determine the state of their 'here'. This requires a teacher to communicate with the student the nature of the CLM, of the CBTM. The student should understand the nature of being in the fight, not acting or reacting, but making conscious decisions based on what is occurring. A teacher might take portions of this book and give it to the student to understand their processes, so they fully comprehend the process. A personal inventory must be taken, if only for the student to understand their current 'here' - and to see its limitations.

A student should not start training from the mat, but from the battlefield of their current point in life. In our classes I was asking so many questions, I created a questionnaire that can be used to guide this disclosure process. In using the questions, many times the 'why' can be determined. Why is the student seeking training? What is their expectation of training, and why is that the student's expectation? In this questionnaire, we search to find what lurks in the past of the student that is creating the 'why' of their training. Once this is done, we must address whatever their why of the past is to transition them to a 'here' without filters.

To do this, a disclosure must take place.

The disclosure a student provides a teacher gives valuable insight into the general state of the student. This disclosure also gives the students insight into where they currently are in relation to their Four Confidences. A student may think themselves capable of fighting, but the personal inventory taken through disclosure often shows otherwise. A student suffering from psychological filters may be a capable fighter, but the unforeseen psychological stimuli in combat may present a large barrier to overcome. Conversely, a student may be psychologically capable but suffering from seen or unseen physical ailments that can cause them to suffer a psychological setback. Discovering these kinds of challenges is the key to the disclosure a student provides. For CBTM, the disclosure is two parts: 'here' and 'there'.

First, a student should provide a personal 'here' disclosure, discovering that when they verbalize what they mentally know they may find challenges previously unseen. This should be discussed with the student and a Strategy for overcoming the challenges created as one would create a workout routine. We do this by utilizing baseline questions.

Baseline questions determine the general state of the individual student. Baseline questions are objective. These questions give insight into the ethical and moral state of the student. Within the answers a teacher can discover how the student views the world, as well as discover deficiencies in the student's thought process that may need correcting to become more efficient in training. Most importantly, answers given may show a teacher the student is not a good candidate for the class.

After the baseline questions are answered an informational question can be asked. The informational question is personal and puts the person in a 'here' or 'there' position where they must answer from experience. The answers should not be compared to the baseline because the experience a student had was only a moment in time. Instead, one should observe the answer of the student and gain insight from the observation. If a student changes their physical demeanor between the baseline and the informational answers, the student may have a conflict. Their beliefs in the baseline may not match their actions described in the informational.

This is not a psychology manual, but instead one that seeks to provide some comprehension and understanding of a student's behavior. If a student says they have no problem with injuring another person and then describes injuring another person with an amount of joy - the teacher may be wary of the student in training. There is belief in the baseline answer and action in the informational answer, but in the end, insight into the student is all that these questions provide. They are not litmus tests for students, they are not a be-all-end-all, instead informational tools to discovering their view of 'here' and 'there'.

Within the disclosure we find weakness many times not evidenced by outward appearance. For example, in the physical disclosure, we find the body is the weakness. In another example, in the experience disclosure where we find that previous teachers may be the root of failures to learn in the present time. Finding these weaknesses and finding the training methods to make strengths of them, means much is expected of the Educator in the CBTM. This begs the question: what does the Educator look for in how they address students within the CBTM and its disclosures?

First, the Educator must convey the terminology in a plain manner. As we discovered earlier in this book - words matter. This is a disclosure, not an assessment or a test. Ensuring the student understands what the disclosure accomplishes is about enabling the Educator to better teach the student and get to the methods that work for them faster. So, let's look at the 'here' disclosure questions, but first, do yourself a favor – fill this out yourself and see how you do before you ask a student, or, if you are in a training group, another student.

Disclosure

- Psychological disclosure - your past is a weakness
    - What about your past brings you to training?

- Physical disclosure - your body is your weakness
  - What about your physical condition brings you to training?
  - What is your purpose in training, what do you want to learn?
- Do you think you are a striker?
- Do you think you are a kicker?
- Do you think you are a grappler?
- How do you learn best?
  - Audio? How do you know?
  - Visual? How do you know?
  - Tactile? How do you know?

- How do you feel about?
  - Public speaking (baseline)?
  - Accidental public embarrassment (baseline)?
  - Have you ever publicly shamed another individual (informational)?
  - Have you ever been publicly being shamed by another individual (informational)?
  - Injury or harm being caused to another person (baseline)?
  - Injury or harm to yourself by another person (baseline)?
  - Have you ever injured another person by accident; how did you feel (informational)?

Experience Disclosure

- How long have you been training in martial art?
- When did you last practice martial art in a classroom environment?
- What is your previous martial art experience?
- What are your thoughts on your previous instructors;
- What are your thoughts on your previous school teachers and instructors;
- When did you submit to teaching versus rebelling against teaching;
- Previous professional experience
- military, law enforcement, EMS/FIRE/first responder, security training
- Previous 'street' experience
  - locations where one grows up in, prior gang or 'misspent youth' experience,
  - previous fights in various locations
- previous weapons experience
  - weapons experience from previous training or experience

Physical Disclosure

- Any known health status that reduces effectiveness in combative encounters?
- Current ailments that are vulnerabilities or 'gaps in your armor'
- Common existing life- injuries
  - Ex., carpal tunnel;
  - Ex., common activity related injuries;
  - Ex., weight lifting, martial art, professional injuries (bad back from duty belt);
- Prior surgeries?
- ACL, MCL injuries?
- Uncommon existing ailments?
- Physical disability (use of a cane, wheelchair, etc.)?
- Spinal deformities?
- Blindness or, extreme optical disability requiring correction?

Physical Attributes

- Particular physical attributes that increase effectiveness in combat?
- Ex., height, reach, weight, hand-eye coordination;
- Particular physical attributes that decrease effectiveness in combat?
- Ex., height, reach, weight, hand-eye coordination;
- Particular psychological attributes that decrease effectiveness in combat?
- Particular psychological attributes that increase effectiveness in combat?

What do you feel is your martial art capability?

- What do you think martial art means in your daily life? (baseline)
- How often have you found yourself using martial art in your daily life? (informational)
- In your mind, what role does physical health play in martial art training? (baseline)
- In your mind, what role does psychological health play in martial art training? (baseline)
- Do you feel you live up to the health and psychological standard you have set for yourself?
- Do you understand the difference between ability and capability?
- What do you feel is a strength in a fight? (baseline)
- What do you feel is a weakness in a fight? (baseline)
- What strengths do you bring to a fight? (informational)
- What weaknesses do you bring to a fight? (informational)
- Do you feel your previous experience serves you well today?
- Do you feel your ability affects your capability in a fight?
- Have you switched training methods in the past due to your abilities?
- What do you think is the easiest way for an opponent to defeat you?
- What is your greatest fear in losing a fight in real life?

Educating the student on the purpose of the disclosure prior is vital to the success of the student. As CLM 3 shows, trust between a student and teacher is paramount to the relationship. As one reads the disclosure questions, there may be some discomfort as the questions are penetrating. Not every student must go through a long, drawn-out questionnaire about their history. Instead, the questionnaire is an active learning eco-system where the teacher finds the answers to 'why' by asking the student questions and forming their training around the answers. This can take place by phone, in person, over a beer, after an introductory class…the last place it should take place is at a desk, the teacher on one side, the student on the other similar to television interrogations, so, leave the hanging light and paper cups of coffee at home and be comfortable with the situation!

The most important discovery of 'why' is determining if the student is in the right class or should be looking elsewhere. A teacher does a student no service by keeping them in a place they will not grow in their learning or facing their fears. In addition, a teacher does no service to the other students by bringing in a student whose 'why' does not match the class. When a student enters your training environment, you must first determine their purpose in training. Here are some questions you can ask a student, or ask yourself, about why you are training:

Why are you training?

- What fights have you had in the past you did not win??
- How were you treated by siblings, parents, friends, and enemies in your past??
- What is your understanding of martial art??
- What is your understanding of the class you are taking and why did you choose it?
- Why did you choose this school?
- What do you know of this school and its instructors?

What is your training purpose:

- What kind of fighter do you think you are in terms of technique?
- Do you know what purpose built is?
    - if you are a striker, you have a particular purpose in your fight;
    - if you are a kicker, you have a particular purpose in your fight;
    - if you are a wrestler, you have a particular purpose in your fight;
    - Why do you feel you are this kind of fighter?
- Conceptual purpose through GSTM:
    - Understands of the GSTM method?
    - Can apply GSTM during pre-interaction?

It's a lot, we know.

Remember, do not consider this an assessment, or use it for any kind of grading.

An assessment means there is a level the student should be at and demonstrate to continue training. It is also a dialogue between student and school, not the teacher. As the teacher, you will not always be present when the student is training and therefore the needs and culture of the school must align with the 'why' that has been determined in this dialogue.

These questions can be used as the basis for first reenacting or addressing the problems from the student's past. We are discovering out information about the student that will explain filters in their training and impede their ability to learn in a class. If a bad teacher is identified, and their quirks or issues divulged, the new teacher should act in such a manner and let the student address it. If it's a fight they fear most, the fight should be simulated, and the student shown their capability if they had been trained. If it is an abuse of some form, the psychological state of the student should be addressed to understand they can't fix what happened, they can only fix their reaction now. If it is job related, then efforts should be made to create a scenario as CLM 2 DPT dictates, where the student is able to be part of the scenario building and the situation confronted. Remember, martial art is a study of life, of survival, and sometimes setting up a mock office and letting a student work through their issues with their boss will save a training partner who becomes the target of frustration.

Part of being in the fight is understanding that the past is the past, the future is the future, and the now in the fight is the now. Nothing will change the past, but decisions made now will affect the outcome in the future. When the disclosure is made, then the student should be given the ability to confront their issues. For example, if the student has had issues with verbal abuse, then the student should be invited to a verbal communication class where communication and de-escalation is the key, and then asked to observe from the sidelines when the physical combat happens. This allows the student to address one fear at a time and become comfortable with their ability to address the primary fear when the student has no training or experience in the class.

There is a tendency at the beginning stages of training to let the student 'jump into the fray' because they want to. A student can still learn while not being in the fray. Sitting on the sidelines, observing the class dynamics and structure, developing a cognitive understanding of the techniques being taught...these are all learning to fight without fighting. While one should not structure an entire class around a new student, but instead can incorporate their fears into the class while not upsetting class structure. If a student has disclosed a certain situation they fear, the class can be structured to this topic. The student can be placed on the sidelines to observe and the other students still get training value from the class as they apply their skill. Within this the student can Observe, Orient, and Decide - and see how others do the same and formulate how to Act.

In a CBTM classroom setting, the Educator can spend more time with the new student, post-disclosure, walking the student around and letting them see what is occurring. This creates a bond between student and teacher that is based on communication and education first. The teacher can take their time to show the student how the class operates, have the student watch pairs, and listen, and then gain valuable feedback from the student on their observations. You will also find that this will ease the student into the setting as one of the great fears of a student as discussed in CLM is the fear of embarrassment.

When a student is unfamiliar with other students, class structure, and subject matter, they learn little. By having an introductory class that is based on the student learning without fighting, the student will be more likely to learn in the next class when they need to perform an action. When the student comes to the next class, they should be expected to be a participant in the learning. Their disclosure done; they have seen the class...now they must become part of the learning environment. This is where the student will be exposed to CBTM in a partner-based environment.

Chapter 34: What does CBTM class look like?

In CBTM there are three roles.

1)Observer - the student who will observe and correct the other student

2)Target - the student who will be the target of observation and correction

3)Educator - the teacher/instructor/coach running the class, setting the rules and topics, acting as the objective reality and the environment.

The Educator should define these roles and the roles should be held throughout an exercise. This can generally be done in small or large groups by 'numbering' the students and matching numbers together. In this case, all Number 1's are 'observer' and all Number 2's are 'targets'. If a student has expressed concern about an opponent, such as taller, then this student may be paired with a student who reflects their concern. Once roles are assigned, they should stay the same until the Educator decides they should be switched. In some regular classes where students are consistent attendees these roles may switch night to night, but rarely in one class. A full study in either role being necessary, a student may stay an Observer for an extended period until they or the Educator feel they are ready to change roles.

In general, the CBTM should cover these Phases:

1. *Stance - first position taken by a student;*
2. *ICM (Initial Combative Movement) - first movements taken by a student post stance;*
3. *Mechanical Connection - first contact made between two students;*
4. *Mechanical Interaction - decisions and movements made during the interaction*
5. *Mechanical Advantage Phase - decision and movements made when one student begins to gain advantage;*
6. *Ending - the decisions and movements that take make full use of the advantage phase to end the fight.*

If a 'target' has been corrected in all 6, then the roles should be switched, or they should switch to another observer. So, we will need a class structure to cover these phases. This structure should be staged, with a student moving from one stage to the next, learning as they go, and being brought back to a previous stage if they need assistance in learning.

CBTM classes are based on five stages:

1. *Identification- identification of vulnerability by the Observer;*
2. *Correction - correction of vulnerability by the Observer;*
3. *Engagement - engagement based on corrected vulnerability;*
4. *Cycle - repeat of Stage 1 - 3 as needed through 6 Phases*
5. *Partner/Role Switch.*

For the first few times running CBTM, we recommend using a simple GSTM. For example, the goal being a control hold after a punch is thrown. Target students will take their initial stance, the Observer will throw a haymaker, and the target will deflect the punch (in Pramek, for example, use a wedge) and move to a takedown, then a control hold on the taken down Observer. This is a simple GSTM, set by the Educator, the Goal being a control hold on the ground, and the student working to it from the thrown haymaker. Each Phase and Stage are clearly defined, easily communicable during the interaction, as the Observer can make corrections.

This is where an Educator must make use of time, stopping the interaction as it goes so the students have a chance to communicate. At first the Educator may just let the students go through the motions, following the example that has been set for the class topic. This allows the students to develop an interactive relationship where the Observer and the Target can experience each other. But, after a few minutes, the Educator can say 'we will work in 10-second intervals, I will call time, and you will have 20 seconds of correction before I call time again.' The students would begin at Phase 1, the stance, and then move to the next based on correction and the Educator's time keeping. The time would be set, and the students work. The Observer teaching the Target as they go through each Phase until all Stages have been completed, and the Target is fully corrected - then, switch roles.

While we've defined CBTM, with roles, phases, and stages, it does not mean the structure of a class must follow this. Once students are familiar with the process and the point of CBTM, an Educator can create classes that attention weights on certain elements. An Educator, for example, may attention weight an entire class on Phase 5 of the Combative Interaction. They may pace students through the five stages of CBTM on only Phase 5, against different body types, and focusing only on bringing these different body types to an Educator defined Goal. With CBTM the class can utilize the entire CLM, moving from EPL to

CBTM, tested in DPT, with varying combinations of each. This provides students something more than just a class - it provides a learning experience they walk away from trusting their 4 Confidences.

Examples of Educator Commands in CBTM

The commands used by the Educator are important within CBTM. They give guidance for the interaction, which provides an environment where both Observer and Target can focus on educating each other. The guidance that an Educator provides is a Statement of Work (SOW) that is clearly understandable by all students regardless of role. The SOW should be guidelines for interactions, with the following elements as the rule:

- *Course of study or topic*
- *Goal (and additional commands, such as focus points)*
- *DPT based stage, resistance, speed of interaction (if applicable)*
- *Position to begin*
- *Defining of attacker and defender*
- *Understanding of rules of engagement*
- *When stop will be called*

Since every class should have a course of study, or topic, this will be the basis for the interaction. If the course of study for the day is a defense against wrist grabs and then executing a specific take-down from the defense against grabs, then each pairing will enact this. Should the Educator wish to provide additional Goals (ex., a focus point like 'focus on your levers') then it should be given within the Goal. This way the student knows they must achieve their Goal and a focus point during the engagement. The Educator should provide the DPT based stage and resistance level as a hard guideline for the training. Educators should try to watch pairings in terms of speed and resistance. There is no excuse for a pair to be working at 100% resistance if the guideline is 50%. Resistance and speed parameters are set for a purpose. A student operating at 90% resistance and 90% speed may not be able to learn from a focus point and this must be considered.

Where to begin interactions

All students in CBTM should start from the stance. Stances are style specific and the correction of a Target's initial stance is based on the observation of their training partner. In Pramek we recommend that the initial stance be Pramek's IFS (Integrated Fighting Stance) which is a completely neutral platform from which one can move. The Observing partner should communicate to their partner the vulnerabilities that they find in a Target's stance. The observer should not say, 'your hands are too low', but should provide feedback about the consequences as well, for example, 'your leg is too wide, and I can tackle it' or, 'your footwork is not lite enough and I can rush you'. This is the very basis of CBTM - for a student to understand what 'there' sees and why it's important. This should not be a conversation as a conversation will engage the ego of the student's 'here' and they may attempt to justify what they are doing. Instead, the student must be humble, and seek humility in following the observation. After the observation, the observer should assist in correcting the stance.

After this, the Educator would then say, 'Take your positions' and then students will square up. At this point the Educator might say, 'Observer correct stance' and the student will correct the other. At this point the point the Educator may say, 'According to the course of action, using the lever, work for a single leg take-down.' At this point, the Observer will identify and explain to the Target everything they see as a vulnerability on the other student in the Correction stage. When this is done, the student may or may not be allowed by Educator command to correct these vulnerabilities. After this period, the Educator will yell a command such as 'Begin!' and the interaction will take place. After the allotted time, the two students will stop, communicate their thoughts in a period, then move to the next timed phase. At some point the student must be allowed to make correction.

After a period, the Educator might command a partner switch and then the process will begin again. This time the student may be facing someone shorter, heavier, different in gender. The process is repeated, over and over, with the identification of vulnerability, the correction, the interaction, the partner switch. This allows the Target student to know they, post-correction, operating from a neutral stance, are not disadvantaged. 90/90 doesn't only apply to the fight and opponents…but the stance itself.

After a few rounds in CBTM a student has had multiple people correct them which means. If done properly, any general problems are corrected.

We generally define rounds as:

- *Round One*
  - *Opponent should be of equal size, equal or higher skill level*
- *Round Two*
  - *Opponent should be bigger, strong, higher level*
- *Round Three*
  - *Opponent should be smaller, equal, or higher level*
- *Round Four*
  - *Student should work at 50% or lower speed with the Educator*

A few rounds can make a world of difference. The student will begin to find aspects of their abilities becoming better as they are corrected over the course of a class. These aspects will become generalized and they can then focus on the fight past the initial stance or ICM. In the real world, this translates to a student whose stance and ICM's are designed around the 90/90 rule. In training, if a taller Observer, then shorter Observe, then similar sized Observer all correct the Target, the result is a stance that is 90/90 proof in terms of height. This is our Goal - a student no longer concerned with the height of an opponent as they have because from the moment they square up their methods that have been corrected by taller, shorter, and similar sized opponents.

The CBTM model can create a student that is 90/90 - no tells, no structural issues, and no vulnerabilities for the majority of fights they will face. The calculated corrections must make sense for the process to be effective, and this is up to the Educator to ensure through common sense. The Educator must be involved, using the EPL, DPT, and CBTM to ensure students are learning from correction. As a student is corrected, they will be a better Observer, and a more adaptable Target as they trust the process. Remember, the Goal of CBTM is not to 'game' the training to win. In most methods of training, a student can 'game' the method - in CBTM, they cannot game it until they are corrected by 'there' so many times they become 'there' instead of 'here'. The true 'win' in CBTM is assisting the training partner to be better.

Time in CBTM

At this point it is important to note why these interactions being timed is so important. Fights do not last forever, and the Phases of Biomechanical Interaction take place in time. Many times, students lose track of time as they work with another student and this is often why students end up losing their GSTM and start 'wrestling around'. Fighting is an exercise in time management. When a student has a concept of time, they can keep on track, to know they are existing in a combative space. The longer the interaction goes, the more there is an opportunity for them to stray away from GSTM and become lost in the fight. Worse, the student who has a GSTM complex, can end up reacting repeatedly, in a reactive feedback loop as they lose track of time.

Time is important, and the presence of time should exist in training. If the scenario is one that is sporting and long in time, training should reflect that, as opposed to reality based quick violent encounters that should have a limited time period. Students should be expected to accomplish their tasks in a defined period. If they are unable, then they should be reset, corrected, and asked to try again. This is the nature of the DPT - accomplish tasks in a period. When time is brought into play early, and not just a bell between rounds, but timing in the interaction, the student is constantly reminded of time. 3 minutes to the bell is too long for a new student to remember the Phases and work toward them. A student should be reminded constantly through short time periods in which they must work, refining their work and going for their Goal faster. Beyond this, the student should be able to work quickly, using OODA to their advantage, and see what is happening in real-time. Not reaction time, not offensive time - real time, as the fight takes place. When a training scenario is broken down by time, the student can dissect their work on the spot and not have to 'remember' everything later - they can see it as it is at the moment, be corrected, or be asked to adjust.

Chapter 35: Compounding Effects of Training

Up to this point we have addressed stances and ICM. Obviously, the training progresses to other phases of combative interaction, from the stance, ICM, to a strike or takedown, to a control hold, etc. Correction should be progressive. The student should begin at adjusting their stance, then parts of their interaction in stages, which is why timing the interaction and calling 'stop' is important. The reason for this is simple: if a student has a poor stance, they will be quickly overcome. Correction should begin at mechanics - the foot position, center mass, shoulder location, head location. Then, onward.

As the student transitions to the next CBTM phase, the learning compounds. Over time the student no longer needs to ask, 'will it work on this guy' or 'does she know what I am about to do', as self-doubt is erased. The student knows the answers because, in training, various Observers have corrected them. But this may only be effective for the student based on the topic of the night. Training must be varied based on course topics. The more iterations of this training, the more situations, the more the Educator runs classes on various kinds of interactions to work with, the more the student will develop methods that are 90/90 corrected and able to be utilized.

The compounding effect of this training methodology cannot be understated. When a student has a stance that works on a taller opponent but not a shorter opponent, the combination of corrections from the different Observers will create a medium. This medium is created because the student will face each again through partner rotation, each time corrected. For as long as the class goes, over and over, the student is corrected until their stance and ICM gives them a position that neither the taller nor shorter opponent identifies vulnerabilities.

But, what about a larger weight opponent that is taller? When a larger opponent is introduced and gives correction, the average between weight sizes is evolved to meet all three. The student will recognize they need to adjust based on the target in front of them, not to the shorter opponent who corrected them. This is when a student begins to think about their stance based on their experience with the CBTM. The Educator running the class may suggest these students face each other with no correction, just to see how the students are progressing. The student may fail initially by using their height-evolved ICM against the heavier weight opponent. After this interaction, and the correction is made, the student is now able to adjust what is already working to what is identified by the larger opponent.

As training progresses, the student will be corrected by the Observer on other fundamentals such as footwork. Footwork against a tall student is different from the footwork needed against a shorter student due to concerns of a lower body attack based on a takedown. A taller student may be less likely to attempt a takedown, but instead will attempt to use range as an attack method. Each opponent requires different kinds of footwork. A student will find some things they only do with a taller student versus a shorter student based on correction and remembering the correction. Some students will create an entirely new stance and ICM's to face both opponents effectively based on the student's GSTM. If a student is confident in their grappling ability, but not their striking, they might create a stance that is based around this that works 90/90. We are looking for a student who is an average - not average in skill, but instead averaged out over several training cycles. Their stance, ICM's, footwork, center mass, hand position, leg and foot position, angle of attack, etc., all become averaged out to work 90/90.

While some students readily may accept feedback, some will not. When it comes the turn of the Target to provide a response, the accuracy of the feedback should not be questioned. Accurate or not, the Target should not be encouraged to filter the feedback through 'here'. What matters is what is another person observes about their 'here', not how they see 'here'.

Here are some questions that can be used to gauge the feedback a Target is given:

- How do you feel about the feedback you have been given?
- Do you feel you can accept the feedback?
- Do you feel you have the capability to accept the feedback?
- Do you feel the feedback will enable you to achieve your Goal?
- How does the feedback fit within your GSTM?
- Test purpose and Goal - do you feel this Goal was right for your abilities/capabilities

- Purpose is multifaceted - what could you do differently base on your capabilities
- Does your purpose address all issues - can you make adjustments that address these?
- Do you plan on implementing the corrections provided to you?
- Do you need extra assistance to correct based on feedback? If so…
- Can the EPL assist you in adjusting to this feedback?
  - (The Educator should determine what phase in the EPL)
- Can the DPT assist you in adjusting to this feedback?
  - (The Educator should determine what phase in the DPT)

The key to effective communication with a student regarding their feedback is to ask them to look at themselves, to look out from 'there' onto their 'here' and think about the possibility that what the Observer has said is applicable. When a student is challenged by feedback, don't ask the student to take on the feedback immediately. Utilize the above questions for reflection and begin to create a plan for change out of the feedback.

Remember, feedback can be taken very personally, and a student should be shown this is a training methodology…not the personal intrusiveness of the Educator. Over time students will not need these questions, they will quickly work with other students and focus in on the most important aspects of feedback. But, in the beginning these questions help a Target sort through what may seem to be a very personal critique. You will find in the CBTM that, if not addressed early, students take interactions personally. They will feel the pull between the Observer, the class, the Educator. They shouldn't – they should understand they are in class to experiment. Unless a class is identified for life or death combatives, everything is exploratory, experience, associative versus cognitive understanding. The student should see this process as one that assists them and give them possibilities…never removing their options.

The DPT removes options through measuring effectiveness…the CBTM increases possibilities by increasing awareness of options.

Post Interaction

After the interaction, the Observer should provide targeted feedback based on the following post-interaction questions. This should be done in a timely, efficient manner, with the Observer expected to give targeted feedback quickly. 'Leave out the bs' as one might say and address what needs to be addressed. After the feedback is provided, the Target can provide their feedback about the feedback, not about the Observer. It is not the role of the Target to provide constructive feedback to the Observer. The Target should listen for information about 'here' in the eyes of 'there'. The Target should then be allowed to adjust based on the criticism if they choose, then reengage in the same scenario. After some time, the Target is then rotated to a new Observer. For smaller classes one person may need to be the Observer for all the students and then rotate into the Target role while another takes their place as a teacher.

Many times, it can be difficult for an Observer to come up with feedback. The following are questions that can be provided to an Observer to assist them in developing feedback for their partner:

Stance

What are your observations about the following:

- placement of feet;
- upper body positioning;
- hand and arm positioning;
- head movement and positioning;
- What does the stance tell you about the student?
- What strengths do you see in the stance?
- What weaknesses do you see in the stance?
- What do you feel would penetrate the stance most effectively?
- Does the Target communicate clearly (if applicable)?
- Did the Target respond to your verbal cues (if applicable)?
- Is the Target easily frustrated in the engagement?
- What do you feel the Target could improve upon most?
- What do you feel the Target's greatest strengths are?
- What do you feel the Target's greatest weakness are?

What are your observations about the following:

- Footwork;
- Hand eye coordination;
- Protection of vital targets (eyes, throat, groin);
- Protection of clothing worn against grabs;
- What are your observations about the following:
- What was your attack or defense;
- What is your ability and capabilities to protect against your attack or defense;
- What is your ability and capability with the following (if applicable):
  - defense against, or use of strikes;
  - defense against, or use of kicks;
  - defense against, or use of elbows;
  - defense against, or use of grabs in the clinch;
  - defense against, or use of throws;
  - defense against, or use of ground methods;
- What do you feel the Target could improve upon most?
- What do you feel the Target's greatest strengths are?
- What do you feel the Target's greatest weakness are?

All these questions do not need to be asked at one time! This is a list of many of the questions one can ask and you may add more as the Educator as you become experienced with CBTM. These questions are to the point, and feedback should be gauged by what the student is able to comprehend. This is a role of the Educator: to determine where the correction should begin in the Target's mechanics. To expect a student to adjust their 'here' based on a laundry list of recommendation is unachievable and will create psychological and neurological confusion.

Creating a 90/90 student is where the Educator becomes key. The Educator must take the average of all interactions, corrections, and modifications taking place and then insert their personal knowledge and experience. There is no point in focusing on a onetime flier mistake a student makes. The average is the key as repeated movements and methods create neuropathways along which bad techniques travel. The Educator is the third party, the environment, seeing what is happening from the outside. The Educator is the room where the 'here' and 'there' exist and provides feedback based on this. But we should not forget, OODA applies to the Educator as well as students. To Observe the interaction, not once, but multiple times. To Orient on the areas where corrections can be made. To Decide at which point the student needs a third party correction, and then to Act in a constructive way that will result in a positive learning experience for the student, so they see value in the process.

Chapter 36: Trusting the process

Training environments change, but in terms of the CLM, processes and roles should not. A student should be able to rely, whenever they are overwhelmed, on the Educator ad process guiding how they train and test. The processes utilized within the training environment, such as the DPT for testing, and the role of Educator of CBTM, should not change. Survival does not bend to the student's aesthetics, so the testing process should not. But the testing process cannot be an arbitrary list of check off boxes and then subjective decision making on if the check box requirements were filled. When the process is about checking the box, objectivity regarding effectiveness is lost and instead the aesthetics are observed.

Olympic diving is a great example of effectiveness versus aesthetics. Anyone can dive, but not everyone can perform a perfect 10 dive in competition. The difference between a 10 and a 9.8 and a 9.2 are so small to the untrained eye that the scoring can seem tedious. The legs spread too wide, the splash too big, the angle of entry slightly different. But if your goal is just to get into the water rapidly and continue moving, diving is just diving, aesthetics be damned. The Goal is to get into the water without hitting one's head or causing damage. Functionally, they are both effective - one just looks cooler or may be more complex than the other. In the end, if someone gets into the water headfirst and doesn't break their neck, the dive was functionally successful.

Similarly, in martial art, regardless if one finishes a scenario with a heart rate of 135 BPM or 201 BPM - they've still gotten out. But how much can they accomplish after? Can they continue fighting others, drag a dummy, or perform non-fighting tests? To test this, in the DPT, an Educator can begin having students play simple games, for example Tic-Tac-Toe or Connect 4, against each other post-interaction. In these simple games, they can see the effects of a combative engagement on their ability and capability to perform basic problem solving. For example, multiplication tables and flashcards are also especially useful in training. These tools demonstrate not only where a student is in their post-engagement problem solving state but can lead to a sense of accomplishment as students increase their capability through answering the questions quicker and more accurately.

In one seminar in Cleveland, which portions are available for viewing on YouTube, I utilized a number of these tools. The ability to perform these tests was directly related to a student's physical conditioning. You'll see that the students who were physically fit, and in this you will have to rely on a comparison in overall weight and stature, completed tasks at a much faster and accurate rate than their less that fit counterparts. These DPT tools teach students in a variety of ways about a variety of lessons, from fitness to problem solving.

This is the purpose of the DPT - to answer, physically, the functional questions regarding what 'works'. Efficiency within martial art increases the ability to perform tasks after the altercation, but the capability is reliant upon the student. Capability, as we have discovered, is different from ability. A student may have the ability to perform a task, but if they are non-functional at high levels of respiration due to lack of conditioning, their capability is reduced. If one is uninjured physically, able to see, and has a relatively even heart and respiratory rate - their capability is increased. By fighting efficiently, one has the capability to perform tasks unrelated to the fight in a faster manner afterwards. Think for a moment about competitive fights you see without of shape people - laying on the ground, gasping for air, highly injured. Now, place them on the street, or put their child into the scenario. Then add their child being injured from the fight and now the fighter needs to carry their child to the hospital 3 blocks away.

This is the reality of combative training.

That is the capability that must be trained for.

It starts in the EPL, it is refined in CBTM, and tested in DPT.

Making CBTM effective

CBTM is only a training tool. It's an arrow in the teaching quiver.

CBTM solely, but instead incorporate it as a training tool. While CBTM may be just a training tool - EPL and DPT are not. EPL is how people learn, and DPT is an organized methodology of testing. These two methods should be the foundation of teaching and testing. While one can fit procedural into the EPL, and belt testing into the DPT…one cannot remove schema from learning and heart rate from testing. There is a tendency to blend teaching methods, blending the science of EPL with what has worked through an instructor's 'experience' and this should be avoided. Experience is subjective – EPL is not. An Educator, a teacher, an instructor – they should first look to the mechanics of learning and adjust the surrounding material, then look to what has 'worked for others' or 'worked in the past'.

As for CBTM, a school may dedicate one night a week to CBTM or use it as a means of addressing certain aspects of the school curriculum. For example, many schools that use CBTM as a training tool may find time to use it limited if the school is using each night of the week to teach a different skill-set, technique, or method. In these situations, CBTM may be utilized for a limited time in class for an organized round robin. Another example is that CBTM may be used to focus in one skill for belt-testing related subjects, or perhaps for only material that students regularly have a difficult time grasping and need different opponents with different body styles to help focus on these difficulties.

In today's environment, with some schools having an open format where a student pays for access to all classes, students can become overwhelmed. They and learn 10 things poorly instead of 1 thing well. In these situations, a school may move to a weekly use of CBTM that is topic based with one topic (ex., gaining mechanical advantage) being the focus for each class all week. In this scenario, the school would have a CBTM night and another night of sparring to test the information learned within CBTM. For a limited usage of CBTM, one idea may be to arrange a topic of the week with CLM methods built into each night. For example, the EPL on the topic as the first class with DPT used as a tester. Subsequently a CBTM class may be used to refine skills, and then another EPL night to adjust what was noticed in the CBTM class. For this a training schedule, this may appear as:

Weekly Topic: Defense against leg-based takedowns

- *Monday - EPL on topic*
- *Tuesday - open*
- *Wednesday - CBTM on topic*
- *Thursday - open*
- *Friday - EPL for CBTM Correction*
- *Saturday - DPT on topic*
- *Sunday – off*

Within this structure the school now has a dedicated night of EPL to discuss the Goals and mechanics, then a night of CBTM interactions. The next CLM night would be correction through the EPL, and finally a DPT night where students can engage in hard testing of the skills learned during the week. With this schedule, the status of students in their Four Confidences will be magnified and flexibility is kept as there are two open nights. It is important to remember CBTM and EPL go together as they build each other and should be used to do so. The lessons learned from CBTM should be refined in the EPL so that bad habits are not accumulated week to week, month to month. When bad habits are accumulated, students do not perform at their optimal level and can become frustrated with the instruction. Eventually they may look elsewhere for training.

In advanced classes, CBTM may be utilized the same night as the EPL, with the EPL being the instruction method, and CBTM moving quickly past stance to the interaction itself. Then, on a second night, students can move through EPL quickly to warm up and straight into DPT stages of training. The important point is this: be creative. Remember that the process exists for the 90/90 rule...you are creating better students through this process.

A student's best teacher is the student in many ways. CBTM promotes reflection, as the 'here' is reflected in the 'there', then the 'here' is made aware of its state and chooses its correction. This process, combined with their own need to become better, peer pressure, failure, and success, will drive a student toward excellence. In CBTM, the ability to master one's self begins not with the student's ability to fight, but with the ability of the student to take correction.

Team learning

CBTM also allows for team learning. Team learning means other members of the class are brought into the interaction for their insights and input. This allows for a completely new 'eye' on interaction and new feedback. By bringing in other members of the class the Educator can foster communication amongst the class. It encourages students to correct in public and assist others by pointing out vulnerabilities and deficiencies. This is often most successful by bringing the whole class into a circle to watch an interaction, then during timed stops having the students act as Observer and provide feedback. This must be controlled, so 'shout out the answer' is not encouraged. The Educator should take care of who asks questions and what feedback they ask for. Due to the number of students an Educator should at first ask for observations but not recommendations. From this an Educator could take a poll on which is the best advice and then giving the student a choice on whether to utilize that advice or not. To add complexity the student may be told they must take the path most voted on. Be creative as team learning benefits all students.

Team learning has additional benefits. These processes allow for sensory usage in combat for the combatants. Humans, as predators, experience predatory responses from the nervous system, such as visual acuity and auditory exclusion during combat. While this may not be a major problem in sport, where the opponent and environment are controlled, in the real-world, tunnel vision and selective hearing can be deadly. A third party may not be seen, or a cry for help from a comrade or spouse may not be heard. By encouraging sensory usage in training, the student learns more about self-control and their abilities. They also learn to control the proverbial 'ego'. When the team is giving feedback, the Target student must listen to it, take it into account, while acting in their 'here' and making decisions.

For the Educator leading team learning the Goal should be identifying when most problems have been corrected and deciding what is the next step for a learning pair or the class. In CBTM, if 80-90% of problems are solved and the lesson plan is done, the Educator will eventually have to ask, 'what's next?' In this case, creativity is needed. Using the DPT to, as the saying goes, up the ante is one option. Making interactions more complex, adding two on one scenarios, blind folding, tying up limbs, etc., may be also employed.

The Goal of the CBTM class is to round robin to correct deficiencies. Once deficiencies are identified there should be no moving to the next subject until all students are correct. One must ask themselves what the point of moving on if a student's basic stance, much less fears, stay unaddressed? Use this Goal as a base level and then work from this as a base level so the student has no general 90/90 problems. The Goal for the Educator should be self-imposed to develop observational skills and classroom control skills.

A better CLM based teacher

A CBTM student is not only a student but trained to become a teacher from the beginning. The student learns to teach by being taught. This is a common misnomer in the martial art world where students learned to teach by watching their teacher and then duplicate the methods. Unfortunately, if there are deficiencies in the teaching method of the teacher, these will be passed on to the student, who will duplicate these in their teaching. This is how martial arts begin to become less 'capable' over time or become unrecognizable in comparison to their original forms.

In the EPL and DPT there is an instructor or teacher who guides the class, teaches the lessons, imparts their experience, and works to make the student better in their martial studies. So, why differentiate in the CBTM and make what would usually be an instructor or teacher into an Educator? CBTM teaches through process and works to remove the 'here' that the Educator has developed through leading classes. It removes the ego that drives them to stand out and guide, relay their experience, and attempt to create a better student. There is nothing wrong with that drive...it's why we strive to teach. But many times that same helpful drive can make one seem beyond correction with experience viewed as the only experience that is worth studying. This takes a person with knowledge, feeds the ego, and makes them more than the person who leads the class. This position, one of leading the class, makes them infallible. Under an infallible teacher a student cannot grow. They will constantly work to emulate the teacher or please the instructor.

We have all seen the super-teacher, a former special forces master of many arts with incredible stories to their name. Many times, the teacher's experience becomes more important than the lessons plan. Within the EPL this tendency is limited by the process of neurology, and within the DPT it is pushed to the side as the guidance and instruction is tested. If the instruction is lacking, the DPT will show it. But, in neither situation is the ego of the class leader completely removed. In CBTM, by taking all focus off what is considered to the teacher, and focusing on the here and there, students are freed up to give the insight required to make each other better. The traditional teacher or instructor still plays a role within CBTM but is challenged in their teaching ability. Sometimes teaching isn't about saying a lot - but saying the right thing at the right time.

Turning the teacher or instructor into the Educator allows them to hone their skills at creating better students. It allows them to conceptualize what is occurring, analyze it according to the EPL, or use phases of the DPT to test instruction. In this state of analysis, they become an Educator, educating the student instead of teaching or instructing. To be an effective Educator means providing an environment where students can learn, and the experience of the teacher can be utilized to its fullest potential. Being the Educator is not asking questions on a list in this book, but instead asking the right questions. CBTM means observing, acting as the room, impartial, viewing what neither Observer nor Target sees. Sure, they can see it, but what they miss is only by a third party viewing the entire interaction objectively. No experience, no ego, only educating based on what occurred. While in CBTM the 'teacher' is everyone, the Educator teaches by seeing what would usually be missed in instruction. An Educator must think of the environment, third parties, missed observations, and asking for disclosure to focus in on what is needed.

Teachers want to teach, but their experience isn't that of the students. CBTM allows the teacher to remove themselves and their ego and see their own challenges in instruction. By utilizing knowledge of the EPL the Educator sees where problems occur, reflecting on their own instruction and identifying trends in student problems. They can identify problems from the moment they begin, and the more times CBTM is used, the faster this identification takes place. They become a better teacher in the non-CBTM class, understanding 'I may need to focus more on differentiation because students are having a hard time at that point'. In their observations, they begin to understand elements such as that students need more time in the fatigue phase of DPT because the CBTM is mentally breaking most students by the fifth round of changes.

CBTM facilitation also means looking at the bigger concepts of a combative engagement. For example, these are questions an Educator may use:

- How does an interaction start? Reminding the Observer to take the time to answer, 'what vulnerabilities do you see in your partner?' Is a Target looking at their 'here' before 'there' every time, or are they jumping straight into every interaction?
- Is a student switching to adjust or did they keep the feedback going-forth? Does a student who refuses feedback have other issues in their life affecting classes? Should a class be given on changing one thing for everyone and forcing them to keep that change?
- Are problems persisting that should be corrected by the third or fourth corrective feedback? If so, what is causing students to not correct

'here'? Are there other students in the class who are causing the process to be slowed? Is DPT needed to force students to look at their vulnerabilities?

CBTM also allows for engaging in instructional interaction. For example, using timed 'stops' to ask questions and point out vulnerabilities that the Educator sees. During the interaction, the Educator may call a stop to a learning pair and begin communicating with them. This allows a third party interaction that adds insight to an important point in the interaction, such as a transition from a hold to a submission. 'Stops' also fosters discussion from the information gained in such a stop, such as asking 'Stop' questions. An Educator should be comfortable asking 'what are you thinking about doing'; 'what move can you set up right now'; 'what do you think your opponent is going to do next?'; or 'is your next move worth the risks it could bring?'

I have taught Pramek around the globe, I never have enough time with the students. To me, just like any teacher, an eight-hour seminar is never enough so I try to impart as much knowledge to a student in a foreign land I may not see for another year as I do at my own training school. At a certain point, I found myself interjecting my own experience into the student's experience. In doing this, I realized at a certain point the student stops having their experience and instead has mine. They work from my viewpoint, not their own. I began asking these questions during 'stops' because I realized that I was not being the Educator but trying to teach. What I want them to do is irrelevant if they do not see why I am seeing what I see.

When a teacher injects too much, students what the teacher would do instead of what they would find within the interaction. I found many times what I was identifying and asking them to do was beyond their capability had I not pointed it out. This engaged a cognitive learning state in the student, but they would not move to associative - as they did not have the skill beyond my directing them. We must strive to have a student in a training interaction work to the best of their ability and what they can do at the time, their 'here', not our ability. If we wish to have them do something we would do, as teachers, this should be separated into another training evolution. The focus must be on their skill and making the most of it at that point in time. Asking these kinds of stop question is an ego-check, it takes your ability out of the interaction and instead focuses the student on their fulfilling their capability.

Finding Action in CBTM

CBTM teaches the student to control action. Within action we find time and with time being our most valuable ally in a fight, the more that we control time the more effective we become. To control time, one must control their perception of it and see if for what it is, distance, and means to achieve their Goals. One of the most valuable tools in giving access to control is to remove the fear that is created by facing an opponent. Fear creates a delay between each stage of OODA and the faster a student arrives at an effective Action, the faster the challenge they face is overcome. CBTM allows for a student to begin the process of removing fear through a structured study. Remember, an instructor or teacher looms as large in a classroom as the feeling of fear and self-doubt a student has. By removing this third party pressure, and focusing on student based instruction, this filter of fear is removed, and the student is freed to focus on their actions based on what 'there' sees, not what the instructor or teacher wants.

Chapter 37: Going forward

This manual originally had four more sections, sections like 'Finding Being in the CBTM', 'Correcting Mechanics Using CBTM', and two others. I tied them all together, a nice little bow on a wonderful package for you the reader. As I wrote them, I realized I was becoming the teacher and not the Educator. I removed them and in doing so, I removed my ability to force you to do it the teacher's way. 'Finding Being in the CBTM' will occur naturally, and Mechanics is an EPL training element, not one of the CBTM. At some point you, the reader, must create your own chapter through your own experience.

The EPL was written to bring us all back to the basics of how people learn and how to teach using this knowledge. DPT was written because tests can be so arbitrary that I felt Pramek classes, and martial art, needed an objective standard for testing skill. CLM 3 was written because I know firsthand the challenges of the teacher and student relationship and how uplifting, and damaging, they can be.

We live in a time where media and culture has shown us the abuse inflicted by those who are in the position of authority in terms of knowledge. We also live in a time where people gather more and more without teachers. In garages and parks around the globe, the interconnectedness of our world means that learning via the internet and through other's experience means 'black belts' and 'gurus' are needed less and less; and the communication and caring that happens between training partners is needed more and more. Each time I have written a CLM book I have endeavored to ensure that a long-term trend is defined, redefined, then structured so that the martial art world can make the most of what is either human behavior and communication. We are after-all, beings, and whether it's a village in Thailand or a park in Denver, people wishing to learn to defend themselves will gather to learn from each other whether someone of informational authority is there or not.

I believe, and hope, that more and more people will leave their teachers and look to other students to learn with. Thus, in CBTM, I wanted to kill the concept of the instructor or teacher, to show that today, it isn't needed…if you don't want it. Teachers cloud the marketplace of ideas, they dominate the spotlight, they make what is so beautiful about martial art a little less bright in their shadow. If you want it, it's no longer needed, not in the way you've experienced it.

If you want it, to stop with the idea of 'my teacher' or 'my guru', you need to discover your why and find worth outside of the teacher's eye. Once you do this, you are ready to take instruction from anyone you believe is worthy, without regret or shame. You can trust someone to show you things about your 'here' and 'there' without them controlling your being or telling you what your 'here' is.

This isn't to say that teachers and instructors aren't needed…far from it.

In competition-based arts, for example, an experienced hand is needed. But some people don't want that – some people just want to learn everything they can learn and don't want to pay to be taught by a master, or perhaps, can't afford anything other than a donation of a six pack of beer for someone's garage to be used. Some people want to be like a fisherman at the river…picking out what you need and leaving for another creek if you think it meets the criteria of your 'why'.

I also wanted to make sure that those who are abused by a teacher have a method of learning that doesn't force them back into another teacher's hand. The abuse I suffered at the hands of one of my teachers would have forced me from martial art forever had I not found the logic I found in Krasnodar. Those men and women in Krasnodar were the first educators I met. They all had PhD's, teaching positions in universities. Their approach was so drastically different than what I had been through that, all these years later, I look for educators and shun teachers. So, with this book, I set out to find the middle ground…something a teacher wanting to be better could utilize, or a teacher-less group could use. The Educator role of CBTM doesn't require a black belt or a history of winning competitions…it requires organization, an eye for detail, and a willingness to just help others learn.

But CBTM was only a portion of this book. It's a concept rooted in the concept of Being, our existing within the fight. It's about a realization of why we are studying, why we are here…and the things that bind us to ways that don't benefit us. So, for a moment, let me be your Observer, and let me tell you what I found outside of the cave that Plato described.

I know, in my core, I am different than most teachers or instructors. I love to teach, I love to educate, and see the light in a student's eyes when they do something they have never done. I also know that power it creates, and I avoid it. I shun it. I teach what people need to hear, not what they want. I tried that once, it only led me to look elsewhere than martial art to find something that interested me. The pressure to be in the spotlight, to grab that power, to be a counter to the other personalities…the pressure was so great, and I dislike it so much, I lost total interest in teaching or learning martial art. I wrote other books, I released other videos, I did other interviews. I started a company, opened shops. I worked hard at my career. I hiked 2500 miles.

But martial skill is found in the strangest of places and it always calls you back if you genuinely love it. From a fitness gym teaching proper mechanics, a yogi teaching a pose, or a firearms instructor explaining how the eyes work under stress…I see martial art. I see the relation back to survival, life, martial art is there. We all know that our art, our style or system, isn't all there is. It's about finding a way to see our art, style, or system in the things that aren't them. Knowledge is infinite, but our time in this cycle of our existence isn't. We should look to find an equilibrium between our martial pursuits and the other pursuits of life. It's why I focus on internalizing and making martial art a part of life and why Pramek was designed to be about theory first and embodying that theory in our movement to create an application. I realized over time that I would never be able to study all the arts I wanted, not only due to time, but also due to interest. I have many pursuits, most not martial art, but all are deeply affected by my martial art experience.

So, if I may, let me make some corrections to your life stance. I encourage you, if you pick up anything from this book, to look at life as a training ground. Approach every challenge, obstacle, and adversity as if it is an opponent. Ask what the universe sees in your 'here' and find what you see in 'there'. Uniformity has a beauty all its own and I can find nothing more effective in facing life's struggles than taking the martial art lessons and making them the way you approach life. Ask yourself, if you love martial art so much, why not make it a way of seeing life? Before you take on the opponent that is life, first take your stance. Understand what is 'there' and where your 'here' is. If living a great life is your Goal, then Observe what you face, Orient on it. Think about what Theory applies to it, develop a Strategy, Decide your Tactics and Methods to face it. Act willfully, confidently, using your abilities and capabilities, leveraging your knowledge. And if you need advice, perhaps you'll call a teacher. If you do, call them as a peer that you wish to pick their brain, not as a student needing to learn. You have the answers, sometimes you just need someone else to help you find where it is instead of telling it to you.

Plato's Allegory of the Cave, from The Republic, is a story I hold dear. If you don't know the story, go look it up, read it. It took me a long time to recognize it was time to leave the martial art world 'cave'. Sure, I snuck out to the entrance a few times, but I always walked back in, sat down, and put my chains back on. Then, one day, I crossed the threshold.

When I walked out of the cave, and left all the students, masters, and teachers, the sun that is the public burned my eyes and scorched my skin. I was in pain, scared, what would I be without my teachers? Who would people think I was? But something interesting happened, like the prisoner in Plato's allegory of the cave when he saw his true surroundings. The shadows on the wall that my mind made into giants were merely old men with drinking problems. The great animals I was sure would eat me were trolls on the internet, bolstered by followings but small in purpose. All the objects like belts and certifications that were made into shadows on the wall…they were held up by those who only wished to fool me to keep me in that cave. That fire, the thing in the center that made it all possible…it was me.

My study of martial art gave me the life I have, from my career to friends, opportunities to being well known in the circles I want to be well known in. But my martial art path has taken much from me. I'm childless, no wife, more concussions, and injuries from my early days than I can count. Yet, when I think about the other path, the easy path, to go back to join my fellow martial artists…I can only quote Plato here, from Plato's The Republic, when Socrates asks Glaucon about the prisoner, who has left the cave and thinking of going back to his comrades:

> "And if they were in the habit of conferring honours among themselves on those who were quickest to observer the passing shadows and to remark which of them went before, and which followed, and which were together; and who were therefore best able to draw conclusions as to the future, do you that he would care for such honours and glories, or envy the possessors of them? Would he not say with Home, 'Better to be the poor servant of a poor master,' and to endure anything, rather than think as they do and live after their manner?"

Yes, Glaucon said, 'I think that he would rather suffer anything than entertain these false notions and live in this miserable manner.' (Plato 516d)

Now you know my 'why'.

If it's only to glance the sun that is your 'why' then you quit forever, step out of the cave…

You won't walk back in…trust me.

####

Appendix

Appendix 1: ISBN Information

Pramek CLM manuals were published between 2012 and 2018.

Manual One: Efficient Perceptual Learning: ISBN-13: 978-0-9883216-1-8

Manual 2: Directed Perceptual Testing: ISBN-13: 978-0-9883216-2-5

Manual Three: 'The Teacher and The Student'; The Learning and Teaching Relationship: ISBN:978-0-9883216-4-9

CLM 4 The State of Action Training 'Being' and 'Existence' in Martial Art: ISBN-13: 978-0-9883216-8-7

Appendix 2: CLM 1 Dedication

This manual and series would not have been possible without help...

Laine, taking on the role of editor, for her tireless work on these. Who would have known in college we would still be talking today?

John M. Landry, Ph.D. for the final edit...it's amazing what a little correction can do.

To all the Pramek folks world-wide, thanks for sticking in and letting me share this knowledge with you all. It is an honor to wake up every morning knowing that all of you support me and Pramek and want to help and make this something bigger than me. From the support team for web and film, to students in Atlanta and Europe and across the world, I hope you all appreciate this series.

My family and friends for always being there and making fun of me when I need it, giving some encouragement when I was down, and always believing in what I do.

Sunny, Audie, Phoenix, and Bandito - my faithful pets who always seem to know when I need to take a break - I know you'll never read this, but I respect you enough to say thank you.

Pramek is the result of my teachers and mentors, some even when they did not know standing in the room as I taught them, they taught me. To Victor Zavgorodnij and Dr. Shvets - the best teachers a student could ever have, Mr. Kadochnikov and Arkadij, Alla Akrimova, Alex & Sasha, Al Retuinskih, Scott Sonnon, Ben Brackbill, Scott Fabel, Mike Elk, Alexei Ovtchinnikov, Victor Block, Boris J, Avery Mitchell, John Cornetta, Michael Martin, Leigh Culver, David Dempsey, Scot Mann, Juri 'Juricaine' Tchazuk, Dave 'Mongoose' Hicks, Brent 'Cash Faction' Cash, Aaron Cowan, Walter Barber, Drew Jackson (the best attorney ever), Walter Jermakow, Craig, Chief Norwood for the opportunity afforded to few, James, Jeff Bramsteadt, Mike Hager, Stephen Lardieri, Martyn Bliss, Dennis Z, Chris Bridges and Chaka Zulu, and countless others...

And you the reader...thanks for reading.

Appendix 3: CLM 2 Dedication

CLM 2 had no dedication

Appendix 4: CLM 3 Dedication

This manual is dedicated to the memory of my best pit-bull friends, Audie and Sunny.

After a combined 23 years of friendship, I lost them both during two long weeks in February 2013.

They are missed daily when the lines start to blur, my fingers grow tired, and sometimes I no longer can tell the page numbers and I need a good run to clear my head.

These were toughest words in the whole manual to write.

- Matt

Appendix 5: CLM 4 Dedication

I dedicate this book to the student who wants to question, to rebel, to be different.

I dedicate this to the student who wants to make science a master to bow before.

I dedicate this book to the student who wants to make biomechanics his Gracie.

I dedicate this book to the student who wants to make kinematics her Rousey.

I dedicate this book to the student who wants to make mechanics his Lee.

I dedicate this book to the student who wants to make psychology her Inosanto.

I dedicate this book to the student who wants to make physics his Vasiliev.

I dedicate this book to the student who wants to make neurology her Hatsumi.

I dedicate this to every student who is out there like I was at 19.

I walked out of Plato's Cave, you can too.

-

To Patton and Phoenix and Bandito: thanks for staring at me all the long nights I worked on this between Georgia, Florida, Colorado, and New Mexico. We missed a lot of walks while I wrote this and for that I'm sorry.

-Matt